HV 640 O45 2010 c.1.

Defying Displacement

The banner proclaims the determination of residents to continue their protest to protect the Xingu River in Brazil. Photograph by Glenn Switkes

Defying Displacement

Grassroots Resistance and the Critique of Development

ANTHONY OLIVER-SMITH

University of Texas Press ⟨⟩ *Austin*

Requests for permission to reproduce material from this work should be sent to:
Permissions
University of Texas Press
P.O. Box 7819
Austin, TX 78713-7819
www.utexas.edu/utpress/about/bpermission.html

♾ The paper used in this book meets the minimum requirements of ANSI/NISO
z39.48-1992 (R1997) (Permanence of Paper).

Library of Congress Cataloging-in-Publication Data
Oliver-Smith, Anthony.
Defying displacement : grassroots resistance and the critique of development /
Anthony Oliver-Smith. — 1st ed.
    p.   cm.
Includes bibliographical references and index.
ISBN 978-0-292-71763-3 (cloth : alk. paper)
1. Forced migration.   2. Land settlement.   3. Protest movements.   4. Infrastructure
(Economics)—Social aspects.   I. Title.
HV640.O45   2010
325—dc22

                                                      2010006152

Portions of Chapter Four are reprinted by permission from Anthony Oliver-Smith,
"Evicted from Eden: Conservation and the Displacement of Indigenous and
Traditional Peoples," in *Development and Dispossession: The Crisis of Forced Displacement
and Resettlement,* edited by Anthony Oliver-Smith. Copyright © 2008 by the School
for Advanced Research, Santa Fe, New Mexico. Other materials were previously
published in Anthony Oliver-Smith, "Applied Anthropology and Development-
Induced Displacement and Resettlement," in *Applied Anthropology,* edited by Satish
Kedia and John van Willigan. Copyright © 2005 by Satish Kedia and John van
Willigan. Reprinted by permission of Greenwood Publishing Group, Inc.,
Westport, CT.

Contents

Preface

I first became aware of the importance of place in peoples' lives and the tenacity with which they generally resist being uprooted not in the context of a development project, but in the aftermath of a disaster of enormous proportions. In May of 1970, a huge earthquake devastated an area in the north central coastal and Andean region of Peru. The impacted area was larger than Belgium, Holland, and Denmark combined. The disaster killed roughly 65,000 people and destroyed 86 percent of all buildings in the region. One of the central tragedies of that event took place in the city of Yungay, which was located below and with a spectacular view of Huascaran, which, at 22,190 feet, is Peru's highest mountain. The earthquake shook loose a massive piece of Huascaran's peak, over 800 meters wide and 1.2 kilometers long, that dropped a vertical mile before colliding with a glacier and quadrupling in volume. This enormous mass of ice, rock, and mud careened down the slopes of the mountain, ultimately to engulf and devour the city of Yungay, killing 95 percent of its inhabitants and leaving only four palm trees and the church bell tower from the main plaza protruding from the surface of the avalanche.

Several months after the disaster, I began a study of recovery and social reconstruction in Yungay that was to last 10 years (Oliver-Smith 1992). The surviving Yungainos, grouped in a makeshift camp just north of the avalanche, faced the daunting task of constructing a new city and reconstituting a decimated community. To compound the losses experienced in the disaster, the government, for reasons of geologic safety, announced plans to resettle the survivors some fifteen kilometers to the south in a town called Tingua, which was intended to become the provincial capital. To the Yungainos, this was seen as the final blow, the potential death knell of Yungaino existence and identity. What nature had started, the government would finish. The Yungainos were adamant in their refusal to relocate. Thus began a collective effort to resist the government's plan to resettle their community. Meetings were held, always introduced by fervent declarations of fidelity to the tradition of the lost city: "We will not abandon our dead!" Allies in the capital city of Lima were sought out for assistance in the struggle. Visits to the offices of reconstruction authorities were strategized. Marches were planned and carried out. Banners were strung across local streets, proclaiming, "Yungay will be reborn here!"

In effect, the announcement of the resettlement plan galvanized the surviving Yungainos—and the hundreds of other disaster victims who joined them in their camp just north of the buried city—into a single body united around a single theme: the rebirth of Yungay in its place next to the avalanche. In their fury over the relocation plan, the survivors were forging a continuity for their community and molding new, meaningful identities and purposes for themselves. Their misery in the aftermath acquired a purpose, the resistance to resettlement and the defense of their home, their place in the world. And they could newly affirm and heal themselves in enacting it and making it known in the world, recapturing a sense of meaning to return from despair and to reengage life.

Their resistance and their final victory over resettlement were both evidence and a continuation of the healing process that persists to this day. Working with the Yungainos over those years between 1970 and 1980 impressed upon me the emotional power of ties to one's place in the world. But in addition, witnessing and documenting the strategies and tactics they worked out to achieve their goal in the face of a military dictatorship helped me to gain a broader understanding of and appreciation for the importance of local grassroots movements and their allies for achieving more participatory, more democratic policies.

The fervent resistance of the Yungainos to the government's relocation plan was fresh in my mind when I returned to the United States. Very quickly I began to meet colleagues who were working with people who had been displaced by other causes, such as war and civil unrest, but most especially development projects. I learned that the development process displaced millions of people a year, often consigning them to misery in ill-conceived resettlements or migration to urban slums. Not surprisingly, many communities around the world were beginning to resist, fighting the same battles that the Yungainos had waged. In hearing about these cases, I found that the sentiments and strategies of the Yungainos were being echoed all over the world by people threatened with or afflicted by development-forced displacement. They too evoked the same deeply felt ties to the environment, the economic importance of local resources, the importance of community, the fidelity to tradition, and the outrage at the disempowerment that the displacement and resettlement process consistently imposed. Moreover, their resistance to the process of displacement and resettlement not only was gaining attention around the world, it was gaining ground, becoming part of a growing global democratization movement.

Discovering that the processes that I had carefully documented in my research in Yungay were part of a global phenomenon provided me with a research task that has proved both exciting and daunting. The excitement lies in the evidence from communities around the world that local efforts to achieve more democratic, more sustainable ways of living are still viable within our globalized world. The challenge lies in attempting to comprehend the vast array of resistance movements in all their cultural diversity, social complexity, and political dynamism. As I write these words, vast new projects to transform environments around the world are being planned, most with little heed for the costs that will be borne by the communities, sometimes the entire cultures, that will be uprooted. Every day, resistance movements spark confrontations in villages, at construction sites, in offices, and in front of legislatures and capitol buildings around the world. The conflict between big development and local communities has sharpened, particularly in the current climate of economic distress that is being experienced globally. Attempting to understand, even in broad strokes, the dynamic identities and interests that are at stake in these local conflicts, conflicts that express ever more sharply the tensions within our globalized world, has been both enormously challenging and rewarding. One can never really finish a book, I'm told. Never was that truer than for this book. The struggles that I attempt to document continue. The participants, their identities and their interests, their strategies and their tactics are evolving constantly. And new struggles emerge daily. These conflicts will continue as the contradictions between current approaches to development collide with the environmental concerns and human rights of local communities.

Acknowledgments

If one pursues a project over a certain number of years, in this case close to ten, the list of people that have contributed to the final product can be quite long. Almost as long can be the list of ways that people have helped, sometimes without realizing it, ranging from providing places to stay to great conversations filled with valuable insights over beer or coffee to reading suggestions to careful readings and incisive critiques.

There are people who have been working in the field of development forced displacement and resettlement as long or longer than I have who encouraged this project from the beginning, when I began to look at the connections between the "disasters of nature" and the "disasters of development." The three earliest, to whom I owe great thanks, are Art Hansen, Elizabeth Colson, and Ted Scudder. I am also very grateful for the participants in the annual Latin American Conference on Development and Displacement at the University of Florida in 1980, especially Scott Robinson, Gustavo Lins Ribeiro, and Teresa Serra.

In 1995 at the First International Conference on Development-Induced Displacement and Resettlement at the University of Oxford's Refugee Studies Programme, I was fortunate in meeting Chris McDowell, Andrew Grey, Darrell Posey, Alicia Barabas, Miguel Bartolome, Walter Fernandes, Hari Mohan Mathur, and Susan Tamondong, all of whom personally or through their work contributed to this effort. The core document on which this larger work is based was produced as part of a project at the Refugee Studies Programme [now Refugee Studies Centre (RSC)] entitled Improving Outcomes in Development Induced Displacement and Resettlement Projects, which was organized by Chris de Wet (Oliver-Smith 2001; see also Oliver-Smith 2006). The participants, Chris de Wet, Alan Rew, Eleanor Fisher, Balaji Pandey, Dolores Koenig, and the various consultants to the project, including

Dan Gibson, S. Parasuraman, and Warren Waters, as well as David Turton and Sean Loughna from the RSC, are all gratefully acknowledged. Several of the case studies and other materials I use first appeared in that project document and in *Applied Anthropology: Domains of Application,* edited by Satish Kedia and John van Willigen, Praeger Press 2005.

Over the years the leadership and staff of the International Rivers Network, now known as International Rivers, have assisted and supported this work in many ways, ranging from places to stay while researching in Brazil to unlimited use of their extraordinary library to the invitation to observe the second International Meeting of Dam Affected People and their Allies in Rasi Salai, Thailand, in 2003. In particular I am very grateful to Patrick McCully, Aviva Imhoff, Monti Aguirre, Glenn Switkes, and Selma Barros.

Most recently, assistance and support for this project came from the members of an Advanced Seminar on Development Forced Displacement and Resettlement that I organized at the School of American Research in Santa Fe, New Mexico, in 2005. Gregory Button, Michael Cernea, Dana Clark, Ted Downing, William F. Fisher, Barbara Rose Johnston, Satish Kedia, Dolores Koenig, Ted Scudder and Chris de Wet all produced superb papers for that event and our recent book (Oliver-Smith 2009b). Moreover, their support, encouragement, and assistance have been very important in the development and completion of this present effort. Most of us have known each other for many years, and while we don't always agree, we've been a congenial group, and our conversations in many contexts over those years constitute a rich vein that I have and will continue to mine as our work in this field proceeds. I am deeply grateful to them all.

I also want to express my great thanks to Dana Clark, Ted Downing, Barbara Rose Johnston, Monica Montalvo, Scott Robinson, Renzo Rosales, Glenn Switkes, and Kayana Szymczak for the generous contribution of their excellent photographs for this book. The cover image was inspired by *The Woods Within,* a sculpture by Alison Saar.

And, finally, I would like to thank my family. My sons Daniel and John, teenagers when this project began and today young men engaging with energy and vision the challenges of this complex world, supported my efforts cheerfully during the ten years of work on this project. And to my wife Kerry, who has sustained this project with her wisdom and humor, my love and thanks.

Defying Displacement

CHAPTER ONE

Disasters of Development

Development Forced Displacement and Resettlement

Introduction

At the end of the twentieth century, following the collapse of its socialist challenger, the dominant Western model of development stood triumphant as the guide to improving human welfare. However, even as the socialist model began its precipitous decline, alternative interpretations of development had begun to emerge. These new approaches were not based on class conflict, although in some sense they included it, but on the discourses of the environment and human rights. Confronting the current neo-liberal version of the dominant model, voices articulating other interpretations and practices of development and advocating greater emphasis on social justice and environmental sustainability have appeared among many regions and peoples who have been forced to deal with a wide variety of losses, costs, and calamities brought about by misguided policies and projects. As Coronil points out, "In social spaces organized under neo-liberal global conditions, collective identities are being constructed in unprecedented ways through a complex articulation of such sources of identification as religion, territoriality, race, class, ethnicity, gender and nationality, but now informed by universal discourses of human rights, international law, ecology, feminism, cultural rights and other means of respecting difference within equality" (2001, p. 82).

In the past several years, violent and nonviolent demonstrations have disrupted successive meetings of the World Trade Organization; also, well-organized campaigns protesting the imposition of structural adjustment and privatization programs dictated by the International Monetary Fund (IMF) have been frequent occurrences in many venues around the world.

Increasingly over the last twenty-five years, the grassroots protests against and resistance to what some have called "big development" and others have labeled "development aggression" (Heijmans, 2001, p. 5) are being heard. This approach to development is chiefly characterized by capital-intensive, high-technology, large-scale development projects that convert farmlands, fishing grounds, forests, and homes into dam-created reservoirs, irrigation schemes, mining operations, plantations, colonization projects, highways, industrial complexes, tourist resorts, and other large-scale forms of use favoring national or global interests over those of people at the local level. Putatively designed to spur economic growth and spread general welfare, many of these projects have left local people displaced, disempowered, and destitute. People around the world, from many different societies and cultures, urban and rural, proximate and remote, are raising their voices and taking action against development forced displacement and resettlement (DFDR), which was characterized recently as "development cleansing" that is analogous to the ethnic cleansing inflicted on minority populations by the Bosnian government (Rajagopal, 2001).* Media coverage of the major violations of human and environmental rights, as well as of the protests themselves, have given some of these projects, like the Three Gorges or the Sardar Sarovar dam projects, a high public profile and have embarrassed developers, governments, and multilateral funding agencies. The struggles of these local communities against their national governments and international capital have thrust them into the midst of global development politics.

Uprooting and displacement have long been among the privations associated with development and modernity. Indeed, the economic model on which modern society is essentially organized articulates and requires both a social and spatial mobility as essential to the circulation of commodities, currency, and labor that vitalizes the model itself. The core concept and element of the Western model, capital, in its circulation and reproduction drives a process of continual social transformation that we have ideologically glossed at the individual level as freedom and self-realization. Displacement, virtually accepted as a way of life by First World elites, is disguised as natural, simply

---

*For roughly the last twenty years, involuntary displacement and resettlement has been referred to as Development Induced Displacement and Resettlement (DIDR). However, a number of researchers and practitioners now suggest "induced" is not descriptive of the process because it suggests that people may be convinced by arguments or rewards to be resettled (Oliver-Smith, 2009c). When such is the case, resettlement becomes voluntary, not forced or imposed. But "induced" is not an appropriate term for a process that is determined by fiat, decided and planned out in advance (Cernea, personal communication, September 2005). Therefore I have chosen to employ the term Development Forced Displacement and Resettlement (DFDR).

the workings out of the market, when in fact it is actually a form of structural violence (Farmer, 2004; Kothari & Harcourt, 2004). The means and context of transformation, also understood as the concept of progress, are encompassed in the process of ever-expanding production for realizing exchange value in markets.

Indeed, there are many social and economic processes that set people in motion, and many of them involve a degree of volition. According to varying conditions, people move to change or improve their lives. They move with the idea that things can be better somewhere else. The extraordinary processes of migration and urbanization of the nineteenth and twentieth centuries attest to the degree to which people will set themselves in motion and will embrace changes. Of course, the degree of coercion experienced by many "voluntary" migrants should not go unrecognized. The successive waves of migration that arrived on North American shores in the nineteenth and early twentieth centuries were partly the outcome of a series of environmental, political, and economic disasters in Europe. Recent migratory patterns from the south to the northern industrialized nations are equally the result of stressful economic and political conditions, often the direct or indirect outcome of intentional policy decisions. Recently, the United States has gone to considerable effort to enact a somewhat contorted distinction between so-called voluntary "economic migrants" and involuntary "political refugees," a distinction that largely depends on the political character of the regime of the sending country. Thus, Cubans are automatically refugees while Haitians are economic migrants and therefore subject to return (Holman, 1996).

Certainly, we all currently confront a myriad of globalized forms of change and may sometimes be obliged to move, adjust, and reinvent ourselves as individuals, sometimes with dislocations and discontinuities of varying intensity. Indeed, as Lifton suggested more than thirty years ago, the rapidly changing circumstances of technological and social change virtually oblige everyone to engage this process of reinvention of the self (1970). However, the radical changes confronting people uprooted by development are of a different order. Development forced displacement and resettlement requires a reinvention of self and community that is far more profound than what we face under the "normal" pace of rapid social and cultural change.

The central problem of displacement and resettlement is essentially the uprooting of people and the destruction of homes and communities in the name of progress. However, for all people, self-determination and sovereignty over their natural resources are rights that are recognized by international law. The fact that these rights are also claimed by states, along with rights to

develop resources for the national interest, poses a difficult problem to reconcile, particularly within the framework of international norms, which say
that development should not be undertaken at the expense of human rights
(Caruso, Colchester, Mackat, Hilyard, & Nettleton, 2003, p. 3). Nonetheless,
opposition to such development processes is still seen as tantamount to standing in the way of progress and national security, a position that is attributed
to those threatened with displacement not only for their actions but often for
their very identity as well.

The idea of progress is intimately woven into the cultural fabric of the
West, providing a major ideological justification of colonialism and other
forms of economic expansion. In the modern worldview, human beings and
their conditions of life are both improvable and amenable to the ministra-
tions of science and rationality. Implicit in this perspective's most overtly
racist forms in nineteenth century social Darwinism, certain populations and
cultures were seen as representing obstacles to progress. The subjugation or
disappearance of such peoples was considered to be an acceptable price for the
overall progress, the upward movement, of human culture and society. Such
attitudes still lie just under the surface of many development agendas today,
which have been described as driven by "an ideology of high modernism"
(Scott, 1998, p. 4).

However, the sacrifices made in the name of progress have also been
noticed. In the early nineteenth century the great German poet and playwright
Goethe, witnessing the increasing contradictions of contemporary European
technological and economic expansion, captured the moral complexities of
development and displacement even up to this day and age in his epic drama,
Faust. In a penetrating critique of the psychological and social costs of the
development process, Goethe's hero, Faust, sells his soul to Mephistopheles
for the God-like power and knowledge to create, to develop. Mephistopheles
tells Faust that it is only through destruction that anything is created in the
world and that there is no morality in this process of destruction-creation,
so assuming blame for the loss inflicted is pointless. Life is both destruction
and creation and therefore the truly creative can be rid of guilt and act freely
(Berman, 1982, p. 48).

As Faust begins his final triumphant project, an elderly couple, Philemon
and Baucis, refuse to be relocated to make way for its construction and block
his progress. To entice them to move from their coastal homesite, Faust offers
the aged couple a cash settlement or resettlement to a new home. However,
they refuse his offers, preferring to remain where they can continue to live
meaningful lives by providing service to shipwrecked sailors and wanderers.
Frustrated by their refusal to be moved, Faust mutters:

Resistance and such stubbornness
Thwart the most glorious success,
Till in the end, to one's disgust
One would as soon no more be just.
(Goethe, 1963, p. 445)

In the end, the power of the developer is served, and the resistance of the elderly couple is overcome. Moreover, Faust simply orders their removal, not wishing to be involved or to know how it is done. He is interested only in the end result. The land must be cleared by the next morning so construction can proceed. As Berman notes, this approaches a modern, delegated form of evil; it is impersonal, for perpetrator and victim are separated by bureaucratic roles and the internal complexity of modern organizations (Bauman, 1989; Berman, 1982, p. 67). The following day Mephistopheles jovially informs Faust that he and his henchmen have murdered the old couple and burned their house down. Faust is horrified by the violence that he protests he had no intention of initiating. The chorus mockingly intones:

The Ancient word still makes good sense:
Succumb at once to violence!
If you are bold and don't give in,
Then risk your house and home and — skin.
(Goethe, 1963, p. 453)

The Concept of Development

Examining the many and diverse forms of projects that involve displacement and resettlement (and resistance) inevitably thrusts one into the midst of the debate on development itself. Behind the concept of development lie some of our most fundamental notions about the world, about growth, about progress, about nature, and perhaps from the point of view of social implications, about race and class as well. Development as a concept first emerged, becoming a major theme in international economic and political discourse, in the post–World War II era.

The Second World War radically altered the structure of international relations, shifting power away from Western Europe toward the United States and the Soviet Union. The role of the United States in shaping post-war international politics is well known. The creation of the United Nations, the formation of the Bretton Woods institutions (the World Bank, the IMF, and subsequent agencies), and the Marshall Plan for the reconstruction of Europe all resulted from the efforts of and expressed the political interests of the United States (Rist, 1997). In the rapidly changing post-war international climate of independence movements and increasing Soviet bloc power, President Truman's inaugural address of 1949 laid out four fundamental points that would come to characterize post-war international relations: support for the new organization called the United Nations; the reconstruction of Europe through the Marshall Plan; the formation of a military alliance (NATO) to confront the Soviets; and aid to the poor nations of the world, especially those who would soon emerge from colonial status to nationhood. With these four points the American president articulated the structure of international relations for the next half century, which would be dominated by the ideological and political agenda of the world's most powerful nation (Rist, 1997, pp. 73–75). Development became part of the American post-war political agenda.

Regarding the fourth point: as Truman phrased it, ". . . we must embark on a bold new program for making the benefits of our scientific advances and industrial progress available for the improvement and growth of underdeveloped areas" (Public Papers of the Presidents, January 20, 1949, pp. 114–115, as cited in Rist, 1997, p. 71). The key term in Truman's speech, which defined what came to be known as the Point Four Program, is, of course, "underdeveloped." Although not unheard of, the term as used in that context replaced the colonizer/colonized opposition, once defined by the now-depleted political power of a fallen Europe, with a new dichotomy of developed/underdeveloped, which was defined in economic terms by the overwhelming political and economic power of the United States. As Rist notes, "Point Four simply imposed a new standard whereby the United States stood at the top: Gross National Product" (1997, p. 76). Using this yardstick, and conveniently forgetting the entire history of European colonialism, if a nation was underdeveloped, it could become developed by adopting U.S. scientific knowledge and technology, intensifying production, and expanding international trade, allegedly replicating the process through which developed nations had passed. Development, in effect, became a model for achieving progress through ever-expanding growth and consumption fueled by public and private investment in infrastructure, production capability, and expanding markets.

Between 1945 and 1960, the Point Four Program and its successor plans for the underdeveloped world, along with the Marshall Plan for Europe, articulated a core concept—development—around which a new framework for international relations would be shaped, a set of institutions (the World Bank, IMF, the United Nations Development Programme, the International Finance Corporation, etc.) established to further the development paradigm, and new markets opened up and expanded for U.S. enterprises. National governments eventually added their own agencies designed to assist developing nations enter the development age. Consistently framing development as a model of economic growth based on the application of scientific knowledge, increases in productivity, and expansion of international trade for the common good, the post-war development paradigm was ultimately the expression of U.S. ideology, influence, and interests (Rist, 1997, p. 78). American politicians and scholars would play significant roles in the emergence and expansion of development discourse both intellectually, in terms of modernization theory, and programmatically, in the financing and delivery of various forms of assistance.

Over the next quarter century, in the context of continuing tensions between the West (led by the United States) and the East (led by the Soviet Union), development discourse took on the form of a debate between the model of growth based on capitalist development and the model of revolution based on radical redistribution of power and wealth (Berger, 1976). Development investment in infrastructure, but most especially in the formation of economic and financial structures and organizations in developing nations, reflected Western geopolitical priorities. Both models, however, shared similar emphases on the expansion of productive and systemic infrastructure and promised the Third World, as it came to be known, that development would be the outcome of their respective policies. As the ideological conflict and competition between the capitalist West and the socialist East sharpened over the direction the emerging nations of the post-colonial era would take, promised development became both the means and the goal for global ideological victory in the cold war. For the post-colonial states, development models and strategies from both camps became legitimizing ideologies that justified, indeed demanded, that the state produce the institutional conditions and infrastructure for development (A. D. Smith, 1986, as cited in C. Smith, 1996, p. 27). The all-but-complete demise of the socialist model of development has done little to alter that emphasis. Today, in the current trend toward privatization of infrastructural projects, capital still looks to the state for institutional support and frequently for financial guarantees. The state, for its part, increasingly seeks to engage the vaunted efficiency and cost effectiveness of the private sector, as well as to transfer responsibility for outcomes and impacts.

Despite the increasingly insistent call from many sectors of global society for redefining development in broader terms of social and environmental justice, other than the inclusion of a rhetoric of sustainability, economic definitions and approaches largely continue to both orient and mobilize resources and actions in pursuit of other goals. Development continues to be defined by those with the power to implement their ideas, for whom it is the process through which the productive forces of economies and supporting infrastructures are improved through public and private investment with eventual benefits ensuing for broader sectors of the population through the functioning of labor and commodity markets. The model also implies that economies of scale are a more efficient use of resources, thereby justifying increases in scope and cost of ever larger projects.

Although increasingly contested, big development still involves the frequently large-scale transformation of both natural and built environments through construction of such projects as dams, roads, irrigation systems, pipelines, and energy resources, aimed eventually at generating and supporting both agricultural and industrial growth, and with them, increased national and per capita incomes. Furthermore, with the newly appreciated value of biodiversity as a sustaining element of natural cycles of renewability, the development process also involves the establishment of national parks and reserves. Escobar, however, has mordantly noted that biodiversity becomes a development issue when it is constructed as a sustaining element in the reproduction of capital (1999). Environments that have been previously seen as hopelessly remote and useless acquire value as the source of exchangeable commodities and are reconfigured by human institutions and human technology. Thus, biodiversity, fundamental as it is to the reproduction of life, can also be easily transformed by development into a commodity in the pursuit of capital. These largely economic definitions and approaches to the development process are ideologically consistent with predominately Western cultural models that privilege economic rationality and productionist goals. The expansion of infrastructure is considered virtually synonymous with development and has been a paramount goal of nations past and present seeking economic growth.

Generally, infrastructural and productive development is considered to produce benefits that far outweigh any costs that such processes might entail. Here economics is seen to contain its own internal morality in terms of benefits outweighing costs. Economic development therefore becomes "doing good." In many ways, any costs occasioned by infrastructural and productive development have been externalized, to be absorbed either by the environment through resource exploitation and waste processing or by the general population when social, cultural, and economic disadvantages occur. The effects of the externalization of the costs of development are realized in serious impacts on the environment and in a transformation of people through the reduction of an enormous diversity of life ways into a significantly reduced set of social, cultural, and economic relationships that are compatible with the industrialized forms of production that form the basis of current development models.

While the paths that this process follows at the ground level are numerous and varied, at the institutional level they can generally be subsumed into the two large-scale transformative trajectories of increased integration into the state and the market. People who remain outside or only partially within the threshold of these institutions are considered underdeveloped, or, at best, undeveloped. There is an assumption that such a condition is unacceptable and that an obligation exists to develop such people, however the process may be defined.

Although some consider development to be the central organizing concept of our time (Cowen & Shenton, 1996, p. 27), the increasingly contested status of the term now calls into question not only its definition, but the extent of the organization it allegedly engenders. Despite some superficial consensus that development should refer to some idea of progress or improvement, the concept has come to mean many things to many people. Twenty-five years ago Peter Berger noted that development had become a kind of myth of redemptive transformation (1976). "Development" was the label that was given to the wished-for state of the future, what you wanted to become. The term became a kind of window through which a promised land might be glimpsed. Once glimpsed, such a vision could be used as justification for a variety of means.

There is no question about the power of the concept, however it is defined, to mobilize people, resources, and institutions. But today, perhaps more than an organizing concept, development has become the major arena for discussion of the serious political, economic, social, and environmental questions that currently energize debates about the nature of society. The substance of those debates is the basic qualities of development itself. In many ways, rather than being an end state or condition for a society to strive for, development has become the focus of a debate about society, about what a society should be and what it should provide and require of its members. Because there are few uniform responses to these queries, development is becoming more of an interpretive frame within which societies debate the kind of future they want and construct images of what they wish to be rather than a set of concrete goals.

Consequently, the social, economic, political, and environmental features that characterize development are now at play. The means and the methods of attaining these features form the core of global debate, even to the extent that the goal of development is being questioned by approaches that suggest that there might be alternatives to development. Such approaches contend that development, as it has been defined by dominant nations, in-

stitutions, and organizations, does not bring the kind of results that are sat-
isfying and fulfilling to all people. Those that question the dominant models
of development do not reject the need to alleviate the grinding poverty that
afflicts roughly half the globe, but neither do they embrace the consumer-
ism and accumulation that characterize "modern" societies, particularly at
the expense of the social, cultural, and environmental integrity that these
elements undermine. Development elites, the experts and professionals from
non-governmental organizations (NGOs), governments, multilateral organizations, now find themselves enmeshed in debates that fundamentally question not only their right to define development as well as the wisdom and
ethics of their formulations, but also the very epistemological grounding that
their definitions and formulations are based upon. The substance of these debates revolves around the destruction that certain forms of development bring
about.

The Costs of Development

Goethe's narrative of the demise of Philemon and Baucis allowed him to
launch a bitter commentary on events of his own time and on things to come.
For two hundred years before Goethe and for nearly two hundred years after
him, myriad cultures have succumbed and environments have been swept
away in the name of development, always justified by some idea of progress, of
greater good for greater numbers. The old but quintessentially modernist saying, "If you want to make an omelet, you've got to break some eggs" has often
been used to justify the costs that certain forms of development impose. Unfortunately, the phrase tends to gloss over the fact that those with the fewest
eggs too frequently see them get broken for the development omelet. Nor
does it reveal what kind of eggs get broken for the development omelet. And,
not to beat the metaphor to death, frequently reasonable and sustainable eggs
get broken while the omelets that get made are all too often inedible, if not
downright poisonous. When people are displaced by development projects of
whatever stripe or order, the disruption and trauma that are inflicted may be
profound, an unintentional result perhaps, but one that has been considered
by decision-makers to be an acceptable risk or cost, whether or not efforts are
made to mitigate it.

People displaced by development, now many millions a year, face enormous material losses, as well as the radical necessity of reinvention of self and
community. Resettlement imposes forces and conditions on people that may
completely transform their lives, evoking profound changes in environment,

in productive activities, in social organization and interaction, in leadership and political structure, and in world view and ideology. Resettlement means uprooting people from the environments in which the vast majority of their meaningful activities have taken place and on which much of their understanding of life is based. They may be relocated in a new place about which they have little firsthand knowledge and experience.

Place and space are key concepts in the problem of resettlement. A sense of place plays a central role in individual and collective identity formation, in the way time and history are encoded and contextualized, and in interpersonal, community, and intercultural relations (Altman & Low, 1992; Malkki, 1992; Rodman, 1992). The feelings of loss associated with displacement and resettlement reveal how important a sense of place is in the creation of an "environment of trust" in which space, kin relations, local communities, cosmology, and tradition are linked (Giddens, 1990, p. 102, as cited in Rodman, 1992, p. 648). The human need for an environment of trust is fundamental to the sense of order and predictability implied by culture, and threats of removal from these spatial and symbolic environments are profoundly disrupting. Under these circumstances, it is not surprising that resistance or hostility to the idea of resettlement has been characterized as "normal and . . . expected," indeed, virtually inevitable (Cernea, 1988, p. 15).

The strategic displacement of peoples for purposes of various public policies is documented in historical sources as ancient as Herodotus and the Bible. The expropriation and appropriation of territory for economic goals has an almost equally antique tradition. Although displacement of people for public goals probably emerged with the expansion of prehistoric states roughly six thousand years ago, some have speculated that displacement of communities that is driven by the goal of economic growth perhaps first appeared in the process of the English enclosure movement of the thirteenth century, during which estate common lands were privatized and peasant farmers were thrown off the land to make way for more lucrative sheep ranching (Drydyk & Elliott, 2001). The expansion of European colonialism from the sixteenth through the twentieth centuries saw many examples of forced displacement of subordinated populations to further the expansion of market exchange and capitalist production, as plantations, farms, and ranches were staked out, forests felled, mines excavated, canals dug, and roads laid. Much of the history of Native American–white contact and interaction involves white land appropriation and resettlement schemes, both violent and nonviolent, and subsequent Native American responses to these efforts (Fixico, 1990; S. Levine & Lurie, 1968).

Post-colonial elites, in rejecting European political hegemony, nonetheless have in large measure heartily embraced the spatial and temporal scales and forms of Western development models and the resulting projects that necessitate the displacement of thousands, even millions of people (Nandy, 1998). Although considered a shockingly conservative estimate, the World Bank calculated that publicly and privately funded development projects, ranging in scale from the Three Gorges Dam in China (1.3 million to be uprooted) to dislocation of sections of urban communities by roadway or building construction, displaced approximately 10 million people a year in the 1990s (McDowell, 1996, p. 2). Michael Cernea, former chief sociologist for the World Bank, now asserts that the figure is closer to 15 million people displaced by development projects each year (Cernea, personal communication, September 26, 2005). It must be recognized that the great majority of these people in being uprooted have suffered some form of violation of their basic human and environmental rights. They have been uprooted against their will, and their communities have been destroyed, often before their eyes, by forms of development ranging from tourist resorts to hydropower and urban renewal. The century we are now beginning promises much more of the same.

Development and Democracy

The transformative processes entailed by development in general do not occur without considerable cultural and social discontinuity and quite often conflict (B. Moore, 1966; Wolf, 1982). As socioculturally diverse peoples around the world are subsumed into globalized forms of governance and exchange, their economies, societies, and cultures are profoundly transformed. While such transformations may be welcomed and readily adapted to in some cases, the ensuing shift in economics, politics, and culture may prove profoundly disturbing. The change from diversified production for use to monocropping production for exchange and the sale of labor alter basic economic relations. The increased presence of the state in the form of regulation, control, and taxation may simply bring new forms of oppression. The general commodification and monetization of life, with all the related cultural changes in values, consumption patterns, gender and power relations, and a myriad of other domains, may be tenaciously resisted. These changes are experienced as losses of resources, culture, identity, and autonomy and as violations of basic human rights.

The discussion surrounding these necessary transformations has included the perspective that democratic regimes are not necessarily the most efficient means of achieving development (Haggard, 1990; Khagram, 1999). All societies construct social arrangements for the allocation of goods and resources. Regardless of the character of the society, this allocation is to a great extent a function of the distribution of power in the society. Consequently, the form and means through which power is generated and distributed will greatly condition the production and distribution of resources, particularly in the service of development. Since one aspect of development is that it requires investment of surpluses in the construction of infrastructure, such expenditures preclude the use of funds to address immediate needs. A central proposition of democracy is that government policies and expenditures should reflect the public will. Democratic regimes are thus subject to pressures to allocate resources for consumption needs at the expense of investment for growth and development. For this reason, authoritarian regimes are, some have argued, more efficient in allocating resources for growth since they are unhampered by pressures to distribute surpluses for immediate consumption needs. Authoritarian regimes are also freer to restrict the activities of opponents to their ideologies and policies (Haggard, 1990; Khagram, 1999). The recent robust growth rates of Asian economies such as those in Malaysia and Singapore have been cited as examples of successful development in which authoritarian regimes have placed development goals over individual rights and democracy (Ignatieff, 2001, p. 62).

Conversely, democratic regimes have been considered more favorable for other approaches to development, such as those that favor public investment in human capital. Within approaches favoring investment in infrastructure, education, training, and health were often categorized as forms of consumption to be postponed, but they are now seen as important for development, even when narrowly defined in terms of economic growth (Khagram, 1999, p. 36). However, the existence of democratic regimes does not guarantee that the development process will respond more directly to immediate human needs. Powerful interest groups within democratic societies have frequently been able to direct the development process toward ends that compete with immediate public needs, but in democracies there is, at least, greater room for debate over these allocations.

The question of development and democracy takes on considerable importance in relation to DFDR because the forms of development that generate projects that require DFDR are generally large-scale infrastructural projects that absorb from national treasuries enormous amounts of economic resources that might otherwise be employed to address immediate needs. In its crudest form, political power can be thought of as the ability to move people and things about the landscape in any way you see fit. When one considers the whole phenomenon of development-forced resettlement, that perspective, crude as it may be, is remarkably apt. Development-forced resettlement is, in many ways, the ultimate expression of a state's monopoly on the management of violence in conjunction with ambitious engineering projects, freed from all other nonpolitical power and institutions of social self-management and able to exert ultimate control over the location of people and things within its territory (Bauman, 1989, p. xiii). Conversely, to be resettled is one of the most acute expressions of powerlessness because it constitutes a loss of control over one's physical space. The only thing left is the loss of the body. As Margaret Rodman so cogently notes, "The most powerless people have no place at all" (1992, p. 650).

The process of DFDR, when undertaken despite the opposition of affected peoples or when accomplished without participation by and benefits for affected peoples, calls into question the entire relationship between this form of development and democracy, particularly democracy as expressed through respect for human and civil rights. Furthermore, the capacity of people to protest, resist, and influence DFDR policies and projects may constitute an important test of the democratic character of a particular regime.

In current debates alternative approaches to development favor environmental and ethical considerations revolving around notions of sustainability as well as human and environmental rights. Indeed, this form of development discourse now questions the fundamental social, cultural, and economic assumptions of development and purports to offer alternative conceptualizations that produce benefits and reduce costs at specific local levels, as opposed to large-scale efforts for more generalized beneficiary populations who assume fewer risks and costs. The fundamental position adopted by these opponents of current development practice is an ethical one based on a concept of human rights.

Ethics, Global Norms, and Transnational Civil Society

Development and human rights discourses both emerged as important issues of public discourse and debate in the post–World War II era. Development became one theme in the ideological debate between the capitalist and socialist worlds, with both sides placing the concept of human rights at the forefront of their arguments. In their assertions, each side adopted a moral position that its model, as opposed to the alternative, provided for and guaranteed certain basic human rights. One camp privileged the civil and political rights (freedom of expression, movement, congregation); the other foregrounded economic and social rights (freedom from want, freedom from exploitation

and appropriation). Clearly, the emphasis on one kind of rights did not preclude attention to other kinds of rights, such as in the security of private or
public property. In effect, each model claimed that by following its guidelines,
political and economic rights would be both protected and developed for the
general well-being of national populations. In effect, each side justified its
theoretical constructs and its practical strategies for the development of societies, particularly those of the post-colonial world, on the basis of a concept
of rights.

Out of these differing concepts of rights, and most especially out of the
ideological struggle between the two interpretations, emerged a generalized
moral obligation to develop post-colonial societies in ways that would enhance and develop human rights, particularly those privileged by each model.
The moral obligation to develop is based on a number of ethical principles
regarding human relationships and the relationship between people and resources. Generally speaking, development as a goal of public policy is aimed
at improving the levels of welfare of the global population. Well-being and
poverty are clearly distributed unequally among the world's populations. Thus,
it is a generally held moral principle that the levels of impoverishment enormous numbers of people around the world currently endure are intolerable
and morally unacceptable and require directed action to reduce and ultimately
eradicate. There are two general routes toward the reduction of these morally
unacceptable conditions: addressing resource distribution inequities and enhancing productive capability. Generally speaking, reigning economic models
and policies—created and applied by hegemonic national governments and
multilateral development agencies through various forms of discipline, such
as loan conditionalities, Structural Adjustment Programs (SAP), etc.—have
so shaped local realities that redistributional options have been excluded in
favor of concerted efforts at enhancing productive capacity on the theory that
increased production and income will filter through the system to enhance
general patterns of consumption and well-being. Enhanced productive capacity is based on a principle of efficient use of resources to render their maximum value, defined largely in terms of consumer preferences domestically and
earnings potential in international exchange (Penz, 1992, p. 107).

It is this principle of resource use efficiency that generally energizes nations
to initiate projects that displace people. At the most fundamental level, a
judgment is made that a more efficient, that is, a greater value-producing,
use for resources than may currently be operating can be achieved. In essence,
national governments and private developers see resources as underutilized
by local populations, prompting the elaboration of projects to more efficiently
exploit the economic potential of those resources. The origin of the efficiency

argument is deeply embedded in the history of Western imperialism. It is first found in the arguments of Sir John Davies, who argued in 1610 regarding the eviction of Irish countrymen that if land is left in a wilderness condition, the king may lawfully grant it to people who will make it productive. John Winthrop, the first governor of Massachusetts, similarly asserted in 1629 that since the indigenous people of New England did not improve their land according to God's will, it could be lawfully taken from them, as long as they were left a little to survive on. In 1690, John Locke enshrined this idea in his principle of improvement as the origin of property rights. That is, the natural right of property is derived from its productive use (Wood, 2002, pp. 157–159).

Thus, the argument is made that if resources possessed by particular communities can be more efficiently used to produce a greater value that will be enjoyed by the general population, thus enhancing their level of development, the resources may be lawfully taken. Public and private developers ethically justify their actions in diverting such resources from inefficient use toward more value-producing outcomes with the belief that greater production will increase consumption and well-being at all levels of society. Such development goals provide a moral obligation, and greater value production provides an ethical justification for a wide variety of interventions around the world.

From this moral obligation emerged what James Ferguson has referred to as a "development industry" with major political and economic agendas to reproduce an idealized form of society (1990, p. 8). While the socialist model and agenda, which were both productionist and redistributional, have, with some few exceptions, fallen by the wayside, the capitalist model, with its agenda of transformation toward an intensified production capability stimulated by modern industrial market economies and justified morally as the best means to combat poverty and raise standards of living on a global scale, is clearly ascendant.

The moral agenda now involves not just the obligation to develop, but the right to develop as well. Both the obligation and the right to develop have involved discourses that have been heartily embraced by a majority, if not in fact the entirety, of the post-colonial world elites. Adopting both the rhetoric and practice of the development industry, post-colonial nations have worked assiduously to expand the influence of both the state and the market through major investments in infrastructure to address national priorities that are based on the ideological constructions of a utilitarian nature, private property, and a mass society based primarily on the identity of national citizenship. As a citizen of one of these nations, one has the right to development through these institutions.

Article 1, Clause 3, of the United Nations General Assembly Declaration on the Right to Development (adopted by General Assembly Resolution 41/128 of December 4, 1986) established that "States have the right and the duty to formulate appropriate natural development policies that aim at the constant improvement of the well being of the entire population of individuals" (Office of the High Commissioner on Human Rights, 1986). This concept is in some form replicated in numerous national constitutions around the world, establishing the state's right and duty to expand its capacity to serve the needs of its population. When the expression of national purpose involves infrastructural development that displaces people, the state's right of eminent domain allows for the acquisition of the necessary land, with adequate compensation to the owners. There is an assumption that such development will produce benefits for all, not just a particular community or sector within the society. There is also an implicit expectation in these assertions that the state, in asserting its right to develop, will act in an ethical fashion that respects the principles of democracy and the human rights of the people involved.

Reigning development models, promoting large-scale infrastructural projects, transform social and physical environments and espouse the concept of "the greatest good for the greatest number" rather than the rights of the less numerous and the less powerful. Although the record does not reflect it entirely, such a position assumes that the less powerful will benefit eventually, through the project itself or through a well-designed and well-implemented resettlement program. For some observers, given the current framework of economic structures and conditions, realism dictates acceptance of this development ideology. Many of these conceptualizations are based on a foundation of ethical or normative positions that are, in Western models, generally thought to be inherent in the development process, most specifically the understanding that production stimulated through market demand will improve levels of well-being for more people.

Since the 1960s, a small but persistent group of scholars and activists have insisted that, rather than possessing an inherent ethical foundation, theories and models of development must have ethical or valuational components specifically inserted in policy and project design and implementation (Crocker, 1991, p. 457). Starting in the 1970s, Goulet argued that development theory, planning, and practice must be accountable from more than a purely economic basis (1971). Peter Berger subsequently critiqued both market-driven and command approaches to development for ignoring two elements he called the calculus of pain and the calculus of meaning. Berger contended that elites from both the capitalist and socialist development models have often blithely written off the pain experienced by the poor, the displaced, and people in opposition as part of "the acceptable costs of development." The calculus of pain involves the high infant mortality, malnutrition, displacement, home-lessness, social disarticulation, and political and social death that frequently accompany the different models. Attendant to those losses is the loss of a structure of meaning in which to frame and live a life that is experienced as beliefs about human relations, the environment, and the cosmos, all of which are cast away or commodified in the transformation. Considered equally as important as the scientific elements of development, development ethics addresses the definitions, goals, and means that are employed in development work, calling for "the normative or ethical assessment of the ends and means of Third World and global development" (Crocker, 1991, p. 457).

As opposed to a general understanding of development as operating within an assumed ethical framework because it was intended to do "good," the specific connection between development and ethics has also recently been apprehended by policy makers and development professionals. Some have recognized that, while traditionally defined economic development was still, in their eyes, necessary to bring about human development, there are urgent ethical problems that globalization, technology, and development produce, as shown by the persistence of the poverty in which vast sectors of the population remain submerged. The perceived failure of dominant models to address these inequalities places in doubt the goals of development and the priorities, means, and characteristics of a desirable society (Kliksberg, 2001).

While there is little questioning of the economic model in these and similar formulations, some awareness has emerged that the benefits of development have not been equitably shared nor the costs equitably borne. Critiques of the World Bank and the IMF by high-profile individuals (some of them ex–World Bank insiders) appalled at the devastating impacts these institutions' policies have had on general populations have focused on the negative impacts on overall economies, such as Third World debt and the grievous Structural Adjustment Programs and monetary policies imposed on the populations of developing nations (Goodland, 2007; Soros, 1998; Stiglitz, 2002). There is concern that IMF loan conditionalities coerce nations to accept trade, investment, financial deregulation, and privatization policies regardless of their impacts on local populations. The imposition of these forms of capitalist discipline by the World Bank and the IMF serves, some argue, to undermine the state's sovereignty and capacity to be the primary guarantor of fundamental rights and provider of basic services such as education and health. And much of the criticism of the World Bank focuses on its financing of large infrastructural projects without regard for their social and environmental impacts (Bretton Woods Project).

While these critiques are long overdue and confirm what protesters around the world have been contending for more than a decade, it remains to be seen how they will ultimately affect infrastructural development strategies that displace people in specific nations. Robert Goodland, the chief environmental advisor to the Bank, resigned in protest in 2007 over the policies implemented in recent years by bank presidents Wolfowitz and Zoellick that privilege large multinational corporations in their extraction of resources in developing nations, with little attention to major environmental and social damage. George Soros saw some encouraging signs in the 1990s in the criticisms of dependence on quantitative indicators of development outcomes (1998), but recent policies seem solidly directed toward financing high-risk projects that generate maximum GNP (see Conclusions, Chapter 8, for more information).

These critiques and earlier concerns have been interpreted by some as forming part of a shift in world politics away from struggles over power and wealth toward struggles over normative issues (Wilmer, 1993, p. 40). Almost simultaneous with the initiation of discussions of development, concern over the enormous violations of human rights that took place during World War II led to efforts to establish international standards and norms regarding the rights not only of states (and corporations), but of individual human beings. Since the end of World War II, there has been a relatively continuous spread and institutionalization of global norms and principles of various types—regulatory, constitutive, practical, and evaluative (Khagram, 1999, p. 23). Under the broad rubric of human rights, two specific applications—the environment, and the rights of indigenous peoples—have seen particularly extensive growth and diffusion to many nations around the world.

An analysis of 140 constitutions of independent countries, written in the century between 1870 and 1970, revealed a major increase in the number of states formally committed to ensuring a broad set of human rights, including civil rights, such as free speech and due process; political rights, such as the vote; and social or economic rights, such as unemployment insurance and social security. In recent years research by the United Nations Commission on Human Rights, the International Labour Organization, and national and international environmental advocates reveals similar steps in the constitutions that have emerged from the wave of democratization since the 1970s and that include an even greater enumeration of rights, such as those pertaining to gender justice, indigenous peoples, and other ethnic minorities. Internationally, human rights norms were among the formative principles behind the organization of the United Nations. Before the founding of the United Nations in 1948, there were no international organizations focused on human rights, but by 1990 there were 27 formally dedicated to furthering human rights (Khagram, 1999, p. 27). The diffusion of international human rights norms is critically linked to the establishment and sustainability of networks of transnational actors who can connect with international regimes to alert the public and generate opposition to situations in which rights are in jeopardy, particularly situations in the West (Risse & Sikkink, 1999, p. 3).

Similarly, a global normative framework of principles and organizations has taken shape around the issue of the environment. National environmental agencies were virtually unheard of before the United Nations Conference on the Human Environment was held in Stockholm in 1972. Since that time environmental agencies, including ministries, have been forming rapidly. By 1988 approximately 60 had been created, and roughly 40 more were developed in the period around the 1992 United Nations Conference on Environment and Development. National legislation related to and regulation of environmental practice has expanded along with the growth of these organizations. Internationally, environmental norms have seen a similar expansion in the form of such organizations as the United Nations Environment Program, the Office of Environmental and Scientific Affairs (OESA) of the World Bank, the United Nations Commission on Sustainable Development, and the Global Environmental Facility (Khagram, 1999, p. 25).

Organizations promoting the rights of indigenous peoples are far from new in specific nations, but the worldwide expansion of an indigenous movement only began to occur in the 1960s. The enormous challenges and problems faced by indigenous peoples around the world, including discrimination, confiscation of territory, violation of treaties, and exploitation and extraction of resources, have given rise to literally thousands of organizations, particularly in the post-war period of decolonization. The rise to prominence of civil rights issues and the resources to promote them in many of the industrialized nations have contributed to the emergence of a global indigenous movement, spreading from Europe and North America in the late 1960s to Latin America in the 1970s, Asia and the Pacific in the 1980s and to Africa and the former Soviet Union in the 1990s. Of the thousands of indigenous organizations, some have created national federations to address the problems that are faced at the national level. Indigenous peoples bring their concerns over rights to land and territories, the right to social and cultural freedom of expression, the right to be represented by their own institutions, and the right to consent and control over development into national and international forums, including the United Nations, the various continental associations such as the Organization of American States, and the International Labour Organization (Gray, 1996, p. 113). Increasingly, amendments safeguarding the rights of indigenous peoples are being added to national constitutions around the world. Consequently, it is in this broader context of an emerging transnational civil society—more specifically, in a transnational political economy of development addressing such issues as general human rights, the environment, and the rights of indigenous peoples—that the people and organizations resisting DFDR act and in which the conflictive and cooperative relations they engage in are played out.

The dire problems confronting people who experience development-forced resettlement are central to the concerns that this expanding front of human rights, indigenous peoples, and environmental organizations is addressing. In essence, the entire topic of development forced displacement and resettlement is fraught with ethical dangers. Specific ethical formulations regarding DFDR revolve around the open contradiction between projects designed to improve development levels and the abject misery that the vast majority of them have created. Cernea's landmark article modeling the eight resettlement risks of landlessness, homelessness, joblessness, marginalization, increased morbidity, food insecurity, loss of access to common property, and social disarticulation speaks volumes about the outcomes of most resettlement projects (1997). Such projects are often justified by their capacity to stimulate economic development and improve living standards for regions or nations. The ethical dilemma posed by DFDR projects was captured succinctly by Adam Curle in discussing the removal of the Chakma people for the Kaptai Dam in Bangladesh. As he put it, there is ". . . a moral problem. How much suffering for how many may be justified by how much good for how many?" (1971, p. 105).

Early efforts to address the extremely negative outcomes of most resettlement projects began in the World Bank in the 1970s. Michael Cernea, the senior sociologist at the World Bank, asked pioneer researcher Thayer Scudder to give to Bank staff a presentation entitled "Some Policy Implications of Compulsory Relocation in Connection with River Basin Development and Other Projects: Impact Upon Low Income Populations." Scudder recommended that appraisal of resettlement needs be done by social scientists during the feasibility study stage. The requirement was subsequently included in the first resettlement guidelines in 1980, drafted by Michael Cernea (Johnston, 2005, pp. 22–23). Shortly thereafter, the Organization for Economic Cooperation and Development (OECD), the Asian Development Bank (ADB), and the Inter-American Development Bank (IADB) developed similar guidelines to regulate their own participation in and to minimize the adverse effects of such projects. These initial guidelines, however, left much to be desired; they allowed borrowing countries to merely restore the living standards of resettled people rather than improve their well-being through development (Scudder, 2005, p. 278). The World Bank continued efforts to refine resettlement guidelines in Operational Directive 4.30: Involuntary Re-settlement (World Bank, 1990), which is the strongest policy the Bank has yet produced. O.D. 4.30 called for minimizing resettlement; improving or restoring living standards, earning capacity, and production levels; resettler participation in project activities; a resettlement plan; and valuation of and compensation for assets lost (World Bank, 1990, pp. 1–2), but it still allowed borrowers the cost-reducing option of simply restoring living standards. The 2001 iterations of Operational Policies/Best Practices (OP/BP) 4.12 were subsequently weakened, providing compensation only to landholders with formal legal title and neglecting to cover a wide range of cultural and psychological impacts (Scudder, 2005, p. 281). Nonetheless, in the opinion of many, the World Bank guidelines came to serve as a standard by which to assess the adequacy of other institutional guidelines as well as actual projects (Koenig, 2001, p. 16). There is also little question that deficient though they may be in many respects, the World Bank guidelines have helped to improve resettlement planning and implementation and to reduce the numbers of people affected by projects. However, as Scudder points out, even the Bank would not claim that income earning capacity and living standards of displaced peoples have been restored (2005, p. 278).

The motivation for the development of these guidelines can be debated. Clearly, the ethical inconsistency of development projects that generated impoverishment demanded resolution. The initiative to develop guidelines paralleled the Bank's overall interest in projects that addressed rural poverty in general (Shihata, 1993). However, the interest in safeguards was surely prompted by a number of key processes and events that took place in the 1970s. The passage, in the U.S. Congress, of the National Environmental Protection Act (NEPA) in 1970, along with subsequent bills for clean water and clean air, inspired U.S. and international environmental activists to urge that NEPA should apply to situations in which U.S. aid was funding development projects internationally. The Carter administration, which had foregrounded human rights as a major pillar in its foreign policy, supported the effort by urging the passage of and then signing the International Financial Institutions Act of 1977, mandating U.S. opposition to loans to governments that routinely commit gross violations of human rights. The act specifically directs U.S. directors of international financial institutions to vote against loans to foreign governments or agencies that the U.S. president has found to be responsible for human rights violations (Johnston, 2005, p. 22; Kapur, Lewis, & Webb, 1997, pp. 477, 760). Since the World Bank president is always a U.S. citizen, voting for loans to governments that commit human rights violations places him in legal peril and opens the door to civil action.

However, according to Escobar, the interest in establishing guidelines was due more to rural protest and resistance and the failure of modernization theories than any transformation in the Bank's thinking (1991, p. 664). While he has a point, Suzanne Autumn cogently points out that, since institutions are rarely gifted with "either superhuman prescience or unalloyed altruism," changes in institutional policy are usually responses to changes in the real world (1994, p. 34). Certainly, the legislative and legal actions taken in the 1970s, particularly by the Carter administration, and the increasing media attention to and public recognition of resistance by local peoples to large development projects constituted just such real world changes. These changes, coupled with sharp criticism of bank financing of environmentally destructive projects by NGOs and other organizations, stimulated efforts to formulate a set of resettlement policy guidelines within the Bank (cf. Clark, Fox, & Treakle, 2003; Fox & Brown, 1998; Rich, 1994).

Based on the research and experience of multilateral staff as well as the work of independent researchers, these guidelines have recently been the subject of examination by researchers concerned with the ethics of development. Ethical scrutiny of resettlement guidelines is centered primarily around the aspects of the projects where ethical errors transpire. For development projects that displace people, Drydyk and Elliot consider the areas of greatest risk of ethical blunders to be (1) the extent of displacement, (2) equity, (3) voluntariness, (4) the consent of indigenous peoples, (5) other human rights, (6) environmental protection, (7) cultural heritage sites, and (8) compliance (2001, pp. 4–5).

While within each of these areas there are many specific concerns that focus on the role of guidelines in safeguarding the rights of people facing resettlement, Drydyk and Elliot are particularly concerned with issues that are not addressed or on which there is less than clear direction or guidance. Despite the fact that these concerns primarily involve problems that the guidelines, which focus on the project level, do not address, they also clearly involve ethical issues beyond the level of specific projects that reveal serious ethical dilemmas at the level of policy and society. These gaps, as Drydyk and Elliot call them, require further discussion.

The baseline concept against which policies and projects that displace people and communities may be assessed ethically is the human right to development, which is most clearly articulated in the United Nations General Assembly resolution 41/128 of 4 December 1986, "Declaration on the Right to Development." This document establishes in general terms an approach to development that goes beyond the economic confines of building productive infrastructure and capacity to which the concept has largely been limited in practice. The declaration adopts a broader and more normatively conceived approach directed at enhancing the well-being of the entire population. In essence, development is conceived as providing the best context "in which all human rights and fundamental freedoms can be realized." Paragraph two of the declaration states that

> development is a comprehensive economic, social, cultural and political process which aims at the constant improvement of the well-being of the entire population and of all individuals on the basis of their active, free and meaningful participation in development and in the fair distribution of the benefits resulting therefrom.

Furthermore, Article 8 asserts

> States should undertake, at the national level, all necessary measures for the realization of the right to development and shall ensure, inter alia, equality of opportunity for all in their access to basic resources, education, health services, food, housing, employment, and the fair distribution of income. (Office of the High Commissioner on Human Rights, 1986)

Under these conditions, it becomes fairly clear that the vast majority of projects that displace and resettle people enter into perilous ethical terrain. As de Wet points out, such projects "simultaneously promote and undermine human well-being" (2009, p. 79). Development projects that displace people are generally narrowly conceived in terms of specific economic returns, whether in terms of electricity generated, water for agriculture, transportation efficiency, or other productivity-related goals, rather than the broader distributive orientation recommended by the United Nations. As opposed to having an emphasis on equity, participation, and well-being of all the population, most projects, until relatively recently, have been characterized by a general disregard for the dislocated population. Even in circumstances in which a resettlement plan has been provided to the people facing dislocation, the vast majority of such undertakings have fallen woefully short of achieving anything like equity, participation, and well-being for the "beneficiary" population.

Thus, besides the issues of guidelines and ethics, we also have to address the issue of limits of competence. In the best of cases, adequate resettlement has been only partially achieved, and those cases are miniscule in number in comparison to the truly awful failures. Guidelines, well intentioned though they might be, will not help if we really do not know how to carry out resettlement projects that benefit the people. There is more than a fair amount of hubris involved in the idea of resettlement. "We" think "we" can do it. But resettlement is not just picking up communities and setting them down somewhere else. It really is trying to replace what has been a historical process of community evolution with an administrative process. In point of fact, resettlement (and the reconstruction of community) may not be something that is entirely amenable to administrative processes. Are there ethical constraints against engaging in actions for which the competence to achieve successful outcomes does not exist? Surely there are in medicine, engineering, law, and other professions and trades in which examinations and licenses establish competence. But competence in DFDR is still informally established. Do guidelines point toward what works or what we should avoid? How do we know "best practices" are best if a good track record of success does not exist? Given that there is a scant established canon based on successful cases, can current projects be considered a form of experimentation masked as development projects? Are there not ethical guidelines regarding experimentation in cases where we are not sure that procedures actually work? Are issues of informed consent as required of scientific research with human subjects not relevant here? Visvinathan, writing on what he calls "the laboratory state," suggests that development becomes a vast scientific experiment energized by the imperative of progress that legitimizes the use of social engineering on all objects defined as backward or retarded. The suffering that such "objects" experience in the process emerges from "the vivisectional mandate" that justifies inflicting pain in the name of scientific progress (1990).

In the matter of "informed consent," the Asian Development Bank's *Handbook on Resettlement* (1998) calls for resettlement and compensation decisions to be preceded by a social preparation phase to build up the capacity of the vulnerable people to deal with the issues. How is this done? How do you prepare people for this? By giving them full information, of course, but does that really prepare them for the trauma of being uprooted and the problems they will encounter in resettlement? There seems to be an unwarranted assumption in the field that the competence exists to carry out these functions. If we do know how to do this well, why have we in fact rarely done it well?

Asking why resettlement so often goes wrong, de Wet (2006) sees two broad approaches to responding to the question. The first he calls the "inadequate inputs" approach, which argues that resettlement projects fail because of a lack of appropriate inputs: national legal frameworks and policies, political will, funding, predisplacement research, careful implementation, and monitoring. Optimistic in tenor, the inadequate inputs approach posits that the risks and injuries of resettlement can be controlled and mitigated by appropriate policies and practices. De Wet, on the other hand, finds himself moving toward what he calls the "inherent complexity" approach. He argues that there is a complexity in resettlement that is inherent in "the interrelatedness of a range of factors of different orders: cultural, social, environmental, economic, institutional and political—all of which are taking place in the context of imposed space change and of local level responses and initiatives" (de Wet, 2006, p. 190). Moreover, these factors are operating simultaneously in an interlinked and mutually influencing process of transformation. And further, these internal factors from the displacement process are also influenced by and respond to external sources of power, as well as the initiatives of local actors. Therefore, the resettlement process emerges out of the complex interaction of all these factors in ways that are not predictable and that do not seem amenable to a rational planning approach (de Wet, 2006, p. 190).

De Wet suggests that a more comprehensive and open-ended approach than the predominantly economic and operational perspective of the inadequate inputs approach is necessary to understand, adapt to, and take advantage of the opportunities presented by the inherent complexity of the displacement and resettlement process. While some might see this perspective as unduly pessimistic, the fact that authorities are limited in the degree of control they can exercise over a project creates a space for resettlers to take greater control over the process. The challenge thus becomes the development of policy that supports a genuine participatory and open-ended approach to resettlement planning and decision-making (de Wet, 2006).

Another major ethical concern, one largely unaddressed by the various sets of guidelines, is displacement by agencies and actions that are not associated with specific projects. Development activities involve many forms and actions beyond specific projects. Government and multilateral bank policies, private sector initiatives, technological innovation, and other agents or forces can result in what has been called "indirect displacement." This form of displacement occurs when the results of policies or actions render it irrational or intolerable for people to continue to live in a home environment (Drydyk & Elliot, 2001, p. 10). Such indirect displacement is often the outcome of market consequences as well, for example, the closing of factories in industrial towns in the United States (Bensman & Lynch, 1987). Closing a factory in one of these towns creates a major crisis, resulting in significant losses, economic hardship, social and psychological stress, and displacement and migration, yet such difficulties are always justified in terms of the workings of the market (for labor, raw materials, transportation, etc.) and the responsibility to company stockholders. The market mechanism is, in some sense, ideologically constructed to contain its own morality, always seen to be operating for the "larger" good but outside the normative constraints that pertain to noneconomic processes. Thus, if people and communities are displaced spatially or structurally by the workings of the market, is there an ethical failure, or is the market ideologically exempt from this judgment? Drydyk and Elliot reason that if project-specific displacement is to be minimized on ethical grounds, it is ethically inconsistent not to demand that indirect displacement, private sector displacement, and policy-induced displacement also be minimized (2001, p. 10). It is likely that advocates of national sovereignty, property rights, and free market efficiency would not be particularly receptive to limitations on agency in these domains because of indirect displacement, particularly in this age of ideology-driven globalization.

However, if current models include within their outcomes direct and indirect displacement as part of the acceptable costs of economic development, such approaches can be seen as ethically compromised. Referring to the human capacity for social cognition, that is, the capacity to imagine the experience of the other, de Wet asserts that forced resettlement has been a massive failure of the imagination. "If the capacity to imagine the other and to make space for the other is at the heart of the capacity to be moral, then forced resettlement has also been a moral failure" (de Wet, 2009, p. 95).

Alternative constructions of the right to development stress smaller-scale undertakings that have less environmental impact, address local priorities, and respect local cultural autonomy and rights. Under these models, one's rights as a citizen include participation in the decision-making that impacts one's life and community. These views tend to emphasize the rights of the less powerful and the significance of cultural diversity over what they consider to be ecologically risky and economically questionable projects.

While the rhetoric that accompanies large-scale development projects frequently makes references to benefits for a general public, those who must suffer the costs that these projects entail tend to be quite specific communities. The costs that these communities are required to bear are often overwhelmingly heavy and at times virtually unmitigatable, given current levels of expertise and competence. It is the fundamental failure of the state and increasingly the private sector to undertake these projects in an ethical and competent fashion that produces conditions generating major forms of resistance.

DFDR Resistance

At some fundamental level, DFDR resistance is a discourse about rights. DFDR pits the rights of the state and, increasingly, private capital to develop against the rights of specific peoples targeted for displacement and possibly resettle-ment. The rights of the state and private capital to displace and resettle have come under increasing scrutiny across a broad front of issues lately. The ques-tion of eminent domain has been subjected to serious scrutiny, particularly in the United States, as local and city governments have met resistance in their attempts to condemn homes and neighborhoods for public purposes only to sell them subsequently to private developers (Carpenter & Ross, 2007). The concept of "national purpose," so frequently invoked to justify the sacrifices of a few for the benefit of an unspecified many is being increasingly questioned as a vague and nebulous concept. The invocation of "compelling and over-riding public interests" provides a loophole of enormous proportions and sub-ject to equally enormous abuses, and many are beginning to ask: Who defines the public interest? Who is the public? How is their interest determined? The need to address these questions has created some strange bedfellows in the politics of DFDR. Libertarians espousing radical individualism and commu-nitarians with more socially based values have occasionally found themselves on the same side of this particular fence.

Human rights groups have challenged the idea that national purpose can continue to be taken at face value. They question whether decisions arrived at through techno-managerial forms of cost-benefit analysis should set priori-ties rather than other standards of judgment such as distributive justice, the right to adequate livelihood, or the right to human dignity (Colchester, 1999, p. 13), particularly when national laws frequently determine, in ways both inadequate and inappropriate, compensation levels for land taken by eminent domain. Many indigenous groups consider themselves to be sovereign peoples whose prior rights over their territories exempt them from eminent domain or at least should provide veto power over development projects on their lands (Colchester, 1999, p. 13).

Since resistance to development-forced resettlement essentially challenges the state and its hegemony over the territory and people within its borders, it may have profound implications for policy at local, national, and international levels. In the sense that involuntary migration and resettlement are part of the means or outcomes of intentional, usually state-driven, development projects and strategies, the phenomenon of resettlement is, therefore, fundamentally a political one, a clash of contesting interests involving the use of power by one party to relocate another.

When people facing DFDR have raised objections, their voices have rarely reached beyond their local contexts—until very recently. People have clearly seen the disruptions and costs that development interventions have signi-fied for their communities, but their objections, even when successful, have often been dismissed as the irrational conservatism of the peasant and the risk avoidance of the poor. Consultation with people to be relocated, prior to initiating planning and design phases of projects, has been perfunctory or nonexistent until very recently, and even then only in exceptional cases. Rarely were the local protests of people included against their will in development initiatives given much credence or respect. In many cases, their protests were denigrated as the ungrateful whining of the selfish who are unwilling to sacrifice for the benefit of the nation (Hilhorst, 2000). Their appeals for less destructive routes toward development essentially fell on deaf ears. Development projects were to benefit all, regardless of what was actually experienced by local people.

Thus, for much of the past 40 years most of the conversations about development, both pro and con, have essentially taken place among elites. However, the counterdiscourse that has emerged in that same period comes from a substantially broader and more diverse base. To some extent, both sides of the discussion share similar rhetorics of social justice and material well-being, but they differ markedly on the deeper philosophical meaning of development as a social goal and the means by which that goal should be achieved. The meanings, means, and implications of development within the discussion reflect the internal heterogeneity of both the development industry and those who propose alternative visions (W. F. Fisher, 1995, p. 8). Emphatically, however, the discussion about development is no longer a top-down monologue by elites, but rather an argument in which many voices from many sectors and many regions are speaking out in protest and resistance. In this era of global communications enabled, in fact, by an expansive technological development, these voices from soon-to-be uprooted villages and neighborhoods now can reach into the halls of power, acquiring allies and challenging proponents of macrodevelopment models that would erase their homes and livelihoods. Some have referred to this process as "globalization from below" (Brecher, Costello, & Smith, 1999).

As I noted earlier, the experience of development has meant for millions of people around the world a separation of local life from a sense of place. Recently, the discourses of triumphant globalization have hailed the emergence of global spaces and the increasing irrelevance of local places (Kearney, 1995). Interestingly, in the midst of the preeminence of the global, there is also an increasing incidence of social movements that maintain strong references to place and territory (Escobar, 2000, p. 141). The uprooted and the social movements and organizations that have taken up their cause under the various banners of human rights, environment, indigenous peoples, and other related issues are now in the forefront of what some have referred to as an emerging transnational civil society (e.g., Fox & Brown, 1998). Posited as an increasingly common feature of world politics, transnational civil society is composed mainly of NGOs and social movements from around the world that focus on a broad spectrum of issues such as trade, democratization, human rights, indigenous peoples, gender, security, and the environment, often in support of local populations and in opposition to the state and private capital (Khagram, 1999). Development projects have increasingly become the sites at which these interests and issues are contested and played out through different models of development and involving individuals and groups from a variety of communities, both local and nonlocal. In the face of efforts to displace them, the poor, indigenous peoples, and other marginalized groups are increasingly choosing to resist in the hope it will prove more effective in protecting their long-term interests than cooperation (W. F. Fisher, 1999).

The uprooted and the resettled have been joined by allies at national and international levels, from communities of activists from human rights, environmental, gender, and indigenous peoples organizations around the world. Indeed, corresponding to the wide array of activities undertaken in the name of development around the world, many of the issues raised by these organizations interweave with resistance to development forced displacement and resettlement and involve an extremely wide range of peoples, organizations, levels, contexts, and relationships that call for greater democratization and more participation of local populations in the decisions and projects affecting them. The argument advanced by these communities and their allies contends, in its most radical form, that large-scale development projects are basically designed to enhance the power of the state and private capital and are incapable of representing or serving the interests of the vast majority of the population.

Since population removal has long been a much-employed strategy of conquest, pacification, and territorial appropriation throughout history, resistance in some form also has an equally long history. Certainly, for as long as dislocation has been an outcome of both public policy and private expansion, there has also been significant resistance. However, the kinds of DFDR resistance that I am most concerned with emerge and assume forms that are uniquely a part of the ideological, organizational, and political climates and discourses of the late twentieth century. Twentieth-century DFDR is distinctive from similar processes in history for a number of reasons.

Certainly unique to the late twentieth century is that DFDR is articulated within the framework of development. That is, displacement and resettlement of specific populations are seen to be essential to the progress of a consciously and "scientifically" based development process. The distinction between development defined in terms of economic growth as opposed to development defined in terms of the expansion of social, economic, and political rights and power to broader sectors of the population has been mentioned. Development clearly involves a continuum of forms or expressions. There are publicly funded projects designed to provide goods and services to a general public. National and state parks and reserves are intended primarily to conserve publicly valued resources. Public funds are used to guarantee loans for private development of natural resources and environments. Wholly privately financed enterprises, such as mines or tourist resorts, are intended to reproduce capital. Moreover, the nature of a given development undertaking is inextricably entwined with the voluntary or involuntary nature of the displacement and migration.

A quick glance at the literature reveals that the vast majority of work in the field of DFDR has been focused on publicly funded, government-driven projects whose aim is to improve the economic and social conditions of variously defined groups of people. The resulting displacement from publicly funded projects is voluntary in some cases and involuntary in others. When the public sector requires land or other resources for public purposes, it is conventionally bound by law to compensate or otherwise provide for those whose land and other resources are being taken. The acceptance of compensation for losses does not necessarily warrant any conclusion about the voluntariness of resettlement. Recently, the greater involvement of private capital in large-scale development projects, sometimes alone and sometimes in joint ventures with the public sector, has been noted and indeed has become the aim of much public policy at both international and national levels.

The involvement of private capital shifts the goal of projects from improving social and economic conditions to enhancing the reproduction of capital in the form of profit, which is also considered to enhance the well-being of the society. Such enterprises are primarily intended to increase the accumulation of capital by private interests, but they constitute and are interpreted and assisted administratively and fiscally by governments as a form of economic development as well. The market and public administration have on occasion acted together to force the displacement of populations. As land occupied by low-income communities increases in value because of surrounding development, the tax rates increase as well. Individual owners may find themselves unable to pay the increased taxes and be forced to forfeit their land or sell to developers at reduced prices. The construction, for example, of large-scale tourist resorts, oil exploration and extraction sites, pipelines, or mines in rural areas often occasions the displacement and resettlement of numerous communities. Such enterprises usually rely on the market to establish land prices that are to serve as compensation for those displaced, although there are cases, such as that of the Rio Tinto Corporation, in which developers have undertaken resettlement projects for communities to be displaced by their mining operations (Rio Tinto, 2001). Where communities are displaced by contamination or other unacceptable conditions created by the enterprise, other forms of compensation may be provided, either voluntarily or through legal mandate.

Generally, people displaced by private development are considered to be voluntary migrants, having accepted a sum of money in exchange for their land. In the dominant ideology, market transactions are seen as being entered into voluntarily by free economic actors. But market transactions often have the effect of disguising the difference between voluntary migration and involuntary displacement. Many factors may influence a decision to accept payment or other forms of compensation for land, not the least of which—in both public and privately driven displacement—are various forms of coercion. Private enterprise projects, with or without government assistance or collusion, may, without legal sanction, withhold crucial information from rural dwellers, depriving them of making informed economic decisions regarding their land. And not infrequently, various forms of violence and other coercive measures are inflicted by private interests, often with the collusion or willful ignorance of governments, on individuals and communities that display reluctance to surrender their land and resources to these private undertakings. For example, a consortium made up of Unocal, Total of France, the Petroleum Authority of Thailand, and the Myanmar Oil and Gas Corporation has employed the military to forcibly relocate people who occupy land in order to completely control the region through which a pipeline will be constructed (Free Burma Coalition, n.d.). The fate of the displaced in these cases is often identical to the fate of those displaced by publicly funded projects with little or inadequate resettlement components. Such a fate is being increasingly resisted by local community organizations in various localities around the world (see Hacienda Looc case study, Chapter 5). Other government organized resettlement projects, although generally better funded than involuntary projects (Cernea, 1999; J. H. Eriksen, 1999), also reveal a variation of degree in regard to the voluntary nature of resettlement. In Bolivia, the U.S.-organized and -funded Zero Option project to combat coca production called for the voluntary resettlement of the peasant population of the Chapare region to other parts of the country, the complete eradication of all coca fields, and the closing of the region to any further colonization (Sanabria, 1993, p. 190). In response, the five tropical federations of Cochabamba organized a 1994 national march from Villa Tunari in the Chapare Valley to the center of La Paz to protest the project (Contreras, 1995, p. 22). Clearly, resistance movements call into question the voluntary nature of much of this "voluntary" displacement. Therefore, the nature of the development project will lead to a determination of the displacement process as either voluntary or involuntary. I would suggest that the forms of resistance that are undertaken by communities be employed as one measure by which the voluntary or involuntary nature of the displacement process is assessed (Oliver-Smith, 2005a, 2006).

The conceptual issue to be addressed here is how resistance is to be defined. The phenomenon of resistance has emerged as a major interest of social science and humanistic research over the past twenty years. As Ortner notes, resistance at one time was a fairly unambiguous concept, connoting an oppositional response to the exercise of domination, which itself was seen unproblematically as a fixed and institutionalized form of power (1995, p. 174). Foucaultian interpretations of less formalized, more pervasive and everyday forms of power and James Scott's work (1985, 1990) on equally "everyday forms of resistance" have complicated the delineation of what is or is not resistance.

Although an explicitly Foucaultian approach to resistance is not adopted here, his work unquestionably informs much of contemporary understanding of power and resistance. Probably the clearest exposition of Foucault's understanding of resistance, at least in his early work, comes from his discussion of power in *The History of Sexuality*. Foucault holds that power is something that pervades all social relations, not just those involving the state or law, which he terms "the terminal forms that power takes" (1990, p. 92). Power is "the moving substrate of force relations which, by virtue of their inequality, constantly engender states of power, but the latter are always local and unstable" (Foucault, 1990, p. 93). While he recognizes that the juridico-discursive form of power is real, he does not think that it encompasses the microlevel complex of power relations that make possible the centralized and repressive forms (Sawicki, 1991, p. 20).

For Foucault, "where there is power, there is resistance," and "this resistance is never in a position of exteriority to power" (1990, p. 93). Just as "power is exercised from innumerable points" (1990, p. 94), there is also a "plurality of resistances," some spontaneous and violent, some interested, compromising, or sacrificial (1990, p. 96), all reflecting the internal diversity of all social groups. Resistances are inscribed in relations of power as "an irreducible opposite." Points of resistance congeal irregularly at varying densities, producing cleavages in both individuals and societies, sometimes mobilizing, sometimes fracturing unities (1990, p. 96), a dimension of DFDR that will become apparent in subsequent discussions. Foucault's later work continues his focus on power and resistance, but also develops a concept of agency and the potential for social change in resistance (Hartmann, 2003; Sawicki, 1991,

p. 100). That is, resistance is not just the irreducible opposite of power, but contains the potential for free subjects to "traverse a field of action in new and creative ways," thus generating and changing consciousness (Hartmann, 2003, p. 10; Fantasia, 1988).

By the same token, James Scott, who acknowledges an implicit dialogue with the work of Foucault (among others) on the normalization or natural-ization of power (1990, p. xv), addresses the "arts of resistance" of subaltern peoples to a public transcript of institutionalized material appropriation, ritu-als of hierarchy, deference, speech, humiliation, punishment, and ideological justification for inequalities (1990, p. 111). In their opposition to the public transcript of domination, subaltern peoples develop a "hidden transcript" to negate and neutralize the material, social, and psychological effects of the public transcript. While Scott in no way diminishes the impact and meaning of the material appropriation, either at the individual or group level, his focus is on the continual humiliations that are suffered by individuals in domi-nated social groups and through which those appropriations are extracted. He wishes to focus on the personal experience of domination and the forms of resistance developed by the powerless.

The hidden transcript of negation and resistance is played out only in the safety to be found among one's peers, who suffer the same indignities. The hidden transcript provides the dominated with a frame in which a sense of order and justice can be reasserted, but it may not be articulated in larger public realms. If the forms of negation in the hidden transcript were expressed publicly, that is, in the presence of the dominant group, it would constitute an act of resistance, even rebellion (J. Scott, 1990, p. 115). Scott's concept of public and hidden transcripts helps illuminate the social and cultural dynam-ics of domination and resistance. The state or, increasingly, private capital, in its very conceptualization of projects that displace communities, expresses its power and its right to exercise that power over affected people. The public transcript of domination is manifest to all, but most especially to those who will be displaced. By the same token, the responses to the public transcript of domination emerge from a violated sense of order, justice, and meaning (Ortner, 1995, p. 180). However, projects that plan displacement often provide contexts for transcripts of negation and neutralization, long hidden in insti-tutionalized patterns of domination, to emerge as forms of active resistance.

Such has been the popularity of resistance in the social sciences, history, literature, cultural studies, etc., that acts of resistance have been imputed to a very wide variety of cultural expressions. Authors far too numerous to men-tion here, construct typologies of, question the authenticity of, dispute the importance of intention in, and explore the social ambiguity and psychological ambivalence of resistance (Ortner, 1995, pp. 175–176). Resistance to DFDR, as will be shown, contains many of the ambiguities and generates ambivalences similar to those of the hidden transcripts. However, it also confronts Foucault's terminal forms of power in no uncertain terms, engaging concrete institutional forms such as the state and market, as well as actual communities and social movements. The social relations of resistance to DFDR revolve around specific, local community issues, although in their evolution they may come to engage with both individual interests and broader, more ideological agendas. DFDR, as will be shown, also involves a continuum of forms, ranging from passive foot-dragging, nonappearance at official sites and times, inability to understand instructions, and other "weapons of the weak" so ably described by Scott (1985) to more overt protest meetings and civil disobedience to outright rebellion and warfare. An important point to realize here is that between the poles of complete passivity (that is, no resistance at all) and active resistance, a variety of motivations, goals, and actions may be present. The lack of overt resistance does not indicate that displacement is at all voluntary. Where governments have a history of abuse and coercion, displacement may be accepted as the only survivable alternative, but it is hardly voluntary and is deeply resented in Scott's hidden transcript. By the same token, there are instances in which active resistance does not indicate a primary agenda of reluctance to relocate. In these instances, resistance becomes a tool of negotiation to increase the levels of compensation.

Research on DFDR Resistance

As diverse as the sites, actions, and people involved in DFDR resistance are, the vast majority of attention has been focused on resistance to publicly funded hydropower projects. The centrality of dams to DFDR research is based on three major factors. First, dams are frequently perceived as the clearest expression of the Western, technologically driven form of development. These "temples of modern India," as Jawaharlal Nehru once referred to them, embody the aggressive, activist spirit of modern society, subduing and harnessing natural forces for the "greater good." Second, large dams perpetrate like few other phenomena a radical alteration, if not the complete destruction, of environments and community sites. The closing of the flood gates of a large dam signals the creation of a large reservoir that deeply impacts or even destroys geological and hydrological regimes both upstream and downstream and disturbs botanical and biological communities in its immediate and extended regions. Human communities are left radically altered, their relationship to their environment disturbed, their livelihoods changed, their lands inundated, and their social fabric disrupted. Finally, dams are expensive. They require enormous investments of capital that usually must be obtained by diverting resources from other forms of consumption and by loans from multilateral, public, and private sources. Financing dams tends to place large burdens on national treasuries, increasing national debts and exacerbating long-term dependency relations. Thus, their modernist cultural centrality and their physical and economic dimensions and impacts have earned dams the vast majority of serious examinations of displacement and resettlement.

By the same token, these same characteristics have also generated significant resistance to dam construction, producing over time large social movements and the most formally constituted resistance organizations. In like measure, then, the most detailed descriptions and analyses of resistance movements have been similarly focused on those confronting dam construction and the resultant displacement and resettlement. Moreover, among dam resistance movements, one in particular, the Narmada Bachao Andolan (NBA) in India, has garnered more attention by far than any other around the world (see case study, Chapter 7). Numerous studies, books, dissertations, and articles, not to mention websites, email list managers, films, and videos, focus exclusively on the NBA and the Sardar Sarovar Project, dwarfing in comparison the discussion of resistance in the rest of the world. The discussion of DFDR resistance to dams and other development projects elsewhere is perhaps most concentrated on Latin America and, to some degree, Southeast Asia. While some documentation exists for Europe and Africa, the volume of materials on DFDR resistance in these sites does not compare with either India or Latin America, particularly Argentina, Brazil, and Mexico. Recent controversies over the construction of the Three Gorges Dam on the Yangtze River in China have generated significant resistance movements both locally and internationally, producing protest movements, pamphlets, books, and websites that articulate opposition to what will be the world's largest dam.

The development impetus in large industrializing nations such as India, China, Brazil, Mexico, and Argentina has led to particularly aggressive programs of dam construction that have, until confronted by concerted resistance movements, run roughshod over the human and environmental rights of affected communities. For example, it is estimated that fully 75 percent of all the people displaced by India's dam construction have not been resettled nor have they received any compensation for their losses (Cernea & McDowell, 2000). Resistance to large dam projects in these nations has tended to garner greater attention because of the scale of the projects, the size of the nations involved, and the democratic forms of governance of those societies, with the exception of China, that give greater opportunity for protest. Large dams have and are being constructed in many other nations, but the attention of both researchers and the media has been limited by such factors as accessibility, the lack of a democratic administration, and the relatively minor political importance on the world stage of the nations involved. In the case of China, whose development projects have displaced millions since 1948 and whose geopolitical importance is undisputed, the relatively small amount of research on resistance to DFDR, in comparison with, for example, India or Brazil, is a function both of the lack of opportunity for protest and the lack of accessibility and available information under the current regime.

Dams, in effect, have become one of the core issues in the debate over human rights and the environment in development. In some sense, dams and the anti-dam movement play an emblematic role for the entire resettlement problem, much as rain forests have for the environmental movement. It is around the issue of dams that a formidable set of multilevel alliances has become organized, capable of creating institutions, challenging governments, and reforming multilateral development institutions. The expansion and success of the global anti-dam movement have led many to consider it as a model or prototype for other forms of resistance. While resistance to other forms of DFDR may learn much from the anti-dam movement, the symbolic and physical centrality of dams to the development process may have made social mobilization against dam construction easier than mobilization around other issues. That notwithstanding, dams share with other forms of infrastructural development a number of core issues of human rights and the environment around which social mobilization can be undertaken for resistance.

Other forms of development-forced displacement, such as conservation, urban renewal, mining, public use complexes, transportation, and pipelines, have received generally less attention as causes of resettlement, although urban renewal in the developed world has been closely examined since the 1950s (e.g., Fried, 1963; Gans, 1962) and more recently, both mining (Rebbapragada & Kalluri, 2009; Minewatch, 2000; Breaking New Ground, 2002) and conservation-driven resettlement have received considerable attention (Brechin, Wilshusen, Fortwangler, & West, 2002; Oliver-Smith, 2009b; Schwartzman, Moreira, & Nepstad, 2000). Generally, resistance to non-dam forms of DFDR has been consequently less documented and analyzed. With the resistance against dams gaining greater support in many contexts, development resources are being allocated toward other forms of infrastructural projects that also displace people. Therefore, there is considerable need for more research not only on other forms of development-forced displacement, but on resistance to such displacement as well. In particular, much greater attention should be paid to privately funded development projects that force displacement and to the resistance movements that confront them (Oliver-Smith, 2001, 2005a). The significance of this form of research will only increase in the coming decades as privatization of previously publicly provided service increases. Indeed, privately funded development directed toward capital growth presents significantly different challenges to resisters, as will be subsequently discussed.

Notwithstanding the imbalance in the contextual spread of resistance research, several other areas of study provide important insights into the nature of DFDR resistance. Most significantly, the growing body of literature on environmental movements, NGOs, and social movements in general offers an array of conceptual tools with which to contextualize and analyze DFDR resistance movements within the broader framework of rights-based mobilization and democratization. As will be more completely discussed later, DFDR resistance movements frequently become participants in a broader front of organized opposition to development as it has impacted peoples and environments. The publications of these movements and organizations themselves, often in the form of newsletters, bulletins, manifestos, and internal reports, produced to both inform the public and broaden their base, are a rich source of information and analysis. Electronic technology has also facilitated the dissemination of information and analysis about DFDR resistance movements. Email list managers and websites maintained by resistance organizations and allies provide almost same-day coverage of activities and events in resistance campaigns around the world. I have drawn on all these resources, published and unpublished.

Recently, confidence in some web-based material has been questioned for its accuracy and analytical rigor. In cases where accuracy is a concern, attempts have been made to confirm points or issues from other sources as well. However, the question of the objectivity of much of the material associated with these struggles is in some ways irrelevant; it is not intended to be objective but to represent a distinctly political perspective and thus serves as primary data for this study. By the same token, a great deal of research by NGOs and independent scholars has convincingly refuted both data and conclusions arrived at by established authorities representing states and multilateral institutions, thus casting serious doubt on the "objectivity," not to mention the empirical and analytical rigor, of the work produced by such agencies. The World Bank's attempt to establish itself as the "Knowledge Bank" has been met with derision in some sectors. The World Bank is in the business of making loans for development projects and cannot be expected to produce impartial information, but it misrepresents itself as doing so.

In that context, then, I consider all information to be inherently partial and political in nature, as must be this book itself. In so far as the discourse of states, multilateral development banks (MDBs), and corporations regarding DFDR claim authority on the basis of their own self-validating power, one of my purposes in this book is to frame the views of local peoples so they can be seen as legitimate in broader contexts outside their communities. Indeed, this goal is also shared by a wide variety of NGOs, social movements, academics, and other allies, including those within state administrations and MDBs.

The Politics of DFDR Resistance Research

I want to close this chapter with a final question about field research and publication. One of the more difficult issues of social research involves the use of information that is gathered and compiled about the lives and activities of individuals and groups. This problem has a long history, but it has become a significant element in contemporary social and policy research, particularly since the early 1970s when a number of projects, such as the Thailand counterinsurgency research and the Camelot Project, pursued and revealed information about informant communities that proved highly damaging to them. Concerns about risk to informants were expressed by researchers exploring the politics of resistance among such groups as the American Indian Movement (AIM), particularly when potentially illegal acts of disruption were being considered as possible tactics in the struggle. Research among populations involved in various illegal economic activities—such as drug production, distribution, and consumption; smuggling; prostitution; or simple retailing without licenses in the informal economy—has the potential of endangering informant communities with legal sanctions or worse.

Such risks must also be recognized for research among resistance movements of various kinds, particularly DFDR resistance. Currently, pending and already approved antiterrorist legislation in many national deliberative bodies around the world is providing ever broader definitions of terrorism that indicate lower levels of governmental tolerance for dissent of many kinds. Amnesty International has appealed, for example, to India's parliament to discard its Prevention of Terrorism bill because they feel it would lead to rights abuses rather than protection (Subramanyam, 2001). Indeed, NGO activists assisting protesters against resettlement from tribal lands by mining interests in India were fearful that the government could use the threat of terrorism against them. "We were in a situation wherein it was easy for the government to use brutal violence and wipe us out and justify their actions by implicating us as Naxalites [an extremist group]" (Rebbapragada & Kalluri, 2009, p. 260). Similar concerns have been expressed about the so-called Patriot Act in the United States. DFDR resisters today run the risk, through the misapplication of antiterrorist laws, of being labeled terrorists and losing their democratic rights of protest against policies and projects that violate human and environmental rights. As Nussbaum noted in 2007, the political climate provided a pretext to the then-current U.S. administration to apply the word "terrorist" somewhat indiscriminately.

Disclosure of movement formation, leadership, and strategizing carries with it the potential of both compromising specific individuals and providing information useful in co-opting, preempting, or disarming DFDR resistance movements. Although most resistance movements are strategically public in their activities and transparent in their goals, in part to contrast with the often covert agendas of projects, which frequently are unwilling to disclose important information relating to planning and schedules, care must be taken in the analysis of DFDR resistance movements to avoid disclosures that could compromise individuals and organizations.

The avoidance of these kinds of disclosures is paramount. However within this constraint, DFDR resistance research can deepen our understanding of development by articulating the perspectives of people who are the objects, and often the victims, of that process. Information about DFDR resistance movements that reaches the general public, potential allies and other forms of support, and the policy-making and scientific communities can help to alter and amend the destructive features of the development process. DFDR resistance research displays and analyzes the important perspectives and critiques that are provided by resistance for a reworking of a development agenda that has deep and abiding problems. Resistance movements directly and through their allies bring into high relief the serious defects and shortcomings in goals, means, policy frameworks, legal options, assessment and evaluation methodologies, and implementation that plague much of the development effort. The most recent final report of the World Commission on Dams (2000) is only one positive outcome that DFDR resistance movements have contributed to through their mobilization. However, the question of how we can explain the emergence of movements and articulate their points of view without compromising them remains difficult and should be in the forefront of the research concerns.

An extremely wide array of participants, movements, forms, strategies, tactics, and goals has emerged in resistance to development-forced resettlement over the last four decades. My purpose in this book is to explore the rights, claims, and visions of the development process that the complex and multidimensional forms of resistance to DFDR express in their refusal to relocate, as well as how these rights, claims, and visions become part of a multi-level and multisectoral effort to critique and reconceptualize the development process. I have attempted to weave together a holistic view of the meaning and experience of DFDR resistance that identifies a number of conceptual, contextual, and exemplary strands that are repeatedly revisited throughout the book in greater and greater detail. The resulting fabric, I hope, provides a more holistic consideration of the problematic nature of the development process.

CHAPTER TWO

Understanding Resistance

Combating the Violence of Development

The rights, claims, and aspirations of people who resist uprooting by development projects are as multidimensional and complex as the projects that threaten them. The kinds of projects that displace people and communities defy easy categorization. Such projects range from the truly gigantic, such as the Three Gorges Dam that will displace between 1.2 and 1.6 million people, to the small expansion of parking facilities outside a New Jersey casino that will displace a multigenerational family business from a traditional location. Similarly, the kinds of people who have been or will be displaced encompass most of the nations, regions, and cultures of the world. There are few regions of the world, north or south, developed or developing, that are not involved in population displacement to make way for projects that express some notion of "development." The resistance of people displaced or facing displacement by development projects also takes multiple forms, some particular to their cultural identity and others more generalized and expressed through global forms of communication. Moreover, the active participation of nonlocal interests in this process—including regional, national and international NGOs; social movements; and transnational networks; as well as multilateral institutions such as the World Bank, the IMF and regional development banks, export credit agencies, and, increasingly, private interests—creates an arena of contestation that defies facile, linear forms of analysis or the reduction of conflict to simple territorial imperatives.

DFDR Resistance: Diversity, Complexity, and Dynamics

The causes of uprooting and resettlement vary a great deal. The form and development of resistance will be shaped in part by the nature of the force or forces threatening a population with resettlement. Some forces are clearly resistible, others permit the possibility of resistance, and still others preclude resistance altogether. For example, forced removal by wartime military forces is difficult if not impossible to resist for unarmed populations. Many environmental conditions, especially those triggered by natural disasters, result in conditions that require relocation because of sheer destruction or because the environment has been made hazardous. Development projects, however, while frequently massive in scale and formidable in political support, present more variable contexts for the possibility of resistance. Development projects are not forces of nature and, at least initially, tend not to resort to military force and violence to achieve their goals of resettling a population. Many tribal and peasant peoples generally interpret development projects as products of a larger society that is the source of a series of broad-scale problems with which they have had to cope or which they have had resist for some time. In effect, development projects present themselves as a form of gradual onset disaster that offers both time and space for contestation.

The projects that involuntarily resettle and displace individuals, groups, and entire communities of people are numerous and varied. The dams, industries, mines, commercial agriculture and mariculture, communication networks, irrigation systems, pipelines, roads, public use facilities (sports complexes, shopping malls, parks, museums, performing arts centers, etc.), tourist resorts, and the processes of urban renewal and gentrification, as well as conservation measures like national parks and wildlife preserves, that constitute the goals, infrastructure, and outcomes of development, all result in the displacement of large numbers of people from their environments and their livelihoods.

The nature of the impact of each of these and other causes of resettlement will vary a great deal, each eliciting different kinds of responses and resistance goals, strategies, and outcomes. For example, the environmental impacts of projects will differ, and those impacts will affect different populations and subgroups of those populations differently, producing different results and different degrees and forms of resistance. The same resettlement project may affect tribal peoples and peasants in different ways, eliciting varied responses of acceptance or resistance from each, depending on their own organizational structure, their experience of the project, their prior experience with the state, and the nature of the losses that each group suffers. Moreover, resistance to DFDR frequently becomes the lead issue for the expression of protest over a complex of issues. As Acselrad and da Silva note, the struggle against resettlement becomes a complex of struggles against the loss of productive resources, against inadequate compensation, against changed relationships with the environment, against non-compliance with commitments made by project authorities, against violence from host populations, and against disrespect for local culture and knowledge (2000, p. 11).

Although the state has been largely responsible for and perhaps the most visible implementer of projects involving resettlement, the private sector is becoming an increasingly major initiator of projects that displace people. Private interests are taking a greater role in financing and developing large-scale infrastructural programs such as dams, mines, housing projects, tourist resorts, and large, urban public use complexes (stadiums, conference centers, etc.) that frequently displace and resettle people. The involvement of the private sector in development projects that displace people parallels its role in the industrial pollution and environmental degradation as side effects of industrial and agricultural development that also are increasingly displacing people (Edelstein, 1988; K. T. Eriksen, 1994; Hewitt, 1997; A. G. Levine, 1982). In the case of mining, for example, relocation is often necessitated by the contamination caused by mine operations as much as the actual construction of the mine itself. In the vast majority of cases of displacement for environmental causes, little assistance in the form of resettlement is offered, and this lack frequently elicits considerable resistance. Much displacement also takes place as an indirect effect of public and private development, often in combination. For example, two outcomes of the construction of the Kariba Dam in Zambia were increased investment in commercial fishing along the northern shoreline of the lake, displacing local fishermen, and the creation of a large irrigation farm in 1985 that displaced over 1600 people more than 25 years after the construction of the dam (Johnston, 2000, pp. 9–10).

As diverse as the forms of development projects that occasion resettlement are, equally widespread and diverse are the forms of resistance, making a simple inventory of instances meaningless, apart from the basic numbers—if they could in fact be compiled. In summary, different kinds of resettlement will evoke different responses, ranging from acceptance to resistance, and within resistance, very different kinds of strategies, tactics, and goals will emerge.

The Diversity of the Displaced

Although the pattern is not uniform, a significant percentage of those who face removal, whatever the cause, come from the most disadvantaged sectors of society. The privileged or powerful of a society are rarely obliged to abandon their homes and communities because the land is needed for infrastructural, industrial, or public use site development. Generally speaking, the political power of elites precludes the possibility of state claims of eminent domain, and the market price of lands owned by the wealthy diminishes its attractiveness for purchase by public or private developments. Since dislocation resulting from development projects occurs first at the level of local community, the variety of peoples around the world facing this challenge is extremely wide, ranging from remote hunters and gatherers, to peasants whose linkages with the state and market have considerable longevity, to the citizens of regional towns and large cities. Although not invariably the case, the communities that must confront the challenge of dislocation and resettlement are frequently from the ethnic and racial minorities of their nations.

Consequently, when development projects, generated by the state or private interests, displace people and communities, the protests and resistance evoked often come from those sectors of a population least heard in a nation's political discourse. Resistance to resettlement, however, is not limited to people whose lives are directly impacted by projects. In the last three decades, the cause of peoples threatened with or actually impacted by resettlement has been taken up on numerous levels by a wide variety of groups and organizations around the world. Local, regional, national, and international nongovernmental organizations (NGOs) and social movements with a wide variety of missions and agendas have joined and assisted in the struggles of peoples around the world to resist DFDR. From the channels accessed through these organizations, information and economic resources are generated and other allies, sympathetic individuals, and groups, are contacted. These groups provide electronic media, including email list managers and web pages, for disseminating information about important events in the struggles of people to supporters around the world within days, if not hours, of their occurrence. This cyberactivism is an essentially new and absolutely revolutionary feature of grassroots political activism. Electronic forms of communication are now an established feature of DFDR resistance (see The Network to Protest the Weakening of World Bank Resettlement Guidelines case study in this chapter).

Complex Responses

The process of development has always met with mixed responses by those affected, ranging from enthusiastic participation, to cautious compliance, to begrudged acquiescence, to protest and armed resistance. Indeed, the responses of people to resettlement are complex. It is not just an issue of some territorial imperative, of reluctance to move, of place attachment, or of inertia. As resettlement is a totalizing experience in its capacity to impact virtually every domain of individual and community life, the responses and motivations for acceptance or resistance are complex and diverse, spanning the spectrum from purely material considerations to the most deeply felt ideological beliefs and concerns (Oliver-Smith, 1996). Equally as diverse, protests and resistance to resettlement by development projects and practices have taken many forms and expressions—passive obstruction, spontaneous protest, fliers, rallies, sit-ins, construction site occupations, teach-ins, courses, films, videos, folk dramas, stories, puppet shows, media campaigns, training programs, email list managers and web pages, road blocks, law suits, restraining orders, lobbying, political party action, conferences and seminars, declarations, hunger strikes, suicide squads, sabotage, guerrilla warfare, and many other strategies and tactics. Such actions take place in villages and towns, at project sites, in state and national capitals, at the offices of multilateral institutions and international organizations, in cyberspace, and at conferences and seminars in schools and universities around the world. Resistance to resettlement involves a diverse array of political forms, processes, and actions of individuals, groups, communities, regions, nations, and international organizations.

Resistance to resettlement also produces a complex array of purposes and initiatives blending environmental, social, political, cultural, and economic concerns that may focus on resisting specific issues or general models of development. Disentangling resistance to resettlement from resistance to other specific project impacts, as well as from a more general form of resistance to development as currently practiced, is a major challenge, but it may also be a false goal since resistance to resettlement often constitutes a first stage in the evolution of a broader offensive against development practice. Displacement is just one of the insults that people must endure when certain forms of development are imposed upon them. By the same token, as will become apparent, it is frequently difficult to distinguish between people displaced by development projects like dams that alter or destroy environments and those displaced by environmental degradation caused by private sector development (Leiderman, 1995, 1997). The line between someone displaced by the inundation of their home by a dam reservoir and someone displaced because their land or air or water has been made unusable by industrial or mining pollution can be a fine one (Clark, 2003). For example, the flooding of agricultural lands for shrimp cultivation by private enterprise in nations as diverse as Honduras, Indonesia, and India has caused irreversible changes in landscape and displaced thousands, with no resettlement plan at all provided (Chadha, 1999; Stonich & Bailey, 2000). In industrial development, a petrochemical plant in the Raigad district of Maharashtra has so polluted the atmosphere that neighboring villagers have been forced to sell their lands and move into the slums of Mumbai (Chadha, 1999, p. 147). The constraints on livelihood practices imposed on peoples who reside in areas recently designated as national parks and preserves constitute an imposed form of environmental change that can be envisioned as a form of structural displacement. Furthermore, people in Honduras displaced by the expansion of export-based production into the fragile rain forest environment of La Mosquitia then become subject to further displacement for conservation purposes (De Vries, 2000). Resistance to resettlement, then, may contain or overlap with multiple agendas and priorities that embrace issues of national security, sovereignty, indigenous and other minority affairs, environmental destruction, human rights, land and property rights, religion and spirituality, cultural heritage, and economic development, to name just a sample of the issues involved.

DFDR Resistance Dynamics

Resistance to resettlement is also extremely dynamic, both changing with conditions and influencing those individuals, groups, and institutions with which it intersects. Indeed, the relationship resistance has with a displacing development project is long-term and evolves over a long period of time. Resistance, in fact, has often been known to appear decades after displacement and resettlement have been accomplished (Jing, 1999;see Yongjing case study, Chapter 6). When people and their resistance organizations encounter development projects, agencies, and national policies, all participants may initiate a process of coevolution, possibly altering the identities, definitions, categories, strategies, and policies associated with resettlement primarily, and ultimately the development project itself (Dwivedi, 1998; Rapp, 2000). Resistance may lead to important changes in resettlement policy and the practices of institutions and states and ultimately a reframing of fundamental questions in development. Alternatively, it can lead to a hardening of government positions, which can in turn lead to increased repression and more violent resistance. In effect, communities and organizations in resistance evolve in response to national governments and multilateral agencies and may in turn oblige those governments and agencies to evolve. Furthermore, people who resist resettlement and their allies are contributing to important reconceptualizations of the development process in general, toward more sustainable, less disruptive, more socially responsible notions of development. By the same token, as will become apparent, in their emergence and evolution these struggles in themselves contain and express all the complexities, contradictions, and dilemmas that development presents as they interact with both allies and opposing interests at a variety of levels.

The Allies of Local Resistance

In its most contemporary forms, resistance to DFDR must be seen as taking place in an era in which an extraordinary growth of organized social action of a wide variety of identities and forms has evolved. There has been a virtual organizational explosion on a global scale, bringing together in alliances and collaborations the widest possible varieties of peoples at differing scales and contexts, contending with a wide array of challenges and problems. This extraordinary expansion of activism has been in part a response, by people of a vast array of identities, to needs and challenges not met or presented by government. The expansion has unquestionably been facilitated by greater access to transportation and communications technology. Resistance to resettlement in its contemporary forms then takes its place as one aspect or dimension of an increasing grassroots activism in collaboration with nonlocal allies who are currently addressing a broad array of issues around the world. This grassroots activism has frequently become linked to a wide variety of nonlocal and even global allies in networks of collaboration to further both local and nonlocal agendas that may or may not always be identical.

As discussed, this complex of linkages and alliances clustered around a specific issue or cause is frequently referred to as civil society, and when the linkages stretch beyond national borders, transnational civil society. Generally, transnational civil society involves citizen-based organizations rather than government- or business-oriented interest groups. These organizations are linked by a shared body of civil norms and values, such as tolerance, trust, cooperation, nonviolence, inclusion, sustainability, and democratic participation. The goal of these alliances and linkages, then, is to engage in actions that further the institutional expression of these values around a specific issue or set of issues (Batliwala & Brown, 2006, pp. 2–3). The resistance to DFDR has become a major issue around which citizen-based organizations espousing both human rights and the environment have formed alliances and undertaken campaigns over the last 40 years.

Resistance to resettlement thus occurs in multiple contexts and environments, ranging from the local project site to regional, national, and international venues in which the issues of development, displacement, environment, and human rights are debated as issues of policy and practice, culture and identity. The complexity of linkages and relations between collaborating and, occasionally, opposing parties brings to the fore problems of coherence, consistency, representativeness, and competing agendas among cooperating entities. The details of these issues will be discussed in later chapters of this book.

The efforts to resist resettlement thus involve people in pursuit of specific goals in organized action in multitiered levels or spheres of political action. While most social actors will have some kind of presence on the site of the development project that relocates people, many of them will establish links to other social actors at the national and international levels. Outcomes of specific actions to further local interests taken in one sphere or level may resonate in sites very distant from the local context. The levels are linked in complex relationships that generate cooperation and conflict both within and among them and that involve participants of widely differing identities and organizational forms. Generally these connections across levels of the social scale enable local resistance groups to access assistance in the form of financial resources, media campaigns, political pressure, or other forms of aid. On the other hand, these alliances can also generate serious tensions and present severe problems for groups affected by the project. Apart from issues of compatibility of agendas at differing levels, widely disparate resources (for example, between northern and southern NGOs) can lead alternatively to a productive symbiosis or outright domination and paternalism (W. F. Fisher, 2009).

Employing the term "fractal" to describe them, Little indicates that these linkages are not organized or mobilized in any orderly fashion but are most frequently irregular and volatile, varying by the historical moment relating to the issue and the strength and density of contacts (1999, p. 10). The term "fractal" has become a way to describe and think about shapes that are irregular, fragmented, jagged, and broken up but that have an organizing structure that lies hidden within the complications of the shapes themselves (Gleick, 1987, pp. 113–114).

The relationships that are established among social actors in struggles to resist resettlement do in fact take on an irregular and occasionally unpredictable character, but these actors are also brought together by the effort to further their common interests involving human rights and the environment articulated across the different levels of scale. In that sense, while the relationships may be irregular and, to some extent, unpredictable, the compatibility of those interests, whether related to halting displacement, improving resettlement, or urging more sustainable forms of development, helps to organize the groups' interactions and channel their efforts toward goals that are similar or compatible. This compatibility is not inevitable, however. One of the challenges facing these interconnected organizations is articulating a coherent and consistent set of interests with such diverse constituencies. Notwithstanding the irregularity and unpredictability of activation of such linkages, resistance to DFDR joins local people to each other in grassroots organizations (GROS) and to others in many other institutional formats such as social movements, NGOS, regional and national governments, multistakeholder processes, multilateral organizations (World Bank, Inter-American Development Bank, etc.), and international organizations (United Nations, European Union, etc.). The many similar activities undertaken by GROS, NGOS, transnational networks, and multistakeholder processes and their frequent concentration in the same physical or structural spaces can tend to blur the boundaries between these different forms of organization (Oliver-Smith, 2006).

Resistance to development-forced resettlement in most cases takes place not in the context of formally constituted governmental or party structure but in the organized collective action of people in communities and/or in groups both local and extralocal. Such organized activities involving a relative degree of continuity over time are designed to achieve a particular goal or set of goals and are manifested in five major forms: Social Movements, Nongovernmental Organizations (NGOS), Grassroots Organizations (GROS), Transnational Networks, and the recently emerging Multistakeholder Processes. These forms vary widely in structure and goals. In some instances, resettlement resistance movements have become subsumed as aspects or dimensions of larger human-rights-oriented social movements. In other instances, DFDR resistance movements have evolved into social movements or NGOS themselves.

Social Movements

Over the past four decades, social movements have become a particularly important form of collective action to promote or resist change as people act on behalf of common interests or values to which they strongly adhere (McAdam & Snow, 1997, p. xviii). However, the term "social movement" must be employed with caution. There are many kinds of organizational activities of a neighborly or communal character that do not qualify as social movements, although in some cases they may form the base or provide the pre-conditions for the formation of a social movement. Social movements must develop a sense of collective purpose and the kind of political goals that involve interaction with other political actors. The political goals of social movements are expressed as claims to rights or are based on the extension and exercise of rights. The demands of social movements in specific situations thus call upon a common language of rights that contributes to the establishment of alliances among them. This language of rights provides the means to organize the elements of social struggle and has found broad application by many different movements in many different cultures. Since this language has shown itself to be very effective in mobilizing support, there is a kind of strategic economy in its adoption and adaptation. The language of rights thus provides a form of "master frame" for promoting effective social mobilization (Foweraker, 2001, p. 4). Since in the modern era the power to grant or withhold rights is vested primarily in the state, social movements make demands on the state. In that sense, social movements seek to mediate the relationship between the individual and the state, particularly in the protection of the individual from state oppression by defending the rights of individuals (Foweraker, 2001). Unlike NGOs or interest groups, social movements must also mobilize their supporters to pursue their goals, although they stop short of guerrilla activity or armed revolutionary insurrection (Foweraker, 1995, p. 4).

The number and scope of social movements increased in the late 1960s in Europe and the United States among groups such as women, students, and blacks, who were not formally represented by specific parties and fell outside of standard class analysis. Since that time, basically two approaches to the analysis of how social movements form and persist through time have predominated. Both schools have tended to focus on analyzing the reasons for individual participation in social movements, so the debate has relevance for DFDR resistance. The earlier theoretical approach to social movements, the resource mobilization school, based on rational choice theory (Hechter, 1987), holds that it is irrational, or at best nonrational, for an individual to contribute to a collective cause from which he or she will derive no benefit, either material or nonmaterial. People are said to form or become members of solidarity groups because they judge that it is in their individual interest to do so. In sum, an explicit individual cost-benefit calculus is said to exist in social movements. People will associate themselves with social movements when they calculate that individual benefits outweigh the costs of joining (McAdam, McCarthy, & Zald, 1988).

However, one of the most persistent issues in social movement research is the tension between the rational calculus of individual self-interest and the bonds of sentiment, affect, and other gemeinshaft emotions in the formation of solidarity groups. Indeed, one gets the distinct impression that in discovering or laying bare the rational basis individuals have for joining social movements, resource mobilization theorists establish the worthiness of such movements and give their members true scientific justification as rational human beings. In contrast, they seem to consign to a kind of emotional, immature, or primitive state of confusion those for whom no rational calculus of cost-benefit can be discovered. In this way, certain kinds of movements based on concepts of collective identity, spiritual values, or aesthetics, such as many DFDR resistance movements, can be dismissed as patently irrational and given short shrift by policy-makers and other authorities (Ferree, 1992).

However effective rational choice theory may be at explaining or imputing a rational calculus to some forms of solidarity, any understanding of the power of expressed affect, such as common identity, to motivate people to collective action is lost on it. In a sense, there may or may not be a rational cost-benefit equation for the mobilization of resources that accounts for solidarity, but such an equation, even if it does exist, also may or may not provide sufficient energy to coalesce individuals. Nor may such a calculation always move people to action. More fundamentally, rational choice may provide the reason for solidarity, but reason may not always move people to action. Research on social movements reflected the recognition of this feature when it shifted from the resource mobilization model (rational choice theory) toward social constructionist approaches, which emphasize meaning, affect, cultural content, and social context (Mueller, 1992, p. 5). Although much of this new social movement research took place among middle-class movements in the United States and Europe, a significant amount of research also focused on urban, women's, indigenous, and peasant movements in Latin America. Failure to understand and factor into its analysis the mobilizing power of emotion expressed through ritual, symbol, and ideology undermines the explanatory power of the resource mobilization approach.

In many contemporary social movements, including resistance to resettlement, it is more than evident that some attempt at synthesis of these two approaches is needed. Material and practical issues mobilize people but so do concerns of identity and affect. In attempting to explore how a collective actor is formed and maintained, Alberto Melucci asserted "only if an actor can perceive his consistency and his continuity will he be able to construct his own script of the social reality and compare expectations and realizations" (1988, p. 340, as cited in Hilhorst, 2000). However, Hilhorst, recognizing the internal diversity of most social movements, sees a difficulty in assuming a unitary collective identity for everyone in a social movement. She suggests that the concept of identification is more helpful for understanding the highly situational and fluid quality of much adherence to contemporary social movements (2000, p. 36). This focus on identification, while not necessarily excluding the concept of identity, better captures the nature of affiliation of the diverse participants in social movements such as those dedicated to resisting DFDR.

Identification with a social movement is constructed around a shared set of meanings (Batliwala & Brown, 2006). Social movements carry, transmit, mobilize, and produce meanings for participants, antagonists, and observers. In "collective action frames," social movements structure campaigns in terms of meanings that have the power to mobilize because they are based on the multiple forms of experience of participants, such as the economic costs, environmental destruction, and cultural losses that people experience in DFDR. These collectively held meanings, framed in a language of rights, serve to dignify and justify the movement (Snow & Benford, 1988). Movement leaders choose symbols that will resonate with the cultural values of the diverse groups they hope to mobilize as well as with the sources of official culture (Tarrow, 1994, p. 122). Hilhorst, basing her contentions on James Scott's concepts of "hidden transcripts" (1990), contends that the process of meaning formulation is much less carefully plotted by leaders and much more nonlinear, negotiated, multipolar, and not necessarily internally consistent or coherent. Those issues and concepts that provide meaningful symbols and actions to participants are more processual and dynamic than unitary phenomena. Scott's hidden transcripts are the narratives that peers exchange in understanding their situation, and, according to Scott, provide the basis for much of the action undertaken by individuals and groups in political contexts (Hilhorst, 2000, p. 37).

Case Study: The International Anti-Dam Movement

The international anti-dam movement began in Europe and the United States during the 1960s and 1970s, particularly as the environmental impacts of dams built between the 1920s and the 1960s began to be perceived and assessed by the growing environmental movement. The anti-dam movement had considerable success in halting the construction of new dams, partially through its effective campaigns and partially through the dearth of good sites for new dams. The decline of big dam construction in the United States, however, signaled an intensification of dam-building efforts in the developing world. Hydrotechnology had been portrayed to the Third World as a source of clean energy and as an essential dimension of development. In effect, technology that was considered damaging and obsolete in the developed world was being exported to the Third World without regard for the destruction and costs it involved. Resistance in the developing world to dam building and DFDR began growing simultaneously with project planning and construction, resulting in the cancellation of dams on the Silent River in India, the Franklin River in Tasmania, and the Kwai Yai River in Thailand in the early 1980s (P. B. Williams, 1997a).

The international anti-dam movement embraces a wide spectrum of environmental and human rights concerns. For example, in the United States there is a strong emphasis on the ecological integrity of environments that are threatened by dams. In May 1979, an American environmentalist named Mark Dubois, a member of the Save the Stanislaus Campaign, chained himself to a boulder in a hidden spot in a canyon in the Stanislaus River in California. The canyon was soon to be submerged by the filling of the recently finished New Melones Dam. The Save the Stanislaus campaign was organized to save one of the last remaining examples of unspoiled California wilderness. All of the life of the canyon, its wealth of archeological and historical roots, its geological grandeur, and the spiritual values embodied there were the focus of the protest (Guha & Martinez-Alier, 1997, pp. 18–19).

Fourteen years later, on another river on another continent, a woman named Medha Patkar decided to drown herself in the waters filling the huge reservoir of the Sardar Sarovar Dam across the Narmada River (for further discussion, see the Narmada Bachao Andolan case study). She and a number of colleagues disappeared into the surrounding countryside to avoid capture before the undisclosed date and place of their suicide. Whether either of these people had heard of the other is unknown, but the parallels in tactics are compelling. Both were part of the ongoing international social movement against dams. Both were willing to sacrifice their lives when faced with the failure of their organizations to stop the dams. Both were saved from suicide when the political system assented to further discussions. It also should be noted that, while both achieved reprieves for their respective rivers, the dam-related damage they were hoping to prevent did occur. Where Dubois and Patkar differed was in their reasons for halting the filling of the dams. In contrast to the environmental concerns in the United States, Patkar and her organization, the Narmada Bachao Andolan (NBA) wanted not only to save the river, but more importantly to resist the displacement of tens of thousands of peasants. The goals of the NBA were not just environmental protection, but a socially just and ecologically sustainable model of development (Guha & Martinez-Alier, 1997, pp. 18–19).

In a broader context, the international anti-dam movement has worked to unite the vast numbers of peoples and communities threatened by dams around the world. Collaborating institutions, including NGOs and GROs, have organized two gatherings of the International Meeting of Dam Affected Peoples and Their Allies. These meetings are integral to the international social movement but have also become known as "multistakeholder processes" (for further discussion, see Chapter 2). The most recent meeting took place in Rasi Salai, Thailand. In late November 2003, representatives of dam affected communities and their allies from 62 nations met for five days in an encampment constructed on the banks of the Mun River near the village of Rasi Salai. The meeting, entitled "Rivers for Life," the Second International Meeting of Dam Affected People and Their Allies, was organized by the Thai NGO The Assembly of the Poor, The International Rivers Network, and the Southeast Asia Rivers Network. Roughly 300 delegates met to strengthen the movement against large dams, build solidarity among dam affected communities, share experiences, and develop strategies for the defense of rivers, environments, and communities facing displacement by the construction of large dams. Also in attendance were representatives of human rights and environmental NGOs, foundation program officers, human rights and environmental law activists, academic researchers, and two World Commission on Dams commissioners (for further discussion, see Chapter 8).

Non-Governmental Organizations (NGOs)

Many of the specific dimensions of social movements may in fact take the form of non-governmental organizations (NGOs). NGOs are not generally social movements but may become allies or parts of social movements. NGOs have become an integral feature of contemporary development policy and practice. Since the appearance of NGOs in significant numbers in the mid 1970s, they have been variously considered as the best means for the distribution of development resources; as the best providers of development expertise; as covert and not so covert agents of the neo-liberal development agenda; as piratical profit-making parasites on both rich donors and poor recipients; as undemocratic, unaccountable, self-selected representatives who exploit their naïve constituencies for power and profit; and as enlightened organizations devoted to progressive environmental and human rights causes and development alternatives. They are all of these things and more. Indeed, the proliferation of NGOs devoted to an endless array of issues over the last quarter century virtually guarantees that they will be very difficult to characterize in general terms.

From the development perspective, NGOs have frequently been seen as catalysts through which local people could become participants in rather than objects of development efforts (W. F. Fisher, 1997). Characterized by specific activist agendas, NGOs in some cases have been accused of manipulation of local communities to further their own visions of development. In other cases, however, NGOs have adopted local priorities and needs as their own and militated effectively for them. NGOs are generally beholden to two fundamental constituencies: donors and communities. They depend on donors for funding, and they justify their roles and actions by the claim that, as *non-governmental* organizations, they can eliminate many of the problems of inefficiency and corruption considered to be inherent in the bureaucratic functioning of governmental agencies. NGOs depend on communities for legitimacy. Since their fundamental model is participatory, without the active involvement of local people, they lose their raison d'etre and become simply top-down development professionals.

NGOs take different roles in displacement/resettlement work. Some NGOs work for the entity promoting the development project in the planning of resettlement communities. Others work to improve the conditions of those communities that have accepted resettlement or have already been resettled. For example, the Indian NGO Arch-Vahini found total opposition to the Sardar Sarovar Project unrealistic and elected to improve the resettlement policy of the Indian states involved and the resettlement conditions of the communities designated for relocation (Dwivedi, 1998, p. 150). And still others work to assist those communities that have chosen to resist resettlement, providing information, media assistance, organizational capacity, and networking and financial resources. The increasing importance of NGOs in development work, including their access to significant financial resources, has greatly enhanced their participation in the various problems in resettlement in general. The expansion of the number of NGOs working in DFDR resistance is largely among those devoted to environmental and human rights issues (see International Rivers Network case study). The linkage of these two global movements, environmentalism and human rights, with the resistance of people threatened with relocation or suffering from poorly implemented resettlement, entails a critique not only of the model of development that accepts the necessity of relocating people for national priorities, but also a questioning of the scale of development interventions that create major disruption for both people and the environment.

Case Study: The International Rivers Network
(Now International Rivers)

As part of the anti-dam movement, the International Rivers Network (IRN) is among those NGOs that stand out for the leadership role it and its staff and members have played in assisting peoples impacted by large-scale water projects, especially big dams. Based in the United States but with offices and staff in many areas of the world, the IRN began modestly. The increasingly active local, national, and transnational struggles around the world against dams led a California-based hydrologist, Philip B. Williams, who had participated in the U.S. anti-dam movement, to establish a collaborative bimonthly newsletter to chronicle and assist the efforts of "citizens organizations that are working to change policies on large dam construction throughout the world" ("Why This Newsletter?" 1985–86, p. 1). Produced by a volunteer group of environmental activists, concerned professionals, and human rights advocates of different nationalities, the *International Dams Newsletter*'s first issue included articles on the Bakun Dam in Malaysia, the Three Gorges Dam in China, and the Silent River and Sardar Sarovar projects in India, as well as recommended readings and an activists' access section. With support acquired from the Tides Foundation and the NGO Friends of the River, 1500 copies of the newsletter were distributed to individuals and organizations in 56 different nations (Khagram, 1999, p. 271).

Response to the newsletter was extremely positive. With the final issue of 1987, the newsletter became the *World Rivers Review* (WRR), and the group formally took the name International Rivers Network (IRN). In its six issues each year the WWR provides extremely current information on all water projects but tends to focus on dam construction, funding, and planning and DFDR resistance movement developments around the world. With the change to the new name, a shift in focus was also adopted. "It is time for us to stop devoting all our energies to fighting individual projects and start developing and promoting a broadly focused alternative view of water management" ("New Directions for River Protection," 1987, p. 2). The following year the IRN organized a global conference in San Francisco on the costs and failures of big dams, which was attended by 60 anti-dam activists and scholars from 25 countries ("Activists Put IRN on the Map," 1988, p. 1). The participants drew up the San Francisco Declaration and the Watershed Management Declaration, the first of several key declarations on dam construction and DFDR the IRN was to play a role in developing. The San Francisco Declaration called for a moratorium on big dam building that failed to adhere to 17 conditions or provisos, such as veto power over the project for affected people, their inclusion in the planning process, free access to information on the project, and guarantees that the project does not threaten protected areas or areas of scientific or educational importance ("New Directions for River Protection," 1987, p. 7). Other results of the San Francisco conference were to broaden the role of the IRN from information clearinghouse to international secretariat, to form an interim steering committee composed of 12 representatives from nine regions (Latin America, the Caribbean, Africa, South Asia, Southeast Asia, Australia, Middle/Near East, Europe, and North America), to establish program priorities, and to establish a network contact in each region to improve communication between local activists and the secretariat.

Since the late 1980s the IRN has grown, developing a professional staff of activists with training in economics, biology, engineering, hydrology, anthropology, human rights issues, and environmental sciences. The permanent staff now numbers more than 20, and it has created an international network of activists, supporters, funders, advisors, and volunteers. Shifting its main offices from San Francisco to Berkeley, it also began to build an impressive library of published and unpublished materials relating to dams, river development, and displacement and resettlement issues. That library now constitutes a major world resource for researchers and activists working on issues of human rights and the environment. The knowledge base represented by staff expertise and the library is fundamental to IRN strategies in combating dams. Since the IRN frequently engages in debate with institutions with vastly greater resources at their disposal, such as the World Bank, they take great care in getting their facts right. Indeed, the accuracy and completeness of IRN reports is often far superior to that of similar documents produced by much larger institutions. For example, after the World Bank conducted an investigation that exonerated itself of any responsibility for the massacre of over 400 Mayan resisters of the Chixoy Dam in Guatemala, the IRN initiated and helped support the five-volume study (Johnston, 2005) that is helping the affected communities get reparations for their losses. In another context, the IRN critique (McCully, 1997) of the World Bank's review of dam impacts (World Bank Operations Evaluation Department, 1996) seriously questioned the data, arguments, and overall quality of the review, faulting it for lack of data, unsubstantiated claims, lack of evidence, failure to deal with key issues, and misleading statements. The critique proved so effective that it became a major factor in the eventual formation of the World Commission on Dams. *Silenced Rivers* by Patrick McCully (1996), who is currently the director of International Rivers (IR), has also been hailed as one of the most incisive critiques of hydropower development.

IR challenges large-scale water development projects on a wide variety of fronts. It cooperates with numerous other NGOs concerned with environmental issues to further campaigns for more sustainable forms of development. IR also works with other human rights NGOs in campaigns to redress violations of the human rights of displaced groups of people as well as individuals, often NGO and GRO DFDR resistance leaders who have been abused, detained, or imprisoned. It coordinates numerous campaigns, interfacing with local organizations and providing consultation and training in organization and mobilization for local activists throughout all phases of a struggle against a dam ("Guardianes de los rios," 2000a). In the view of some, the IRN's position opposing all large dams was too fundamentalist and unrealistic, ignoring benefits that dams might offer in efforts to alleviate poverty and enhance development (Scudder, 2005, pp. 129–268). The issue of opposition to all dams as opposed to only destructive dams was a topic of some heated discussion at the Second International Meeting of Dam Affected Peoples and Their Allies in Rasi Salai, Thailand (for further discussion, see Chapter 8).

IR also participates in efforts to reform the multilateral development banks (MDBs) that are key funders of dams. The pressures exerted on the MDBs include using public input to improve the internal guidelines and regulations of the particular institutions so as to establish standards to which they may be held accountable, and providing information on negative outcomes of MDB-funded projects to convince national governments to withhold funds to the MDBs for such projects. With the increasing privatization of funding for large infrastructural projects, IR has developed similar strategies to attack funding sources. One campaign called for a boycott of the Discover credit card, whose parent company is assisting the funding of the Three Gorges Dam in China. The campaign featured a tourism-like brochure entitled "Discover Three Gorges," emblazoned with the logo and colors of the Discover credit card issued by Morgan Stanley Dean Witter, one of the world's largest investment bankers (40 billion dollars in capital assets) and a key underwriter of bonds for the China Development Bank, a primary funder of Three Gorges. The brochure contained key information about and photographs of the environmental destruction and enormous displacement of people that the Three Gorges Dam will create in the Yangtze River Valley. In addition, the brochure contained a letter to the CEO of Morgan Stanley Dean Witter announcing the signer's intentions to boycott the Discover card until the company ceases to fund Three Gorges (IRN, 2000). The brochure was part of a larger campaign to stop investment in the Three Gorges Dam and to pressure investment firms to become more environmentally and socially responsible. The website for this campaign was called www.floodwallstreet.org.

In 2007 the IRN changed its name to International Rivers (IR) because, as stated in an email to supporters, they realized that, although originally intended to be a network, the organization had really never been one (http://www.internationalrivers.org/en/new-look-the-song-remains-same). It had always been an individual organization. In addition, as a result of building a dam affected peoples' movement and the work done on the World Commission on Dams process, the organization had moved away from opposition to all dams, preferring to challenge those projects that violate human rights and are environmentally harmful. The spectrum of issues now addressed by IR has also broadened. For example, their current work in China is directed towards improving and implementing safeguards for human and environmental rights on projects within China, as well as working for the application of Chinese human/environmental norms in projects financed abroad (Jun, 2005, p. 12). One of their major issues in 2008 was the Kyoto Protocol's Clean Development Mechanism (CDM), intended to reduce carbon emissions through rewards to countries that invest in clean technologies. IR asserts that the CDM is not only increasing greenhouse gas emissions, but constitutes a handout of billions of dollars to dam, chemical, coal, and oil interests for projects that would have been built anyway.

In slightly less than 25 years International Rivers has become a key contributor in placing the issue of dams and other destructive river development projects in the center of the global environmental debate. Although initially the IRN was mainly an environmental organization, it very rapidly began to appreciate the major human rights violations that accompanied certain forms of river development and soon integrated the human rights issues associated with water projects into its mission and agenda. In many ways, IR is among a few key organizations that stand at the intersection between the environmental and human rights movements, recognizing the important relationship between the two and working simultaneously for both. According to Philip B. Williams, "IRN had evolved into a structured organization and our vision had expanded and changed. While our analysis of the problem remained the same, we now understood that the destruction of rivers was as much a social and human rights issue as environmental. We started to see the importance of dams as centerpieces of an inappropriate development ideology and realized we could use dam fights as important weapons in a larger war against institutions like the World Bank or against dictatorial governments" (1997a).

Grassroots Organizations (GROs)

Grassroots organizations (GROS), also called "base groups," "people's organizations," and "local organizations," are membership organizations dedicated to the improvement of their own communities (J. Fisher, 1996, p. 60). GROS have deep social and cultural roots, many evolving from village councils, burial associations, water boards, religious brotherhoods, and other traditional local organizations. Communal labor exchange institutions such as the *faena* or *minka* of the Andes, *pana-pana* among the Miskito of Nicaragua, *torcapeon* in northern Spain, and others too numerous to mention also may provide the cooperative basis for the creation of more formalized organizations. In the last three decades there has been an extraordinary and worldwide expansion of such groups in response to the worsening social conditions associated with the widening disparity between the rich and poor, environmental destruction, the oppression of women and minorities, the debt crisis, AIDS, and the generalized uprooting of communities by both rural and urban development. Also associated with the growth of GROs are the more acute events such as wars, political oppression, and natural disasters. Not always formed as reactions to calamity, many GROs have taken the form of migrant associations formed to assist the development of home communities. During this period of time, tens of thousands of GROs have been created all over Asia, Latin America, and much of Africa. For example, most of the estimated 30,000 Latin American squatter settlements have each created their own GROs. Estimates put the number of GROs at 12,000–15,000 for the Sahel countries of Africa alone (J. Fisher, 1996, p. 60).

Frequently, new GROs are formed due to the inability of government to provide basic services such as health care, education, roads, or credit. In some cases GROs will address the needs of only a subgroup within a community and hence cannot always be assumed to represent every constituency. In recent years there has been a tendency, particularly for successful GROs, to expand their agendas to include larger, extralocal concerns as well. An important element in the development of new GROs is the increase in the numbers of migrants, sometimes the children of migrants, who acquire education and experience in larger contexts and then return to home communities either to found a GRO or assist an existing one to develop new resources and agendas. Often referred to as "Gramscian organic intellectuals," these individuals play key roles as brokers or bridge people between local organizations and outside sources of support (Rothman & Oliver, 1999, p. 43). GROs have also been known to evolve into both NGOs and social movements.

Case Study: The Movimento de Atingidos por Barragens: From a Local GRO to a National Social Movement

Due to the oil crisis of the early 1970s a great many oil-import dependent countries, Brazil among them, began to explore hydropower projects as a means to both relieve their import burdens and achieve energy self-sufficiency. The context for the beginning of Brazil's hydropower experiments was an authoritarian military government that had been in place since a coup in 1964. The regime was run by an alliance of technocrats and military hardliners who believed that economic growth in the short run could not be achieved in an open political system. The economic model the alliance depended on for developing the nation was based on the centralization of resources in large state enterprises that would produce the infrastructure necessary to attract foreign investment capital. Enormous infrastructural projects such as the Itaipu Dam, the Carajas mining project, and the Trans-Amazon Highway were constructed at the expense of social investments in health, education, and housing and with grievous consequences for populations displaced or otherwise impacted by the projects (McDonald, 1993, p. 82).

Energy development, production, and distribution in Brazil are the responsibility of a state agency, ELETROBRAS (Centrais Eletricas Brasileiras S.A.), which has regional subsidiaries such as ELETRONORTE (Centrais Eletricas do Norte) and ELETROSUL (Centrais Eletricas do Sul). In the late 1970s ELETROSUL, one of the earliest subsidiaries to initiate major projects, proposed a series of 25 dams for the Uruguai River Basin in the southern states of Santa Catarina and Rio Grande do Sul. Initial estimates of population displacement were approximately 36,000 people from mostly small villages and rural areas. The citizens of the region put the estimate closer to 200,000. With assistance from the local university and a union, they asserted that the dams were unnecessary because Brazil was still not consuming all the energy it was producing at the time. In the initial period, ELETROSUL displayed an extreme lack of consideration for local people, refusing to discuss the project with them and disregarding the stress that the prospect of displacement was generating (McDonald, 1993, p. 85).

When it became clear to the people that ELETROSUL did not intend to resettle them, much less have an actual plan, they began to organize meetings to discuss the problem. With the assistance of the Catholic Church, rural union leaders, and some university people who had access to information about the dam projects, roughly 150 meetings were held in communities in the region in 1978 and 1979 (McDonald, 1993, p. 86). The support of religious organizations linked the protesters to two NGOs in Germany, MISEREOR (The Campaign Against Hunger and Disease) and Bread for the World, that offered economic assistance. The meetings eventually coalesced to form a new organization: on April 24, 1979, 350 farmers and the allied representatives of the Catholic Comissão Pastoral da Terra (Pastoral Land Commission), the Evangelical Lutheran church, the rural unions, and the local university created the Comissao Regional dos Atingidos de Barragens, CRAB (Regional Commission of People Affected by Dams). The collective identity of *atingido* was actively constructed and revised throughout the struggle to define who was a member of the affected population and who were allies (Rothman & Oliver, 1999, p. 44).

Initially, the atingidos were not opposed to the dam. They simply wanted to receive fair compensation for their losses. However, ELETROSUL's steadfast refusal to meet with or supply a minimum of information about the project to the people facing resettlement convinced them that further action was necessary. To keep the affected communities informed, CRAB began to publish *A Enchente do Uruguai, (The Flood of the Uruguai)*, a newsletter that appeared irregularly. The newsletter ultimately proved to be an important organizing tool (McDonald, 1993, p. 87).

The consistent failure of ELETROSUL to deal with the public's concerns led the legislative assembly of Rio Grande do Sul to organize a public forum to discuss the Uruguai River Basin project and its impacts. ELETROSUL's representatives again failed to satisfy the queries of the delegates, provoking them to publicly express their opposition to the project. The lack of respect so evident in ELETROSUL's refusal to discuss the project convinced CRAB to raise the intensity of the conflict. CRAB and its members refused to be rendered invisible. The public forum signaled a shift for CRAB from a position favoring negotiation of compensation to outright opposition to the dam. In October 1983 they undertook a petition drive that eventually gathered over 1 million signatures of dam opponents. In the process they acquired other allies, such as the Federation of Agricultural Workers (FETAG). They also began to develop contacts with the victims of other dam projects: Itaipu, Passo Real, Salto Osorio, Salto Santiago, and eventually Paulo Afonso, Moxoto, and Itaparica in the Northeast. The terrible losses of the people affected by Itaipu and Itaparica helped to forge important alliances for CRAB. The video made about the experiences of the people displaced by Itaipu proved to be an important recruiting tool. The strategic posture adopted by CRAB appeared in *A Enchente do Uruguai:*

> It is not enough to promote or participate in negotiations to guarantee our right to remain on the land. It is necessary to broaden the fight, occupying all of the possible spaces in the newspapers, radio, television, local government offices, schools, in conclusion, to take our message everywhere of why we fight against the dams (as cited in McDonald, 1993, p. 89).

Over 100 meetings were held throughout the region to discuss the project and the implications of CRAB's involvement in the struggle. CRAB was intent on building a strong base of support through democratic means. A general assembly was held. CRAB and its member communities began to adopt more aggressive postures in the mid 1980s. Reservoir markers were destroyed in ceremonial bonfires; a coffin full of protest signs was burned; people marched, and highways were blocked. On one occasion 50 farmers from the Ita Dam region entered the worksite of the dam and captured one of the chief engineers, forcing him to stop work for a week (McDonald, 1993, p. 95). Further captures of ELETROSUL workers in the region took place after a July 1987 deadline for a concrete resettlement plan passed without results. Later that month CRAB organized a mass meeting of 5,000–7,000 farmers; they surrounded the ELETROSUL offices in Erexim, demanding that a meeting with the president be scheduled or they would burn the building down. A representative group of atingidos was allowed to speak to the president, and a meeting was scheduled at which a resettlement agreement was eventually signed (McDonald, 1993, p. 96).

Part of CRAB's success was based on the support it had begun to acquire from other peasant movements in the region and from national and international movements. Communication was established with the Movimento sem Terra (the Landless Movement), the Polo Sindical (a rural trade union consortium established to contend with the regional power company building the Itaparica Dam), and through these to the rubber tappers movement (National Council of Rubber Tappers) in the Amazon and the Environmental Defense Fund internationally (Rothman & Oliver, 1999, p. 53). In establishing these ties and linking their class-based land concerns to environmental issues, CRAB positioned their cause as part of a larger struggle for land by rural people confronting the socially and environmentally destructive forces of capitalist expansion (Rothman & Oliver, 1999, p. 41). CRAB took a major role in organizing the First National Congress of People Affected by Dams in Curitibe, Brazil, in 1991. It was at this meeting that the national movement MAB (Movimento Nacional de Atingidos por Barragens [National Movement of People Affected by Dams]) was created. CRAB became one of five regional member organizations and was renamed MAB-Sul (Movement of People Affected by Dams-Southern Region).

Since its successes against ELETROSUL in the 1980s, CRAB (now MAB-Sul) has taken increasingly important roles nationally and internationally in human rights and environmental issues. In 1992 at the United Nations Conference on Environment and Development in Rio de Janeiro, CRAB and other allies persuaded environmentalist organizations to allow organizations without explicit environmental agendas to participate in the forums, thus creating a context for the formation of further alliances between environmental

Protestors march during the First International Meeting of Dam Affected Peoples and Their Allies in Curitiba, Brazil. (photograph by Glenn Switkes)

and class-based organizations (Rothman & Oliver, 1999, p. 54). In 1997 MAB and MAB-Sul collaborated with the International Rivers Network in holding the First International Meeting of Dam Affected Peoples and Their Allies, in Curitiba. MAB and MAB-Sul also participated in planning public hearings held by the World Commission on Dams in Brazil in 1999 (Rothman & Oliver, 1999, p. 53).

Another key element in both the growth in GRO numbers and the expansion of GRO agendas is the increasing availability of outside support from national NGOs and social movements. International aid from governments and multilateral organizations has also been available to support the growth of local organizations. The availability of outside economic support, for example, has made it possible for GRO leaders and members to participate in the many international conferences and meetings held to discuss the problems of development around the world. The spread of computers has made it possible for local organizations to communicate with each other throughout nations and across borders and oceans. Thus, DFDR affected people around the world can now share with each other over the Internet and their websites the knowledge they have gained in land and resource disputes with provincial and national governments. Indeed, communication technology and support for travel have enabled regional networks of individual GROS to form, and, in some cases, such as the aforementioned MAB in Brazil, these networks coalesce and form NGOS or national social movements. And, in turn, the new NGOS and social movements become parts of transnational networks, which constitute a fourth organizational form in which DFDR resistance is carried out.

Transnational Networks

The most recent resettlement resistance organizational form to emerge, networks are composed of dynamic, multiple, reticulated transnational linkages. The term "reticulated" is key here. *Reticulum,* deriving from Latin for *network,* is a biological term referring to cells that form an intricate interstitial network, ramifying through other tissues and organs, connecting many points that are not necessarily of similar identity (Kearney, 1996, p. 127). Facilitated by the rapid expansion of information technology, networks include individuals, NGOS, GROS, and social movements and often blur the distinctions between the sub-national, international, and transnational (Kumar, 1996, p. 42). Networks are most easily formed on the Internet and when they cluster around political issues. In effect, politics takes place in a new venue. The Internet, the global "network of networks," has become both means and context for non-state organizations to pursue their goals in what a Rand Corporation study has referred to as "netwar." Netwar, when it applies to efforts in conflicts between states to disrupt, damage, or change what a population knows or thinks it knows about itself, is in some ways simply high-tech propaganda. However, the Rand Corporation study also suggested that "it (netwar) may be waged against the policies of specific governments by advocacy groups and movements involving, for example, environmental, human rights, or religious issues. The non-state actors may or may not be associated with nations, and in some cases they may be organized into vast transnational networks and coalitions" (Arquilla & Ronfeldt, n.d., as cited in Kumar, 1996). Individuals, interest groups, organizations, and national governments employ the Internet to find each other, communicate information, discuss issues, and press their political agendas, and in doing so, they have helped to change the world system from a traditional "state-centric" world to a "multicentric" world in which governments no longer entirely control specialized information nor entirely set the political agenda (Rosenau, 1991). Particularly in the areas of environment and human rights, networks now play increasingly significant roles in policy discussion and formation.

Networks challenge efforts to formally define or succinctly delineate their characteristics. In some ways, it is helpful to try to define a network in terms of what it is not as much as in terms of what it is. To a certain extent, they resemble social movements in their abilities to mobilize large numbers of people on behalf of their goals. However, networks may include formal organizations and sometimes members of governments. Networks have been referred to as "social movement organizations," but since they lack any vertical structure, any hierarchy of officials or departments, the term is misleading. Networks are composed of horizontal linkages between their members, with no one node in the network having decision-making power over any other. Networks are not social movements either. Social movements generally work to change their society in some fundamental way so as to alter the power structure. Networks, by sharing information and strategies among many people, work toward maintaining a constant capacity for changing specific policies when the need arises. Networks cannot be defined as campaigns either. When a policy debate arises, networks undertake campaigns to address the issues, but the network changes with the issue. Thus, networks cannot be defined solely as issue areas since issues also change (Kumar, 1996, p. 23).

One significant feature of networks, particularly those associated with environmental and human rights issues, is the broad array of constituents that adhere to them. In particular, two different kinds of activists stand out. First, these networks draw upon a community of scholars and experts who employ the scientific and technical knowledge base to broaden the existing discourse on particular problems. Secondly, networks depend on grassroots activists, often members of social movements, NGOs, or GROs, who take more challenging stands on issues and confront powerholders more directly (Kumar, 1996, p. 32). These two groups definitely overlap, with members from each not infrequently taking on the roles and functions of the other.

Still following Kumar (1996), it may be best to define a network in terms of what its constituents are able to do politically. First, network constituents can develop information technology options to transmit information rapidly throughout the network. Second, network constituents can develop media visibility and policy relevance for their issues. Third, network constituents can maintain a coherent structure despite the lack of a hierarchical system of organization. Fourth, network constituents can promote agenda-related changes in the discourses on key issues. And finally, network constituents can promote national and international linkages among diverse issues to build momentum toward their goals (Kumar, 1996, pp. 26–27).

Case Study: The Network to Protest the Weakening of World Bank Resettlement Guidelines

In early 2001 a transnational network formed to protest the weakening of the World Bank guidelines (O.D. 4.30) on resettlement. The draft policy (OP/BP 4.12) was seen to be significantly weaker than the existing guidelines and inconsistent with international human rights and sustainable development standards. The recipients of the email "action alert" were asked to contact the president of the World Bank and the Board of Executive Directors to urge them to reject the draft on the grounds that it weakened the rights of marginalized groups, including indigenous peoples, those affected by parks and protected areas, those who lack nationally recognized title to their lands, and those who suffered from indirect effects of projects. Contact information for the president, vice president for sustainable development, and the executive directors was provided. Leaked drafts of the proposed policy were subsequently provided as well.

When the Bank published the draft on its website in March 2001, it stated that the draft was being posted for information only, not for comment. The Bank expected to send the draft for approval to the full board of executive directors. However, after reading both the leaked copies and the posted draft, NGOs got the word out that the proposed draft would weaken the rights of affected communities, especially indigenous peoples and others who lack nationally recognized title to their lands and resources. Further criticisms included the Bank's emphasis on compensation rather than development, the distinction drawn between direct and indirect costs, and the exclusion of costs "of reintegrating and restarting disrupted economies, social institutions and educational systems" (Downing, 2002, pp. 13–14).

Shortly thereafter, a sign-on letter from the Center for International Environmental Law and the International Rivers Network to the president of the World Bank was sent out, urging people to add their names and organizations to the signatories. The letter detailed the losses experienced by people resettled by World Bank projects and asked for reconsideration of the sections of the draft policy that weakened protections for vulnerable groups, indigenous peoples, people indirectly affected by projects, "voluntary resettlers," and people affected by conservation projects, as well as asserting the inadequacy of income restoration strategies in resettlement projects. The letter was signed by representatives of 125 organizations and 33 distinguished individuals from 26 countries.

Subsequent messages stated that the Bank had been flooded with thousands of letters expressing concern and was being forced to step back from the

March draft. Both the president and vice president made very public statements declaring that the Bank was fully committed to its safeguard policies and that it would not weaken them. On April 26, the vice president stated that the Bank would revise the policy again and send it back to a subcommittee of the board, the Committee on Development Effectiveness, for further work.

Network organizers were cautiously optimistic in urging participants to keep up the pressure, noting that the Bank had refused to consider World Commission on Dams recommendations in either the resettlement policy or the indigenous peoples policy. An August 2001 message urged participants to "capture the attention" of executive directors to demand further substantive changes in the resettlement policy before it was approved. Although the message acknowledged that their efforts had been rewarded with some improvements in the draft, there were still many problems with the policy regarding indigenous peoples and resettlement. In another August 2001 message, the language of the policy was characterized as "implicitly permissive of the displacement of indigenous peoples, even if it threatens their cultural survival and even if replacement land is not offered." In early October 2001 the network published news that the Bank's board of executive directors would consider the new version of the draft policy on October 23. On October 10, 2001, another letter was sent to the new executive director of the Bank, highlighting the problematic areas in the draft revision.

However, despite some success at altering some of the language of the draft policy, the effort met with disappointment when the executive board of the Bank approved the revision of the Bank's resettlement policy on October 23. Resistance in the Bank to changing from income restoration to improvement was based on the failure of the existing guidelines (O.D. 4.30) even to reach the goal of restoration (Scudder, 2005, p. 283). Some borrower nations had also made it known to the board of directors that they felt the tougher guidelines infringed upon their sovereignty. A final message to the network characterized approval of the policy, now known as OP/BP 4.12, as a disappointing outcome but stressed that efforts toward an independent and credible review of resettlement practice would be pursued.

Multistakeholder Processes and Other Initiatives

In the last decade a variety of initiatives to address issues central to displacement/resettlement have emerged from the intersection of numerous communities and institutions. Initiatives such as the World Commission on Dams, the United Nations Permanent Forum on Indigenous Issues, and the Extractive Industries Review draw on international expertise and try to integrate the perspectives of multiple sectors to undertake some kind of process, whether it is knowledge- or action-based, relating to the forms and scale of development, its environmental and social impacts, and the rights and obligations of the parties involved in development-forced resettlement. Often organized and financed by multilateral institutions, such as the World Bank, in response to pressures from NGOs, social movements, transnational networks, and other civil society agents, these multistakeholder processes may focus on a specific industry, sector, or process to document impacts and outcomes and recommend policy options and alternative practices. Other initiatives that have emerged in the last decade include the Equator Principles and the World Bank Inspection Panel (see Chapter 7).

Case Study: The Extractive Industries Review (EIR)

During the annual meetings of the World Bank-International Monetary Fund in Prague in June 2000, a number of NGOs strongly criticized the Bank for its involvement in extractive industries. The response of the president was to suggest the creation of "some mechanism [by which] we can stand back and take a look at the actualities of this extractive industry, the pros, the cons." Roughly a year later the Extractive Industries Review (EIR) was organized by the joint efforts of the International Finance Corporation (IFC), the World Bank Mining Department, and the World Bank Oil, Gas and Chemicals Department. The objectives of the EIR were

1. to better obtain and understand the views of stakeholders about the best future role of the World Bank Group (WBG) in the extractive industries if it is to promote sustainable development and poverty alleviation
2. to identify possible areas of consensus on the role of the WBG and the relevant issues, and to identify significant alternative or dissenting views in this respect
3. to make recommendations on the basis of such better understanding to focus, redesign, or reconsider, as needed, future WBG policies, programs, and processes in the sector (*Striking a Better Balance*, Vol III, 2004, p. 2)

All stakeholders—governments, civil society represented by NGOs, indigenous peoples organizations, affected communities and community based organizations, labor unions, industry (oil, gas, and mining companies), academia, international organizations, and the WBG itself—engaged in a constructive dialogue based on the principles of inclusiveness, transparency, independence, and relevance. The process involved holding a workshop in each of five regions (Latin America and the Caribbean, Eastern Europe and Central Asia, Africa, Asia and the Pacific, and the Middle East and North Africa), each preceded by an open forum in which testimony by representatives of civil society would be offered regarding the human rights and environmental performance and impact of World Bank-funded projects in the extractive industries. A final report was delivered to the WBG president in January 2004. In effect, the EIR was modeled on the World Commission on Dams. It had similar financial support; a review panel that included industry, the financial sector, scientists, affected peoples, and NGOs; and the goal of developing a best practice code that could be adopted by international financial institutions, governments, and industry.

In the final report, the EIR concluded that extractive industry companies are discovering that resettlement is not a good solution but that it is too frequently chosen when communities occupy land to be explored or mined. The report further noted that WBG policies on indigenous peoples and involuntary resettlement permit forced resettlement but that current safeguard policies have been unable to ensure that no harm is done, noting a high level of discontent in all areas but especially among civil society, academic researchers, and indigenous peoples (*Striking a Better Balance*, Vol I, 2004, p. 36). Secure, effective, collective ownership rights of land, territories, and resources for indigenous peoples were seen as particularly important for cultural and physical integrity as well as for poverty alleviation and sustainable development. Noting that indigenous peoples have repeatedly repudiated the WBG revisions of its policy on indigenous peoples, in which WBG staff and borrowers are not required to recognize or respect indigenous peoples' property and other rights (*Striking a Better Balance*, Vol I, 2004, p. 41), the report recommends that the WBG should obtain freely given prior and informed consent before resettlement takes place (*Striking a Better Balance*, Vol I, 2004, p. 55).

The final conclusion of the EIR sustains WBG participation in extractive industries but only in the context of poverty alleviation through sustainable development. Three basic conditions are required to make that process viable: (1) Pro-poor public and corporate governance; (2) more effective social and environmental policies; and (3) respect for human rights (*Striking a Better Balance*, Vol I, 2004, p. xii). However, the EIR further asserts that the WBG is not organized effectively to facilitate and promote poverty alleviation in the extractive industries, faulting the institution for being more committed to the economic aspects of development than to the social or environmental features of the process (*Striking a Better Balance*, Vol I, 2004, p. xii). Despite the criticism of World Bank participation in the extractive industries, the EIR was not met with resounding approval from some sectors of civil society. The review of the EIR by consultants from the Forest Peoples Programme and the Tebtebba Foundation found fundamental problems in the decision-making process within the WBG that lead to lending goals subsuming other objectives. Furthermore, the weakness of WBG safeguards, its institutionalized resistance to invoking human rights standards, and its frequent disregard for its own regulations convinced the consultants that the World Bank should withdraw from participation in the extractive industries sector (Caruso, Colchester, Mackat, Hilyard, & Nettleton, 2003, p. 5).

Resistance to Resettlement as a Complex System

Clearly, the multiplicity of phenomena and processes operating in varying dynamics in resistance to resettlement present a significant challenge to identifying all the different social actors, scales, levels, strategies, and goal structures operating in such contexts and then describing the way they interact with each other in the complex processes of political struggle (Little, 1999). As noted earlier, Little's use of the term "fractal" points to the irregular and volatile fashion in which these linkages are mobilized, varying by the historical moment relating to the issue and the strength and density of contacts (1999, p. 10). A large number of simultaneously acting component participants engage in the politics of resistance to resettlement. They each have a certain degree of local information and influence but are unable by themselves to determine outcomes. Such systems (to use the word very loosely) are thus inherently unstable and their processes of ordering and change basically unpredictable and nonlinear, insofar as the alliances and conflicts that occur are outcomes of local priorities and information that change with circumstances and over time (Possekel, 1999, p. 13). Although the politics of resistance to resettlement cannot be said to constitute a system, they do bear some resemblance to the complex systems discussed by complexity theory. Indeed, the participation of new groups representing interests previously without voice in formal politics and employing new strategies and technologies is altering the structure and character of politics nationally and internationally in ways that resemble the dynamics of complex systems.

Complexity theory, which originated in the 1980s in mathematics and physics, addresses the issues of stability and change in systems consisting of many independent agents that interact with each other in many different ways. The relevance of complexity theory for the social sciences was soon recognized and applied to such widely varying issues as the breakdown of political systems, the behavior of markets, and traffic problems. Complexity theory, rather than being directly applicable to the analysis of resistance politics, provides a language with which to discuss the interaction of a wide array of variables acting in various patterns of alliance or conflict across multiple scales of hierarchy, time, and space, a language that recognizes the basic nonlinearity of the process of alliance formation and the emergence of conflict. Fundamental to all expressions of complexity theory is the idea of self-organization, which refers to the fact that through the interactions of components within and between systems and their environments, systems undergo spontaneous self-organization (Hilhorst, 2004, p. 54).

Stacey, Griffin, and Shaw (2000) identify three strands of complexity theory that underlie this language. Chaos theory refers to the many ways in which different elements of an open system interact upon each other, resulting in unpredictable outcomes. Although the interactions between the components of a system or between subsystems follow predictable patterns, small variations in each of them can accumulate to produce large, fundamentally unpredictable outcomes. The second strand of complexity theory, known as dissipative structures, contributes to developing a language to discuss DFDR resistance by establishing how changing conditions can lead to the spontaneous formation of new structures. The third component of complexity theory, complex adaptive systems, focuses on the capacity of some systems to learn through experience by processing information and adapting accordingly. That is, adaptive systems do not simply respond to events but actively attempt to turn whatever happens to their own advantage, leading to even more unpredictability. The unpredictability of adaptive systems is the outcome of the creative interaction of sense-making and diverse agents. Complexity theory is relevant to DFDR in a number of contexts, most particularly for understanding the politics of resistance, but also in examining the actual processes of resettlement planning and implementation, as illustrated in the work of de Wet (2006) previously discussed in the first chapter.

Political Ecological Frameworks

In the sense that resistance to resettlement concerns conflicts over the complex relationships that involve sets of rights that people have and risks that people take with a physical environment, these issues can best be framed by a political ecological perspective.

"Political ecology" as a term was first used by Eric Wolf in a 1972 article entitled "Ownership and Political Ecology." In the article he suggests that ownership over nature is a power relationship and that human-environment relations cannot be analyzed independently of power as an element in human social relations. That is, basically, that the environment and technology are socially constructed outcomes of production relations between people, rather than empirical givens. This assertion addresses the fact that most production systems today are no longer isolated but operate in terms of competing interests for the same resource (Hjort, 1985). In other words, production, as the process through which humans engage the environment, is a social process occurring between humans for the satisfaction of sometimes conflicting needs and interests. Production is not just a technical response of an undifferentiated population to conditions in a physical environment. It is always internally complex and involves the diverse interests of a differentiated population interacting within both a dynamic physical environment and a socially structured, political-economic environment.

A political-economic analysis examines the interacting roles that international, national, regional, and local institutions play in providing constraints and possibilities that affect the way human beings make decisions that in turn affect both these institutions and the natural environment. This form of analysis is derived from the work of John Bennett, who developed an approach called human systems ecology. This approach emphasizes the institutional arrangements that mediate between human beings and physical factors operating as a single system. Human systems ecology includes a focus on regional systems in which different human groups adapt to environmental features, to one another, to hierarchical market and administrative forces, and to pressure groups and other forms of social and political interests (Bennett, 1996). The advantage of this approach is that it takes into account microlevel decision-making as well as institutional features (pressures, facilities, etc.) and allows for the examination of linkages between the local specifics of human thought and behavior and macrolevel institutions such as markets and government agencies.

One important aspect of political ecology is that in addition to factoring power relations into ecological analysis, it is also political. That is, it has a political agenda. Political ecology blends a focus on the relationship that people have with their environment with attention to the political economic forces characteristic of the society in which they live that shape and condition that relationship. Political ecology largely focuses on the conflicts that emerge over rights to access, ownership, and disposition of resources and environments for which different social groups, often characterized by widely differing sociocultural identities and economic adaptational forms, contend. In DFDR resistance, although the stakes may be expressed in economic, social, and/or cultural terms, the fundamental issue is the contestation over rights to a place or the resources of a place. The subsequent analysis of DFDR resistance, then, will continue to have a political ecological subtext in terms of contestations over rights to places and resources defined largely by differential powerholding but will focus explicitly on how these conflicts are expressed socially, culturally, politically, and ecologically (Oliver-Smith, 2005a, 2006).

Vulnerability and Risk

Within the framework of political ecology, it is possible to develop an approach employing a number of concepts that have emerged over the last twenty years and that offer the means to both identify and analyze the participants, scales and action levels, strategies, and goal structures of DFDR resistance. The core concepts underlying this approach are the linked ideas of vulnerability and risk. Vulnerability was initially employed in disaster research to understand the vast differences among societies in disaster impact from similar agents. Thinking about vulnerability was stimulated by the high correlation between disaster proneness, chronic malnutrition, low income, and famine potential and led to the conclusion that the root causes of disasters lie more in society than in nature. Researchers who adopted this perspective, which emphasizes the role of human relations and actions in generating disaster risk and impact, found that these conditions were best expressed by the concept of vulnerability (Hewitt, 1983).

Vulnerability and risk, therefore, refer to the relationships between people, the environment, and the sociopolitical structures that frame the conditions in which people live. The concept of vulnerability is fundamentally a political ecological concept, integrating not only political economic but also environmental forces in terms of both biophysical and socially constructed risk. This understanding of vulnerability enabled researchers to conceptualize how social systems generate the conditions that place different kinds of people, often differentiated along axes of class, race, ethnicity, gender, and/or age, at different levels of risk. The concepts of socially constructed vulnerability and risk were further developed by Giddens (1990) and Beck (1992, 1995) to address the quality of emerging risks in modern societies. Sometimes socially constructed risk and vulnerability are produced by the policies put in place to serve the agendas of specific parties. For example, IMF and World Bank policies of structural adjustment impose a set of risks on specifically vulnerable populations. In that sense, both vulnerability and risk can be generated or alleviated by the application of specific policies.

Vulnerability and Risk Calculation in Resettlement

Who are the vulnerable in resettlement, and why are they vulnerable? At roughly the same time as disaster researchers were testing the concept of vulnerability, Michael Cernea began to speak of the risks of impoverishment resulting from population displacement from water projects (1990). He subsequently developed his well-known impoverishment risks and reconstruction approach to understanding (and mitigating) the major adverse effects of displacement. He outlined eight basic risks to which displacement subjects people, including landlessness, joblessness, homelessness, marginalization, increased morbidity, food insecurity, loss of access to common property, and social disarticulation (1997; Cernea & McDowell, 2000). Cernea asserts that the probability of these risks producing serious consequences is high in badly planned or unplanned resettlement. He further suggests that the hardship of resettlement may be less responsible for resistance than the fact that policy and legal vacuums leave people little alternative (1993, p. 32). Recently, Dwivedi has contributed several significant refinements to the approach, particularly regarding resistance, by elaborating on the social and political construction of risk. Drawing on Beck (1992), he approaches risk as "a subjective calculation of different groups of people embedded differentially in political-economic and environmental conditions" (Dwivedi, 1999, p. 47).

People in different structural positions define risk differently, and their risk calculations are affected by cultural norms as well as by legal and policy frameworks for compensation (Beck, 1995, p. 43). Risk is calculated on the basis of information that allows people to make judgements about relative degrees of certainty or uncertainty of outcomes. People facing DFDR very often spend a considerable amount of time in conditions of uncertainty in which a lack of information on what is going to happen seriously hampers their ability to assess conditions and act. The lack of information produces perceptions of high risk. Uncertainty and the lack of predictability heighten the perception of risk because without adequate information fewer calculations of losses and benefits are possible (Dwivedi, 1999, p. 47). Most mandated resettlement projects deprive people of control over fundamental features of their lives and have generally been derelict in providing affected populations with the kinds of information necessary to reassert satisfactory control and understanding over the resettlement process or the changed circumstances of their lives. Understanding of and control over circumstances are fundamental for human beings to deal productively and positively with the forces of change. Therefore, if people find that their understanding and control are diminished, change will be characterized by conflict, tension, and perhaps active resistance. The often extremely negative concrete impacts of resettlement projects on affected peoples compound the disorientation generated by the loss of control and understanding and become additional motivations for resistance. Resistance is a reassertion of both a sense of logic and a sense of control (Oliver-Smith, 1996).

Dwivedi asserts that when people feel that the risks associated with displacement and resettlement exceed cultural norms or when compensation is deemed inadequate, resistance will be forthcoming. Dwivedi's approach permits a disaggregation of populations facing DFDR according to the different risks they perceive and, on the basis of those perceptions, their likelihood of resisting. The approach also separates risk into project performance risks in terms of costs and benefits, financial risks in terms of adequate funds for implementation, environmental risks (such as reservoir-induced seismicity, insect plagues, or waterborne diseases), and distributional risks in which benefits, for example, are captured by the rich (Dwivedi, 1999, p. 45). When people assess risk to be more than what is culturally acceptable or when the interventions of action groups produce a redefinition of acceptable risk is, he suggests, when resistance will become acute, and demands for compensations from the state will be sharp as well (Dwivedi, 1997, p. 4). Informed largely by rational choice model approaches, his analysis of the responses of the various populations affected by the construction of the Sardar Sarovar Dam points primarily to risks associated with the loss of economic resources as key in the development of resistance movements (1999). Mediating institutions, such as NGOs, also frame and may politicize uncertainties and risks and may be pivotal in the way people construct risk as well.

Rights And Risks

The World Commission on Dams (WCD) links risk with the concept of rights in advocating that an "approach based on 'recognition of rights' and 'assessment of risks' (particularly rights at risk)" be elaborated to guide future planning and decision-making on dams (2000, p. 206). The two-year WCD process, led by 12 commissioners representing the various communities of interest involved in dams, produced exhaustive reviews of the records of 125 large dams around the world, including detailed case studies of the Grand Coulee (U.S.), the Tarbela (Pakistan), the Aslantas (Turkey), the Kariba (Zambia/ Zimabwe), the Tucurui (Brazil), and the Pak Mun (Thailand) dams. In addition to the dam case studies, there were several country studies and 17 thematic reviews covering social, environmental, economic, technical, and management issues.

The WCD's global review recognized that dams had made important contributions to development, but at an unacceptable and unnecessary cost to displaced people, downstream communities, taxpayers, and the natural environment (2000, p. xxviii). To counter these losses, the WCD stressed the need to address the five values of equity, efficiency, participatory decision-making, sustainability, and accountability as justification for the elaboration of a rights and risks approach to dam construction. Rights that were seen to be relevant in large dam projects included constitutional rights, customary rights, legislated rights, and property rights (of landholders and developers and investors). These rights can be grouped by their legal status, their spatial or temporal reach, or their purpose. In the case of spatial or temporal dimensions, rights of local, regional, or national entities or the rights of present or future generations can be perceived. In terms of purpose, rights pertaining to material resources such as land, water, forests, or pasture are cited, as are rights pertaining to spiritual, moral, or cultural resources such as religion, dignity, and identity (WCD, 2000, p. 206).

In terms of risk analysis, the contribution of the WCD global review lies in distinguishing between risk takers and risk bearers, that is, the voluntary and involuntary assumption of risk. Criticizing the traditional interpretation of risk as being borne solely by developers and investors in terms of return on capital invested, the WCD highlights the differences between these risk takers and those who have risks imposed upon them by others. These risk bearers typically have little or no voice in water or energy policies, the choice of projects, or their design or implementation. The risks they face affect their well-being, livelihoods, standard of living, and cultural identity and cosmology—in sum, their very survival as individuals and as communities (WCD, 2000, p. 207). Thus, the WCD hopes that by combining the consideration of rights and risks in the same approach and by observing the complexity of the considerations involved and the values that societies place on different options, the inadequacies and simplifications of traditional cost-benefit analysis can be avoided and better planning and decision-making can result (WCD, 2000, p. 206). The WCD process became pivotal in reshaping an arena for engagement and providing—through its wide array of careful studies of the environmental, social, and economic performance of large dams as well as a set of strategic priorities for enhancing human development—the data and a framework for social action. Moreover, by basing its approach on rights and risks, the WCD recommendations for a new policy framework provide a template for the assessment of large infrastructural development projects that affect both people and environments in general (WCD, 2000, pp. xxxiv–xxxv).

The WCD is one of the early expressions of an expanded effort to bring rights-based approaches to the fore in DFDR. The strength of rights-based approaches is derived from their roots in international human rights law—such as the UN Universal Declaration of Human Rights of 1948, the UN Declaration of the Rights to Development, and the International Labour Organization conventions 107 and 169 for the protection of the rights of indigenous peoples—that provide for elements of accountability and culpability. Rights-based approaches assert that people's access to basic needs is grounded in law and can be enforced by legal instruments. From a rights perspective, failures of projects to ensure that affected people have that access can thus become the basis for real claims and can mobilize support and resources to redress those claims both locally and internationally. Rights-based approaches are seen as superior to needs-based approaches in that they focus on empowering displaced people with agency to establish what they are entitled to by law under their rights as citizens rather than what their immediate needs are. In that context, rights-based approaches also provide a framework for assessing local and national power relations and institutions as they affect people's access to resources (Grabska & Mehta 2008: p. 12).

However, rights-based approaches bring with them several disadvantages as well. The provision of rights and equal access to rights is seen to be more expensive than the short-term transfer of resources to meet immediate needs. In effect, it is easier to address people's needs through assistance programs. Furthermore the extension of rights and equal access to the often already marginalized groups affected by development projects can be perceived as threatening to local and national elites, eliciting a backlash against efforts to address structural inequalities. Despite their emphasis on achieving access to rights at the local level, rights-based approaches may also be perceived as top-down, reflecting more an elite vision of rights than that of local people who may prioritize different rights at different times. And finally, the locus of responsibility for guaranteeing, providing, and implementing rights and access is not always clear. Currently, there are no legally binding international accords or conventions that pertain to people displaced by development projects. States may lack the resources to enforce rights-based approaches in local contexts or may be reluctant to challenge their own or local structures of domination and inequality. Affected people themselves may be unsure about whom they may appeal to for protection of their rights, particularly when it is the state that is driving the DFDR process (Grabska & Mehta 2008, p. 17–19).

The importance of a rights and risks approach to DFDR is that in addition to including material concerns, it allows for the inclusion of issues of the symbolic and affective domains as well (Mehta, 2008, p. 216). As such, it provides not only an approach to improving planning and decision-making for dam projects, but also the template for an approach to understanding and analyzing resistance to DFDR in general.

Methods for Research and Action

A rights and risk approach to DFDR resistance may be developed through three possible perspectives: advocacy anthropology, stakeholder analysis, and political ecology ethnography, a triad of approaches developed by Paul Little to analyze environmental conflict (1999).

ADVOCACY ANTHROPOLOGY

The advocacy anthropology approach is characterized by an activist stance that privileges a particular group's perspective over competing or contesting positions. This approach has been shown to be particularly valuable in situations where groups, such as the Native Americans of Amazonia, are facing acute sociopolitical forces that may amount to ethnocide, to which DFDR has been likened (M. Bartolome & Barabas, 1973), or even genocide. Little suggests that one limitation of an advocacy approach is that only one point of view of the many that may be present in resettlement issues is presented, eclipsing the possibility of acknowledging that each contesting social actor may have their own sources of legitimacy. Thus, advocacy anthropology may forfeit the analysis of positions taken, for example, by anthropologists within the World Bank on behalf of peoples affected by DFDR. Conversely, it can be equally argued that advocacy anthropology often articulates a view that otherwise might not be heard, thus promoting dialogue and negotiation.

STAKEHOLDER ANALYSIS

Stakeholder analysis is an approach to environmental conflict that has emerged recently to resolve conflicts surrounding attempts to reduce levels of environmentally destructive activities and processes. Stakeholder analysis employs methods of conciliation, negotiation, and mediation for reducing levels of conflict and managing disputes. Such efforts at establishing truly efficacious methods for cross-cultural negotiation in DFDR could play meaningful roles in enhancing the capacity of local peoples to effectively represent their interests. On the other hand, stakeholder analysis frequently assumes that all actors have equal or symmetrical stakes in the conflict, something that is rarely the case. For example, while the loss of home, land, and community may allegedly be compensated at monetary values established by the project, these values are frequently an inadequate reflection of the true nature of the social, spiritual, and emotional losses that are at stake for people facing DFDR. Moreover, stakeholder approaches also assume that all participants in a dispute hold and have the abilities to employ the rights of citizenship within the larger political space of the nation. Again, assumptions of this sort are far from warranted, especially in the case of ethnic minorities or indigenous peoples, whose position in national social and cultural hierarchies generally eliminates the exercise of such basic rights (Little, 1999). Further, in the view of Laura Nader the "neutral" position of stakeholder approaches is largely fictional in that it is ideologically based on a kind of functionalist harmonics which is less about the representation and interplay of diverse interests than about pacification and hegemonic control (Nader, 1996, as cited in Little, 1999).

POLITICAL ECOLOGY ETHNOGRAPHY

Political ecology ethnography is characterized by a focus that privileges research on environmental conflict to generate a social scientific approach that incorporates multiple perspectives. This goal is achieved by methods and tools that are aimed at the inclusion of multiple groups at multiple levels to explore the political dimensions of these conflicts, to bring new participants into the political frame of action, and to initiate new approaches to viewing power relationships across multiple social and natural scales (Little, 1999, p. 4). Importantly, this approach has the potential for creating concepts that may be adopted by the new participants to question established public policy and generate new alternatives for action. The methods that are employed in this approach focus on identification of all the different participants in the conflicts, a task that can be challenging because of their numbers and the diverse historical and cultural traditions that have helped to situate them in the dispute. It is most essential that the task reveal the basic claims to resources and territory that are made by participant social actors and analyze the forms by which such claims are promoted and defended within broader political spheres of action, and this must be done in ways that display the competing discourses of cultural and political legitimacy (Little, 1999, p. 5). In this fashion the disputes over eligibility for DFDR compensation may hinge on the legitimacy of various kinds of claims to land.

Political ecological ethnography also enables the kind of multisited ethnographic approach that is essential for both research and action in contemporary development contexts that entail discourses and actions at multiple levels and in multiple institutional contexts. Development research of any type in today's globalized world must go beyond local impact areas to engage the roles of national and international institutions, NGOs, social movements, transnational networks, multistakeholder processes, and private capital, none of which are necessarily monolithic in form or composition. In terms of DFDR, the forces driving displacement go beyond the specific project to also include the social relations and ideologies of individuals, as well as the institutions, personnel, by-laws, and guidelines of the regional and national governments and the international organizations in which they operate.

All three of these perspectives have significant advantages and disadvantages in approaching resistance to resettlement. In point of fact, unlike Little, I tend to see them as nested, interacting and complementary, rather than as exclusive. Each approach roughly corresponds to a level of action in resettlement politics. As in all research conceptual frameworks and methodologies, there are moments and places of inconsistency or less than perfect fit, even contradiction. In that sense, these methodological approaches reflect the tensions and inconsistencies of relations within and among the various levels of resettlement politics. Advocacy research, stakeholder analysis, and political ecology ethnography focusing on the rights and risks in DFDR resistance correspond to the levels or scales of interaction and conflict. Advocacy anthropology is appropriate for work at the level of the community to be resettled. In some instances, applied social scientists have found themselves carrying out research in the midst of the crisis of resettlement, when people are facing a virtually life-threatening process (Colson, 1971; Oliver-Smith, 1992). In these contexts, researchers adopting an advocacy stance fulfill a necessary function by assisting communities in their efforts to deal with the crisis and in articulating their views in nonlocal contexts.

Similarly, when communities employ resistance to enhance their bargaining position in negotiating with planners and other authorities over the terms and conditions of specific resettlement projects, stakeholder analysis can prove useful both in assisting people in the negotiation process and in demarcating the issues and limits that are "in play" in the process. Enlightened stakeholder analysis can reveal the differentials in value positions that are being negotiated among very disparate participants. Stakeholder analysis that is culturally sensitive can frame the issues in ways that help to balance those situations where, as one historian aptly described the exchanges in the first encounters between Amerindians and Europeans, one party has "a continent to exchange and the other, glass beads."

Finally, a political ecology ethnography of resistance helps to place resistance in the context of global conversations about development. The political ecological perspective reveals the commonalities that local resistance movements share with similar struggles elsewhere, contributing to the emergence of new forms of discourse in the shaping of alternative approaches to development that are less destructive to environments and human rights. By revealing the interplay of multiple interests across scales and levels, political ecology ethnography informs resistance movements of the dimensions and scale of their struggle and their role in the larger conversations, as well as enabling them to expand their agendas and call for more sustainable forms of development (Oliver-Smith, 2005b).

CHAPTER THREE

The People in the Way

Who Are the Displaced?

About the only characteristic the displaced have in common, apart from their humanity, is that they are in the way of someone else's plans for development. The politics of displacement and resettlement, no matter whether in a working-class neighborhood in Boston, a peasant village in the Andes, or a tribal hunter-gatherer group in the Philippines, involve the conflict between some people with power who use it to remove people with less power from land and resources the ownership and use of which are desired. To achieve the goal of acquiring that ownership and use, a number of processes of identification are mobilized. After the land is identified as necessary for a project, a multifaceted process begins in which the people residing on that land not only have to be identified in terms of numbers, but they have to be constructed in terms that make them susceptible to policy frameworks that would take their land. The end result is that the people residing on the land come to be defined as less deserving of that land than those who have decided to take it. Covert and not so covert forms of racism then become interwoven into the discourse of expropriation. In the eyes of post-colonial elites who have embraced Western development models, traditional peoples are portrayed as impediments to development and their cultures devalued as inferior and backward (Joshi, 1991; Nandy, 1998). Thus, in that definitional and devaluational process, space is opened up for dualistic, bureaucratic expressions of racial and ethnic difference to be activated in the form of both policy and practice and their outcomes to be activated by the state or private interests. The choice then becomes, as Lohmann aptly puts it, "either assimilation on the one hand or, on the other, exclusion in one of its multiple forms: segregation, resettlement, repatriation, dispossession, eviction, ethnic immigration controls, repression or extermination" (1999, p. 1).

The ostensible reason for most displacement, as discussed in Chapter 1, is economic; that is, the local residents are seen to be making less efficient use of the land and its resources than those who wish to take it will, whether directly in benefit of the nation or indirectly, as alleged in the case of value production by private capital. There may be other more or less covert reasons for displacing people, including the removal of ethnic populations of suspect national loyalty from border regions or assimilationist projects of differing descriptions. Nonetheless, packed into the economic reasoning, although relatively covertly, are a variety of constructions of those to be replaced. These constructions, frequently based on notions of class, race, or ethnicity, are crucial in the mobilization of the interests that intend to carry out the displacement. The people to be displaced are deemed to be less important and have fewer rights in some scheme of values than the higher purposes of the nation or the benefits of enhanced production. They are said to be underdeveloped, primitive, unsophisticated, savage, forgotten by time, incapable of understanding. If they resist, they are called selfish, narrow, egotistical, small-minded. In any event, they are, the constructions assert, likely to be seen as doomed to be overtaken by the inevitable processes of history and progress that the project is frequently constructed as expressing. For example, because the Kurds oppose the construction of the Ilusu dam, Turkish development elites consider Kurdish ethnic identity to be a traditional obstacle to development that must be overcome by modernization (Morvaridi, 2008). As Joshi notes, "A culture based on lower level of technology and quality of life is bound to give way to a culture with superior technology and higher quality of life. This is what we call 'development'" (Joshi, 1991, p. 68, as cited in W. F. Fisher, 1995, p. 33).

Whatever else they may be, people who face displacement and resettlement are almost always initially incredulous. Their initial reaction is usually disbelief. Their credulity is strained by the idea of resettlement itself. It is basically unthinkable (Scudder & Colson, 1982, pp. 271–272; Wali, 1989, p. 74). Their surprise that such an act would be contemplated may be an indication of their lack of interaction with the external authority of the state. However, even seasoned city dwellers often find difficulty in accepting that the government could contemplate such a step. Sixty years ago, when the Boston Housing Authority officially announced its intentions to redevelop the West End by leveling existing housing, relocating residents, and selling the land to developers for luxury apartment buildings, no one in the neighborhood believed it. Although part of the reason for their disbelief was the lengthy and tortuous eight-year legal process of condemnation and purchase and the sketchy and inaccurate information they received from the press and official agencies, even on the eve of eviction some people could not believe that the destruction of their neighborhood was actually going to happen (Gans, 1962, p. 333).

As communication networks among peoples and communities facing displacement become more dense and active, particularly with state and private interests pressing more intensely to develop, one would expect that levels of disbelief would diminish. The intensification of the drive to develop has been paralleled by the expansion of networks of resistance, one of whose primary functions and goals is to inform communities targeted for development and the larger society of the threats that development projects pose to people. However, recent reports still indicate that many people are taken quite unaware and remain incredulous over long periods of time, even after being informed of project intentions (M. Aguirre, personal communication, November 30, 2000). In essence, the continued incredulity expressed by those facing resettlement is an indication not of their ingenuousness or lack of sophistication, but rather of the sheer scale that such a transformation signifies. Ordinary people do not think on the kind of scale that most of these projects entail and find the total transformation of their lives to be a process both unthinkable and immoral.

From a legal standpoint, the people to be displaced must also be recast from being a subject of rights to an object of rights. Some critics note that despite its good intentions, the World Bank Guidelines for resettlement (OP/BP. 4.12; see Chapter 8 for further discussion) reconstructs the legal characteristics of the role played by those to be displaced (Szablowski, 2004, p. 8). The role normally accorded to "legal persons" by liberal legal systems, which of course do not pertain in all societies, is that the individual is an active, rights-bearing agent, protected from arbitrary government action by the rule of law and principles of procedural fairness. These rights entitle an individual to know the rules that protect against dispossession without the possibility of contestation of the facts and legal arguments of the party intending the dislocation. According to Szablowski, O.D. 4.30 (and the subsequent, weakened versions entitled O.P. 4.12 and B.P. 4.12) circumscribes the role played by local people as active agents and recasts them as passive subjects or perhaps as the objects of policy (2002, p. 252). The fairness and soundness of the project, the local environment, the social and economic structure, the nature and degree of project impact, and the needs and entitlements of local people, that is, the legal "facts" of the case, are all determined by the resettling agent and bank reviewers (Szablowski, 2002, p. 252). The people and their environment are reduced to objects of study. The information and opinions of local people may be used along with other materials, but the interpretive conclusions upon which the fate of individuals and communities are based are the province and domain of experts.

These condescending and negative constructions of the people to be displaced have enabled the displacing interests to rationalize a host of omissions and outright deceptions. The rights that people are entitled to in displacement and resettlement by World Bank Guidelines, for example, are often glossed over or represented as a voluntary gesture by the displacing organization, something that can be withdrawn at any time if the people question too deeply or show signs of resistance. In the case of the Antamina Mine in the north-central Andes, a project with World Bank debt and investment guarantees, villagers to be displaced were systematically denied access to copies of the World Bank resettlement guidelines and were not given any explanation of its contents by the Compañia Minera Antamina (CMA) (Szablowski, 2002, pp. 266–267). Further, CMA, a Canadian-owned company in Peru, did not make public its binding commitment to implement O.D. 4.30. It also did not inform local people of the complaint procedures available to them through the World Bank's Multilateral Investment Guarantee Agency (MIGA). The modus operandi of the CMA was to define and select a group to whom it would grant benefits according to its own criteria, develop a compensation plan, and then consult with the elected group to compel it to accept the plan without further input (Szablowski, 2002, p. 267).

The interests that seek to displace people for development projects also make certain assumptions about peoples' needs and the process of displacement. Drawing uncritically on the migratory experience of the twentieth century and the high mobility of contemporary urban populations, developers have tended to ignore the serious consequences that displacement entails for the uprooted. However, even for Americans, who move an average of six times during their lifetimes and who treat land as a commodity that can be bought and sold, the process of continual mobility may still be traumatic and prove to have long-term consequences. The frequent relocation of home and job that characterizes much of American life, that spatial mobility that is for some a source of pride as proof of our resilience and adaptability, lies at the core of many of the repressed tensions and unresolved conflicts of modern American life (Bellah, Madsen, Sullivan, Swidler, & Tipton, 1985).

The breaking of the connection between place and people can be psychologically traumatic, even in circumstances in which it is seen as not only acceptable but praiseworthy. The work of the psychiatrist and psychohistorian

Robert J. Lifton, mentioned briefly in Chapter 1, is instructive here. In 1970, in an effort to characterize the conditions and challenges facing humanity in the late twentieth century, Lifton coined the term "Protean Man" basing it on Proteus, the shape-changing figure of Greek mythology. Lifton was attempting to describe a consciousness that had become separated from "the vital and nourishing symbols of [their] cultural traditions—symbols revolving around family, idea systems, religions and the life cycle in general . . ." (Lifton, 1970, p. 43) and, I would add, place and community. Lifton was characterizing a form of consciousness that is freed (or torn?) from these traditional anchors of identity and must engage in a continual process of radical reinvention of the self, drawing upon the kaleidoscope of imagery available in modern culture. Lifton stresses that such a psychological style is "by no means pathological as such, and in fact may be one of the functional patterns necessary to life in our times." He does not address the possible pathologies of our times. He does, however, consider something he calls "psychohistorical dislocation" (1970, pp. 43–44), referring to the forces of rapid economic and political change that often involve an uprooting from family and community to move far from familiar landmarks into new and radically different environments. These forces have in many senses dislocated everyone, obliging us all to adopt the consciousness of the constant radical reinvention of the self. In a sense, because it has become part of the way life is lived in the developed world, there is an assumption that all people can uproot themselves or be uprooted without experiencing loss or trauma. We have even become blinded to the traumatic consequences of psychohistorical dislocation that we experience under the "normal" processes of mobility. In our blindness to our own pathologies and our inability to recognize the validity of the active resistance of those who oppose relocation within the developed world, we assume that uprooting will be equally untraumatic for others.

However, the fact that the uprooting process is experienced by millions of willing migrants must be addressed. While all migration is motivated by some combination of "push" factors and "pull" factors, most migrants are not forcibly uprooted against their will. There are many social and economic processes that set people in motion, and most of them involve a degree of volition. People migrate voluntarily very frequently, moving to improve their lives in some way. In fact, they embrace change. The mass migrations of the nineteenth and twentieth centuries are ample evidence of the capacity of people to uproot themselves, move, and change. However, we must also recognize that many of these migrants faced considerable coercion as well.

A crucial issue that is often overlooked in discussing population mobility is autonomy. For many, the migratory process may entail a great many stresses but is still undertaken willingly as a means to an end. The loss of autonomy, that ability to exercise choice and make an independent decision regardless of trying circumstances, is an important distinguishing feature of the migratory process. Those who attribute to all people a facility to uproot and move, regardless of culture and place and based on the vast record of voluntary migration, ignore both the traumas that are experienced even in voluntary migration and the insult to the self and the community resulting from the loss of autonomy that involuntary displacement signifies.

In the process of redefining people and their needs, the land to be seized also undergoes a process of redefinition. Land has to be redefined as un-, under-, or misused. Forests, subsoils, and rivers become "untapped resources." Peasant farms are deemed "inefficient." Common property–use rights over resources, such as fishing grounds, become limitations on free enterprise. Neighborhoods become slums, demanding to be cleared for the welfare of the residents. The connection of people to place becomes negated by the commodification process. The relationship that people have with their environment, particularly land, is generally complex and bound up with relations that in many instances resemble those of kinship rather than ownership (Kirsch, 2001, p. 173). Relations to land are often the basis of social relationships and the means through which such relationships are reproduced in many societies. Moreover, the social identity of land is extended beyond relationships with people to relationships with the spiritual realms. Thus, from its complex, multifaceted identities, in which land is the birthplace of the gods, the abode of the ancestors, the source of spiritual as well as material sustenance, the context of historical tradition, and a provider of a sense of continuity through time, development reduces the identity of land to a single characteristic, its value as resource.

The overwhelming majority of the displaced are members of ethnic minorities, the poor, and other groups marginalized within their societies. However, even in that context, it is risky to attribute any kind of uniformity or homogeneity to populations that have been displaced. For example, those displaced or potentially to be displaced by the Sardar Sarovar Dam project in western India's Narmada Valley include tribal peoples, poor peasant farmers, squatters, and relatively well-off farmers of the Nimad plains (Dwivedi, 1997). Each of these groups, and the varying conditions of individuals and families within the groups, bears a different relationship to the land, which itself varies in quality and quantity, and each experiences the threat of displacement and losses from a different perspective. Similarly, their decisions to participate and how they participate in resistance to DFDR are made from specific kinds of orientations regarding their relationship to land, property, and home.

In addition to questions of class, caste, or ethnicity, these and all other orientations are also reflections of gender and age. Gender and age, based in human biology but socially constructed in the way they are expressed in society, are key relational dimensions of human thought and action (Colson, 1999; Indra, 1999, p. 2). The processes of displacement and resettlement are channeled and expressed always through the factors of gender and age. Most of the literature on DFDR either focuses entirely on men or does not differentiate according to gender in documenting and analyzing the experience and responses of people to DFDR. Each gender experiences the changes imposed by these transformative processes in different ways, just as the changes affect the statuses and roles that are accorded men and women in a particular society differently (see Chapter 7).

The responses of men and women to DFDR will vary according to the resources and power that individuals, families, or communities may possess both before and after the displacement process, but it is clear that those responses will also be gendered (Koenig, 1995; Mehta, 2009; Palit, 2009). And each will experience those changes not only in their own roles and statuses, but also in the changes that the other gender experiences. Thus, as Colson points out in her study of the Gwembe Tonga after resettlement, women felt the loss of familiar surroundings and grieved harder than men. Men, however, felt most acutely "the immediate sting of defeat" since they had failed to stop the displacement, some going to prison or even dying in the attempt to resist. Their powerlessness was amply revealed to all in their inability to protect their families and their land. The intense frustration they felt was acted out frequently in abuse of their wives and children. The wives, who in ordinary circumstances would have been able to seek support from kin, were left without resources to defend their rights after kin groups were resettled apart (Colson, 1971).

Resettlement programs for the displaced frequently leave women much worse off. Indeed, the effects of DFDR on women have generally not been factored into resettlement planning (Mehta 2009; Palit 2009). Although only recently the focus of research, it has become abundantly clear that women understand and experience DFDR very differently from men, largely because of their different statuses and roles within the economy of production and reproduction (Palit, 2009). In particular, the relationship of women to land is based more on their involvement in activities that connect them to the natural environment, such as gathering firewood and fetching water, than on property relations, from which they are often excluded either by custom or by law. Displacement and resettlement may alter women's economic roles and livelihoods much more profoundly than those of men (Palit, 2009, p. 284). Women play key economic roles in traditional land, forest, and maritime livelihoods and have correspondingly higher social status, but they are often relegated to casual construction labor, domestic service, petty traders and hawkers, and commercial sex workers after displacement and resettlement (Rebbapragada & Kalluri, 2009, p. 255). Usually compensation payment is given to heads of households, effectively converting family assets into male assets in both rural and urban contexts. Citing the World Commission on Dams Thematic Review on Social Impacts, Dana Clark notes that compensation in the form of either cash or land is invariably awarded to men since women are not considered to be farmers or house owners. The large amount of literature on women in development has documented similar results for development projects in general; for example, displacement also may have serious impacts on women's earning abilities, but they are seldom compensated for lost livelihoods in resettlement (Mehta, 2009; Clark, 2002). Colson, attempting to sum up the impacts of resettlement on women, asserts that (1) women become more vulnerable to physical violence from husbands and other male kin due to the frustrations awakened by the resettlement process, (2) policy and gender roles may undercut women's traditional rights to property, (3) access to economic resources will be limited by assumptions about appropriate role behavior in new circumstances, (4) gender role definition and relationships will be altered by the new contexts, and (5) the process of renegotiating all of these relationships will be complex and difficult since the status quo may be threatened by resettlement (1999, p. 38).

Even less is documented and analyzed for the impacts of displacement and resettlement on the elderly or the very young than on women. While infants and the very young may be vulnerable to the physical hardships and impoverishment experienced by the displaced, the elderly suffer severely from the dislocation and separation from the familiar environments in which most have lived their entire lives. The changes in environment and social organization that displacement and resettlement entail disrupt traditional forms of knowledge, of which elders are the chief sources and custodians. The loss of relevance of this knowledge caused by new contexts and circumstances can constitute a telling blow to self-esteem and the traditional social prestige that support the elderly in their communities. Moreover, overcoming the violation of norms pertaining to appropriate social and environmental relations is more difficult for someone whose whole life has been organized by them than it is for younger people for whom the socialization process is less deeply absorbed. Such changes and the difficult process of adjustments very often leave the elderly more vulnerable than the young to the physical hardships and to more severe emotional and mental distress. Explanations of morbidity and mortality among the elderly after displacement and resettlement are very often expressed in terms of "dying of a broken heart" or simply giving up and willing oneself to die.

The Resisters

When a development project of whatever stripe confronts a community with the prospect of dislocation, local people will differentiate themselves by their responses. No community is ever entirely homogeneous. Some individuals may acquiesce fatalistically. Some may embrace the project as an opportunity to migrate or to gain resources. And others will resist. In resistance, people are distinguished by their interests as well as their identities, although in many cases the two may be virtually the same. Identifying resisters basically constitutes identifying the interests and identities of those affected peoples who feel that their rights have been infringed upon and who feel that they are being forced to suffer unacceptable risks. Responses will also vary over time as the project and the struggle against it evolves, each in response to the other. Consequently, responses vary for the most part because not everyone in a community, much less a region, will be impacted in the same way at the same time by either resettlement or the alterations in the environment that the project will enact. Moreover, many development projects that displace people and communities are large, and their impacts are felt over a variety of environments and among widely varying populations with different economic and cultural patterns. Such large projects are inherently heterogeneous, although elite constructions of impacts and impacted populations often assume an unwarranted homogeneity.

A variety of factors has proven to be significant in the development of DFDR resistance movements, including the social identity of individuals and the identity and organization of groups within the impacted population. Further, political variables such the general political climate of the nation and the history of state-local relations (see Chapter 7), economic features such as degree of market integration or land tenure patterns (see Chapter 5), and cultural issues such as language, religion, and identity (see Chapter 6) may influence who participates in resistance movements. In many senses, each of these sets of variables is interpenetrating and mutually constitutive of the identities and interests of individuals and groups among a population facing displacement. The project and the resettlement process itself are also factors that will influence in different ways the decisions to accept or resist resettlement.

Neither rural communities, whether tribal, peasant, or fully assimilated members of the national society, nor urban neighborhoods of minority or majority identity are ever entirely homogeneous. There are always differences of social, cultural, political, or economic character. Thus, the degree of internal diversity and the patterns of conflict and consensus, as well as the social, racial, ethnic, and class factors at work in an impacted population, will play an important role in the development of and participation of local people in DFDR resistance movements. Even within small communities, some will resist while others may simply acquiesce and still others will willingly accept resettlement. Levels and forms of social solidarity and internal conflict may be changed. Such differences in response to both resettlement and resistance may have long-term implications for the social organization of a community threatened or affected by DFDR.

Risks and Losses as Indicators

In a series of articles, Dwivedi asks the question, "Why do some resist resettlement and others do not?" (1997, 1998, 1999). In answering that question, a similar question may also be addressed: "Who resists resettlement, and who does not?" I have contended that internal differentiation, a multifaceted relationship to the immediate environment and the state, the availability of local and nonlocal allies, and the quality of the resettlement process itself are crucial factors in assessing why people resist DFDR (1991, 1994). Dwivedi builds upon this perspective to consider resettlement policies and implementation, action-group mediation, and internal differentiation as crucial to the formation of different perceptions and reactions to the risks of displacement and resettlement that underlie the formation of resistance. Dwivedi's approach, as mentioned earlier, is based upon the concept of risk. He contends that those who resist will come from the sectors of the affected populations who perceive that they are placed at greatest risk by the prospect of displacement, the resettlement plan and its implementation, or both. As discussed earlier, his approach asserts that risks are socially and politically constructed and thus will be perceived differently by men, women, the young or elderly, rich farmers, landless laborers, indigenous peoples, peasants, outcast groups, and other subgroups. Thus, within the area of impact of large development projects that occasion DFDR, the perception of risks that are to be encountered because of displacement, resettlement, or both, will be variously perceived, and resistance to them will be a function of those perceptions.

However, actually predicting who will or establishing who does resist resettlement is extremely complex. In general, human motivations are rarely unidimensional, and the motivations behind the decision to resist DFDR present no exception. Furthermore, the task is made even more complex by the introduction of the factor of time. Resettlement projects evolve over time in interaction with mediating action groups and policy adjustments, both of which have the potential for changing the decision-making frameworks of people facing and/or resisting resettlement. In the context of the Sardar Sarovar Project in India's Narmada Valley, Dwivedi largely frames the choices made by people in terms of risks of potential losses of economic resources, namely, loss of lands, both privately owned and encroached upon, and loss of livelihoods related to agriculture. In terms of displacement risks, not all villages will lose the same amounts of land or the same kinds of land. Some may lose formally held "revenue" lands, others Nevad (forested) land, and still others homestead land. Depending on topography, some may lose land in the village and others will not. Moreover, government policy may create a skewed situation. For example, since compensation is limited to no more than eight hectares, the risks of resettlement marginalization are minimized for a farmer from the middle peasantry who loses between 2 and 8 hectares as compared to the risks for a farmer from the upper peasantry who loses more than eight hectares of land. However, these farmers' risk calculations must take into account the quality of the compensation land. Without adequate information on the quality of the compensation land, middle peasantry farmers still risk impoverishment. For the Adivasis (tribals), loss of Nevad (forested and encroached) land is not compensated, meaning almost inevitable marginalization in resettlement. However, pressures from action groups and subsequent policy changes have provided the landless with possible gains in land entitlements. Resettlement acceptance in the Sardar Sarovar Project varied by state among Gujarat, Maharashtra, and Madhya Pradesh according to policy changes for land availability, agency mediation, representation, and the immediacy and threat of submergence. Thus, improving policy had the effect of reducing conflict levels and resistance. Improved policy may actually be the result of peoples' resistance and the intervention of action groups. The resistance dynamic thus emerges as a "trialectic" among the people to be resettled, action-group intervention, and policy and project authorities.

In summary, in the Sardar Sarovar Project it would appear that those who bear the most risk in terms of loss of resources and livelihood are actually the upper peasantry since the compensation package does not guarantee either the restoration of quantity or quality of land. In Dwivedi's scheme, then, those most likely to join resistance movements would be the well-off sectors of the peasantry. Conversely, those least likely to resist would come from those groups for whom the resettlement and compensation package actually improved upon previous holdings, namely the middle peasantry and the tribals. However, Adivasis have actually expressed their resistance to resettlement in an idiom that combines elements of cultural and religious identity (see Chapter 6). Dwivedi either discounts or ignores noneconomic considerations as motivations for resistance or as a means of distinguishing resisters. In the case of the possibility of social disarticulation resulting from resettlement, perceived risks are seen as being tempered by existing feuds and conflicts between villages, hamlets, and kinship groups and even with households. The fact that the Adivasis have both a history of resistance to state intervention and little or no history of reciprocity with the state is recognized but not seen as determining. Cultural discourses around issues of loss of identity, place attachment, or loss of cultural heritage resources are also not seen as significant in Dwivedi's approach for distinguishing or predicting resistance.

Resistance, Social Solidarity, and Internal Conflict

From the standpoint of social organization, resistance efforts often initiate a process of redefinition of a variety of internal and external relationships and institutions. The need to organize for resistance will exert a new form of pressure on the internal organization of a community. The organization of a resistance movement may sharpen both internal and external preexisting conflicts. The existence of patterns of internal differentiation based on ethnicity, caste, or class in a community may constitute obstacles to the formation of the necessary levels of solidarity and cooperation for effective resistance and may require efforts to alter local social structural patterns to enable the formation of an organized movement by isolating or banishing dissidents (Lawrence, 1986). In addition, governments and project authorities may attempt to exploit or even create internal divisions within communities to reduce their capacity to organize and negotiate (Parasuraman, 1999, p. 244).

On the other hand, a successful record of defending local interests, usually based on a long history of internal coherence and solidarity, effective political structure, leadership, and previously existing community organizations that may backstop a resistance movement, may also affect the community's ability to mount and ultimately institutionalize serious resistance efforts (L. Bartolome, 1992; Waldram, 1980; Wali, 1989). In some cases, the threat of resettlement creates a culture of solidarity far more intense than what had existed prior to the project (Rapp, 2000). In terms of external relationships, resistance, on the one hand, requires the intensification of relationships with traditional allies and, on the other hand, the development of new relationships with others, often an entity completely foreign to the local context. For example, in the case of the Tucurui Dam in Brazil, the downstream *caboclos* (peasants) acquired significant allies in a rural workers union and church organizations, articulating the caboclos with the larger community of Amazonian peasants and enabling them to assume new political roles (Magee, 1989) (see Tucurui Dam case study, Chapter 4).

Today many resettlement projects are taking place in situations of extreme asymmetry in social structure and power in which elites are the most capable of expressing their interests and needs. Basically, particular groups, whether defined by class and class alliances, race, ethnicity, religion, or another differentiating factor, may find their interests furthered by certain features of a resettlement project while other groups will see themselves suffering great disadvantage. Furthermore, the state has been known to use the distribution of resettlement benefits to influence community opinion, channeling resources to village heads. This strategy may backfire when not everyone receives similar quantities or qualities of benefits. In the Sardar Sarovar Project "resettlement friends" targeted for benefits for a demonstration effect became known as *dalals* (stooges) when benefit distribution to the majority proved unsatisfactory (Dwivedi, 1997, p. 20). Some may see land compensation as an economic opportunity, while formal sector housing, particularly in urban resettlement, may draw interested people into a project area. Differential costs and benefits from resettlement projects may vary according to land and labor factor markets, social differentiation, or other local features, predisposing some groups to favor resettlement and others to oppose it. Indeed, policy changes by project authorities, as well as what Dwivedi refers to as "resistance fatigue" (often due to state violence and oppression), may split villages into contesting factions (1997, p. 19). Therefore, some caution must be exercised in ascertaining whose interests are indeed being represented in resistance movements (Nachowitz, 1988; Partridge, 1993). Communities threatened with resettlement cannot be assumed to be homogeneous. In resistance movements all players have specific agendas that they attempt to further.

Participation

One of the primary means by which affected people make themselves and their needs known is through their participation in the entire process of the development project. The participation of affected peoples can be expressed through individual and group forms of resistance or through direct negotiation over, planning for, and implementation of the resettlement process itself. The social identity of individuals and groups influences the forms of participation that are elected by people facing resettlement. By the same token, the space for participation will be a function of those identities as well as the management and structure of the project.

One of the goals that many resistance movements seek to achieve is greater participation of the affected people in the decision-making, planning, and implementation of a development project that affects them directly or indirectly. The same requirement of full participation holds also for DFDR projects necessitated by the development project. The goal of participation is consistent with the emphasis on the recognition and restoration of the rights of affected peoples. Participation is a particularly thorny issue in many cases because if authentic participation is achieved, it tends to violate many if not all of the traditional forms of power relations and social interactions in most societies. Projects of whatever sort are characteristically initiated, planned, and implemented by people from various strata of elite groups within the society. Although not without exceptions, those affected tend to be members of subaltern groups who are generally not considered by elites to have the social and cultural tools necessary for executive or even advisory forms of decision-making, planning, and execution that pertain to development projects. For example, the government of India did not bother to inform the tribal peoples of the Narmada Valley of the dam and the resettlement project because it felt that they simply did not have the capability to understand the information (Parasuraman, 1999). Even where their rights have been taken into account and participation is considered to be part of a project, affected people are often still expected to accept the wisdom and decisions of planners.

Since its inception, the concept of participation has become a virtual sine qua non for all development projects. As Cleaver has noted, participation has "become an act of faith in development; something we believe in and rarely question," yet there is little evidence, she claims, of any long-term effectiveness of participation in materially improving the lives of vulnerable people or as a strategy for social change (1999, p. 597). Most development programs have largely been structured with a very particular understanding of participation in mind. The World Bank Operational Directive and its successor documents, for example, rather than granting procedural rights to local people, imposes an obligation on the project to ensure the participation of local people in planning and decision-making (Szablowski, 2002, p. 252). Participation in this light then becomes a bureaucratic function of the project, designed and channeled in "appropriate" ways to further the success of the project. The recent controversy over the issue of "free, prior, and informed consent" versus "free, prior, and informed consultation" expresses precisely the perspectives of the World Bank on the one hand and of the indigenous peoples on the other regarding their participation in development projects (see Chapter 8 for further discussion).

Most resettlement programs in effect become extremely large bureaucratic technical organizations operating with specific models of development and progress. They generally have a clearly defined set of activities focused on quantifiable costs and benefits that are to be carried out under time and budgetary limits. Project goals customarily emphasize meeting practical (i.e., material) rather than strategic needs, instrumentality rather than empowerment (Cleaver, 1999, p. 598). Although "empowerment," as an outcome of participation, has also become a development buzzword, its inclusion in the goals of development programs has fundamentally robbed it of its radical, transformatory edge (Cleaver, 1999, p. 599). Rather than empowering community, there has been a neo-liberal reconceptualization of the idea of it in which the opportunities afforded by the development/reconstruction project are to be used by individuals to better themselves, thus contributing to the betterment of the group.

Furthermore, where collective interests are recognized, the goals of development-resettlement programs emphasize the creation of formalized community organizations that interface well with national bureaucratic structures. In many ways, such programs aim to remake the community along lines that are compatible with the larger system. There is little recognition that many community functions are efficiently and effectively carried out through informal social networks, daily social interaction, and the application of cultural norms (Cleaver, 1999, p. 602). In these contexts, the true substance of strategies of participation, in which individual and community take part, become part of, or share in something, becomes lost. The goal of participation should be to strengthen the self-sustaining capacities of the impacted community by developing its local capabilities. When such programs actually undermine or supplant such facets rather than reinforcing the capabilities to increase autonomy and control process, the community's abilities to control its own life are destroyed, creating dependency and increasing the community's vulnerability (Wilches-Chaux, 1994).

The question of authentic participation has also been raised in regard to NGOs and social movements. One of the persistent tensions in the relationship between GROs, NGOs, and social movements is the degree to which grassroots-level opinion is consulted and factored into decisions taken at higher levels in the struggle. NGOs may claim to represent the interests of the community, but the question of how representative and participatory they really are remains persistent and constitutes the core issue of one of the arguments leveled against them. Governments and MDBs have suggested that NGOs have not been elected by anyone and are misrepresenting themselves if they claim to represent the interests of the people. Indeed, the articulation of all the diverse claims and interests of extremely heterogeneous populations in a way that is still coherent with the NGO's own possible agenda regarding approaches to development is a major challenge facing NGOs assisting communities facing DFDR. NGOs depend on their relationship and credibility with the grass roots and generally must be careful not to misrepresent their interests. Nonetheless, the tension is a continuing issue (see Narmada Bachao Andolan case study, Chapter 7).

Categorical Struggles

Since populations impacted by large-scale development projects tend to be heterogeneous, one of the principal points of contention in DFDR resistance involves the definitions established most frequently by project planners of those people to be included as recipients of resettlement assistance. Projects, like states, categorize people as a means of control and containment (Kearney, 1996; J. Scott, 1998). In the case of DFDR affected people, the categories that are established bring with them bundles of rights that are themselves attached to material and social benefits or costs. Consequently, how one is defined by a project will very often determine one's access to a set of entitlements. For this reason, to be formally defined as a PAP (project-affected person or people), an oustee, an encroacher, a *desplazado* (displaced), an *atingido* (victim), an *afectado* (affected), or other similar labels is to be scheduled for the receipt of compensations or benefits if the development project has a resettlement plan (Rapp, 2000). The cursory nature of many social and environmental impact studies of projects has been responsible for the underestimation of both numbers and categories of groups to be affected by DFDR. Consequently, many struggles are undertaken by local groups and their nonlocal NGO allies to resist exclusion by category from resettlement benefits or compensation. The inclusion or exclusion of certain groups from beneficiary categories in DFDR has also been the source of internal disputes and conflicts. The relative "deservedness" of some groups for compensation is often disputed by others who see themselves as more deserving. The struggle to expand the definition of the affected, often to include many non-land-based occupations such as tailors, carpenters, shopkeepers, and the like is also a priority among many resistance movements.

A frequent focus of this form of dispute has been the tendency for planners to define project-affected peoples solely as those who hold legal title to property and are directly impacted by the project. The lack of a legal title to land that has been customarily used by people, often for generations, especially excludes indigenous people and women, who, because of structured gender inequalities, are not legally allowed to hold formal title in some societies. Other kinds of informal, non-titled land tenure and use rights, such as sharecroppers or people who have rights over trees and forests, are also excluded (Grabska & Mehta, 2008, p. 11). For example, ELETROSUL and CRAB (see case study, Chapter 2) challenged one another continuously over the meaning of the term "atingido." ELETROSUL defined it as an owner-operator with legally established titles to the land. CRAB, on the other hand, wanted the term to include various categories of landless agriculturalists, such as squatters, renters, sharecroppers, and indigenous peoples, as well as the owner-operator's adult children. Furthermore, the definition of what would affect people was debated. CRAB's definition of atingido would include those people impacted not only by water from the reservoir, but also by transmission lines, worker living quarters, and the construction site. The new interpretations of atingido thus broadened the base of the CRAB from the ELETROSUL estimate of 14,500 families to 40,000 families, or 200,000 people (Rothman & Oliver, 1999, p. 50).

The insistence on formal land titles becomes particularly thorny when indigenous groups hold traditional land-use rights but no formally recognized titles. Indeed, the social identity of "indigenous" may be the source of considerable dispute since such a category may have attached to it specific benefits from the state or the project that are not provided to those outside of that category (Bolaños, 2008). Development projects have heightened the cultural significance of indigenous identity for both holders and nonholders of that identity. However, because they lack formal legal title to the land, indigenous peoples and other holders of traditional or communal land-use rights have been frequently omitted from development projects' schedules of people to be compensated for losses of productive assets, thus inspiring significant protest and resistance.

The lack of recognition of larger regional environmental impacts of projects has also led to the exclusion of people whose access to resources essential for livelihood are seriously affected by projects. Although populations living downstream from dams are often severely impacted by dam construction due to water pollution, species depletion, and other environmental damages, they have been excluded from receiving any form of compensation, thus inspiring protest. Numerous cases, such as the Tucurui Dam in Brazil (Magee,

1989) or the Narmada project in India (Dwivedi, 1999), to mention only two, have seen a great deal of protest and resistance organized over the failure to include the downstream populations structurally displaced by dam-induced environmental damage. Kinship categories have also proved to be important in determining the distribution of resettlement benefits. One of the principal features of an early resistance campaign in the Narmada Valley centered around categorizing first sons as independent households to be included in the distribution of replacement land (Dwivedi, 1998).

Resistance to DFDR and Social Change

DFDR resistance may create pressures for social change in a community. When a community decides to resist a DFDR project, that decision engages the community with a process that, even if successful, entails significant internal and external change for the community. It is through the conflict instigated by challenge and resistance that communities themselves initiate changes, regardless of how conservative their reasons for resistance may be. Conflict is an important organizing principle of human behavior. Who a community's true allies and opponents are and what is actually good and bad for the community may become clearer in conditions of conflict. Conflict may clarify the ambiguity of changing conditions. Events may become easier to interpret within the frame of conflict. People may be able to articulate their sense of identity and their positions on issues more exactly (Marris, 1975, p. 159).

Resistance requires action, and consciousness is generated in and changed by social action (Marshall, 1983, as cited in Fantasia, 1988, p. 8). In this sense, society is constantly in the process of reconstituting itself through actions of alignment and disengagement, along the axes of individual, group, ethnicity, age, gender, class, etc, activating a process of continual contestation and interpretation of culture. The threat of resettlement constitutes a crisis of enormous proportions for many communities. Crises are periods of time when customary practices of daily life are suspended and new possibilities of action, alliances, and values are created (Fantasia, 1988, p. 14).

When communities resist the threat of forced resettlement, they become subject to a different set of changes that will come about through their resistance. The initial steps taken in resisting resettlement may have a galvanizing effect on people as they become aware of not only their own resources and capabilities, but the vulnerability of their opponents as well. The construction of the Grand Rapids Dam in Northern Manitoba, Canada, required the resettlement of the Swampy River Cree Reserve and the adjacent Metis community of Chemawawin to a new site (Waldram, 1980). Prior to the construction of the dam and the relocation, traditional leadership patterns among the Cree had been undermined by the institution of the "free trader," a person who resided in the community and acted as a broker between the people and the outside world, which included provincial and national governments as well as the market. The free trader became the de facto leader of the community since he constituted the major focus of economic life in his linkage function between the community and the supply of consumer goods. Although there were elected leaders, in practice they exercised little authority and were subservient and secondary to the free trader.

When negotiations began, in 1962, between the community and the national government for surrender of reserve land, the free trader was legally excluded from participating in the proceedings, and the responsibility fell to the elected leaders. Seriously ill-prepared to deal with the negotiating process and having no understanding of the legality of their position regarding the hydroelectric project, the leaders experienced considerable stress and made a number of serious errors, the most grievous of which was the choice of a new site for the community.

However, as negotiations proceeded over the ensuing six years, a process of political socialization took place. Frustrated by their failure to achieve remotely satisfactory results in their negotiations with the committee representing the hydroelectric project, the leaders retained a lawyer to act on their behalf. Although in the particular instance the negotiations proved fruitless, the Cree were able to see "first hand the extent to which they could rattle the government bureaucracy by merely, and unexpectedly, standing up for their legal rights" (Waldram, 1980, p. 175). The startled reaction of the committee to the Indians' seeking legal counsel convinced the leaders of the vulnerability of their opponent and of their own potential as a force to be reckoned with in their efforts to secure better postresettlement conditions for their people. In effect, as Waldram states,

> The long and complex interaction between the various government officials and the local leaders has made the latter 'politically competent' to utilize modern interest group tactics to achieve their goals. Clearly, they have learned to cope with the national political system, but through practical experience and not through programs sponsored by the very political body responsible for the relocation in the first place (1980, p. 177).

The leaders, and by extension the people, have become politically astute, sophisticated, and skilled in their dealings with the federal government. They acknowledge that many mistakes were made, but they learned a great deal in their experience of negotiating with the relocation authorities. As one former band leader said, "We won't make those mistakes again" (Waldram, 1980, p. 177). Clearly, undertaking resistance to the Grand Rapids Dam, despite their lack of success, began a process of political socialization that enhanced their capabilities for future negotiations with the government. The actions of resistance groups, as well as the group changes set in motion by the requirement of action in resistance, often produce new kinds of alignments and coalitions that may have significant impact on the structure and organization of local social relations. Thus, it is in the social action required by resistance that consciousness and practice become changed.

Why People Resist

Since protest and resistance are mobilized on a number of fronts and at a number of levels to confront a variety of opposing parties, a multiplicity of discourses must be called on to represent the concerns of people resisting DFDR. Furthermore, the protest and resistance may encompass critiques of project implementation, state development programs and strategies, and the general global political economy of development. This diversity of idioms and meanings has been characterized as "syncretic" language and is seen as essential for resistance movements to articulate support at different levels and in different contexts. Indeed, development projects that are backed by interest groups embedded in local and global systems necessitate a syncretization of idioms (Dwivedi, 1998, p. 160).

While they are consistently based on a foundational concept of the defense of human and civil rights, individuals and groups resisting DFDR construct at least seven fundamental themes from which they develop a wide variety of discourses, images, symbols, and representations for the various allies and opponents they encounter at various levels. Depending on the characteristics of the project, the social and environmental context in which it is located, and the risks and losses that affected people will be or are suffering, some themes may be emphasized over others. For example, some DFDR resisters may argue on the basis of justice and human rights, while others call on the spiritual values embodied in the environment that will be destroyed, and still others protest the lack of participation in project design and planning. Any of the discourses may change in the evolution of the struggle. Resisters may begin, for example, with an appeal to spiritual values, then change to environmental destruction, then economics, and then project participation. Different discourses may run simultaneously as well, activated by parties at different levels and contexts of the struggle. The seven themes through which resisters develop the various discourses are (1) the environment, (2) economics (3) culture (4) project risks, (5) governance and administration, (6) approaches to development, and (7) justice and human rights. Each of these discourses of resistance raises or privileges different dimensions of both the identities and the interests of affected people. The discourses are not discrete or compartmentalized, but part of an encompassing protest that reflects the totality of the threat that people face in displacement and resettlement. Clearly some projects threaten people more in one aspect or domain than others, but the need to discuss each in a linear or separate fashion should not disguise the interwoven and synergistic character of this protest and resistance.

CHAPTER FOUR

Contested Landscapes

Development, Ecological Upheaval, and Resistance

At one level, all resistance to DFDR constitutes one side of an environmental conflict. Resistance is a rejection of an attempt by certain interests to transform an environment in some way that requires the displacement of people. As such, environmental conflict is at the center of grassroots and NGO resistance to DFDR. Both the state and private interests, in undertaking large-scale infrastructural development and conservation projects, base their decisions on culturally particular constructions of the environment. Because of the conflicts that such images of nature and the environment produce in their applications in such projects, a brief discussion of their basic tenets is in order.

Constructions of Nature and Society

The dominant Western constructions—also frequently adopted by post-colonial states and elites—of the relationship between human beings and nature have over time fluctuated between opposition and harmony. For most of the twentieth century, nature and society were seen as being in opposition to each other, a perspective that can be traced to classical Greece and Rome. Although many integrative or conservationist attitudes have also been part of Western culture over time, a more utilitarian view of the natural world became dominant in the seventeenth and eighteenth centuries (Redmond, 1999, p. 21). Scientific and philosophical discourses of that period began to see humans as ontologically distinct from nature. Indeed, nature provided a contrasting category against which human identity could be defined as cultural rather than natural in the work of Hobbes, Locke, and Rousseau. This new ideological construction focused on the opposition of nature and society and ultimately on the domination and control of nature by society. It is important to note here that emerging with these ideas on nature was a perspective derived from recent European experience with the non-European world. Some of the newly encountered people generated speculation among Europeans about human life "in a state of nature." Deployed philosophically to explore the origins of society and the state, the concept of humans in a state of nature variously fueled imageries of humans as innately good but corrupted by society (J. J. Rousseau, 2002) or innately evil and generating continual conflict and brutality (Hobbes, 1998).

The shadows of such images still inflect many of the constructions of modern societies in their dealings with people deemed primitive, closer to nature, or underdeveloped, resulting in the tendency of modern societies to romanticize, vilify, or patronize them. Now, as then, certain people get relegated to the "nature" category as the need arises. Those people put in the nature category frequently become the objects of development strategies and projects. Indeed, a frequent subtext of development projects is the acculturation of such people to majority-held culture by obligatory participation, whether through forced displacement and resettlement or some other activity. In effect, the goal of such projects is often to bring these people into the national cultural fold through the process of acculturation. The attitude that such a process is akin to civilizing savages is far from uncommon. Indeed, such a process is often glossed as a benefit since the affected people will supposedly become consumers of state services, regardless of the sociocultural, psychological, and material problems caused (Schkilnyk, 1985).

In the West, nature has been largely constructed as a fund of resources into which human beings, regardless of social context, have not only a right to tap but a right to alter and otherwise dominate in any way they deem fit. Along with the detachment of nature and society achieved by eighteenth-century philosophy and political economy, the fortunes of humanity were specifically linked to a set of material practices largely structured by private property market exchange. The market became constructed as the principal vehicle for individual self-realization and societal welfare. Thus, individuals were now not only free to but were virtually obliged to better themselves with the means that God had provided, namely the natural world. With, on the one hand, the reduction of nature to the status of means to the goal of human welfare and, on the other, the rapid expansion of market exchange driven by a productionist ethic, both the ideological justification and the institutional means were available for a relatively unfettered mastery over and unrestrained exploitation of the natural world. Furthermore, the mutually reinforcing pairing of ideology and science (economics) produced a set of institutionalized material practices through which human beings engaged the object of their domination for their new purposes of emancipation and self-realization.

The Enlightenment ideal of human emancipation and self-realization were closely linked to the idea of control and use. Indeed, it was considered that one of the tyrannies from which humankind would be emancipated was that of nature. Harvey explicitly ties this Enlightenment liberation from nature's oppression to a variety of forms of development: physical, psychological, emotional, economic, political, and intellectual (1996, pp. 121–122). As the basic element of the observable world, nature was thus subject to study and ultimately control through understanding its order and its laws. In brief, human life would progress by dominating the natural world through technology and scientific knowledge.

The belief in the domination of nature continued its evolution in Western thought, ultimately connecting in the nineteenth and twentieth centuries with a growing faith in the power of technology to further control and actually shape nature. Nature came to be seen as plastic, ultimately malleable to the purposes of humankind. The "plasticity myth," as Murphy has termed it, is based on the idea that the relationship between humans and their environments can be reconstructed at will by the application of human reason (1994). The application of human reason is believed to impose order on an essentially malleable nature to bring it into line with human purposes. Thus, humans are "capable of manipulating, domesticating, remolding, reconstructing, and harvesting nature" (Murphy, 1994, p. 5). This perspective is eloquently displayed by Vayk who proclaimed:

> Should we find it desirable, we will be able to turn the Sahara Desert into farms and forests, or remake the landscape of New England, while we create the kind of future we dream . . . We are the legitimate children of Gaia; we need not be ashamed that we are altering the landscapes and ecosystems of Earth (1978, p. 61, as cited in Murphy, 1994, p. 8).

The construction of two particular categories, wilderness (Cronon, 1983) and tropicality (Arnold, 1996), played especially significant roles in the application of this largely utilitarian model of human-environment relations.* William Cronon explored the genealogy of the concept of wilderness. He traces the evolution of the concept from a term denoting, in the eighteenth century, a barren wasteland, with connotations of savagery and desolation.

---

*I am indebted to my colleague Laura Ogden of Florida International University for pointing out the relevance of the work of Cronon and Arnold in this context.

Adam and Eve, created in a paradise, are banished to a wilderness. However, by the end of the nineteenth century there had been a shift in attitude, and "wilderness" began to take on positive characteristics. Ironically, when John Muir, one of the earliest and most famous naturalists and conservationists, spoke out against the building of the Hetch Hetchy Dam, designed to provide water for San Francisco from a river valley in Yosemite, he recalled the imagery of Eden. In arguing against those who supported the dam, he said "Their arguments are curiously like those of the devil, devised for the destruction of the first garden—so much of the very best of Eden fruit going to waste" (as cited in Cronon, 1983). Indeed, wilderness, even when considered dangerous, came to be viewed as sublime, as an opportunity to glimpse the hand of God. Places like Yellowstone, Yosemite, and the Grand Canyon in the United States acquired the air of the sacred. At the same time, wilderness also began to be seen as purifying, as an antidote to the problems that were plaguing the developing society taking shape in the United States. Following closely on the Indian Wars, demands for the protection of such sites resulted in the movement to create national parks and wilderness areas, from which all people, particularly native people, had been removed (Jacoby, 2000). Always associated with the frontier and pioneers, the wilderness became a place where "civilized" men could validate themselves as "authentic" men. The wilderness also began to be experienced as a product, as a place properly without people, where the wealthy urban sportsman could briefly experience on holiday a mythic, pristine nature, the ultimate proving ground for the rugged individualist (R. Williams, 2005).

A similar process drove the idea of tropicality (Arnold, 1996). The term developed as a means of dealing with the ambiguities Europeans felt in their expansion into equatorial proximate zones in the eighteenth century. Commencing with images of fertility and exuberance and references to an earthly paradise free of people, the notion of tropicality attracted painters and writers to represent these regions as Eden, but, again, remarkably free of people. In the nineteenth century, the actual experiences of Europeans in tropical zones—heat beyond their imagination, unknown diseases, dangerous animals, and resistant populations—shifted these representations away from the idyllic to the dangerous and corrupt. The climate came to be seen as physically and morally unhealthy for Europeans. Natives were seen as slothful and incapable of civilized behavior. Constructions of the tropics and tropical people portrayed them as disordered, wasteful, and unhealthy. Such images energized a cultural politics among Western societies that justified the transformation of "the tropics" into plantation economies and the resident peoples into slaves (Arnold, 1996).

Contemporary imagery and attitudes toward nature, whether glossed as wilderness or tropicality, underexploited or uninhabited, owe much to these nineteenth-century ideas, and they are refracted into development policies that are aimed at both ordering nature for human use and assimilating the people of these regions into national logics. Confronting these images and the accompanying norms for action toward nature in DFDR resistance are innumerable alternative constructions of nature held by the enormous variety of peoples around the world. There is no overall generalization that one can make about the vast array of understandings of the relationship between nature and society. However, it is generally acknowledged that many local cultures do not accept the dichotomy between nature and society that has undergirded Western economic positions regarding nature. Moreover, local models are not seen as strictly separating the biophysical, human, and supernatural worlds but as posing a continuity among the three that is established through ritual and symbol and is embedded in social relations. In general, local models of nature are complexes of meanings-usages that cannot be rendered intelligible to modern constructions nor understood without some reference to local culture and place (Escobar, 2000, p. 151).

Local perceptions of the environment are often drawn from long-term experience with and knowledge of that environment, as well as from the relationship between that environment and the supernatural. Local environmental knowledge is based on both extensive practice and the cognitive structures linked to the systems of production. The relationship between the environment and the supernatural is expressed through a network of ritual and symbol, transforming the everyday experience of life into meaningful action (Geertz, 1966). In such a context, nature is appropriated discursively, through both the practical and the spiritual realms, thus blurring the distinction between the material and the sacred. Nature thus becomes both the source and the substance of human creation (Gurung, 1997, p. 27).

Environmental Destruction in DFDR

The unrestrained exploitation of nature as the cause for DFDR runs the gamut from mining to manufacturing waste, from deforestation to oil spills. The enormously destructive combination of dam construction and mining in the Singrauli region of central India serves as a tragic example of the environmental and social consequences of unrestrained development (Clark, 2003). Although the initial transformation of the region and significant population displacement began in 1960 with the Rihand Dam, subsequent environmental destruction and the displacement of ultimately between two and three hundred thousand people, some of them three to five times, have been due to the massive exploitation of large deposits of coal that are found beneath the surface of its land. With World Bank loans, the National Thermal Power Corporation (NTPC) established nine open-pit coal mines, operating 24 hours a day, and constructed the Singrauli Super Thermal Power Plant, the Vindhya-chal Super Thermal Power Plant, and the Rihand Power Plant, all on the banks of the reservoir created by the original Rihand Dam. Although not run by the NTPC, three other power plants have been added close by. The power plants subsequently attracted hundreds of factories, as well as chemical, aluminum, cement, and other forms of industrial production.

Local people were relocated into resettlement colonies as their agricultural land was appropriated for the dam and reservoir and then for the coal mines, power plants, and roads, in addition to the markets, homes, and recreational grounds for NTPC workers. Ninety percent of the local people have been relocated at least once and 34 percent have been uprooted several times as development in the region has expanded. A study commissioned by the World Bank and the NTPC found that resettlement projects in the region were unsuccessful, in almost all cases failing to provide adequate facilities and equipment for water supply, sewage treatment, schools, education, and medical care. Moreover, industry-driven air, water, and soil pollution have seriously contaminated the food chain and compromised the health of the population consigned to the resettlement colonies. Displacement has forced formerly self-sufficient agriculturalists to become beggars who seek occasional labor in the industrial complex. The livelihoods and way of life of the resettled communities have been utterly destroyed, and neither the NTPC nor the local government have been willing to assume responsibility for their losses. Now known as the energy capital of India, Singrauli has also been compared to "the lower reaches of Dante's Inferno" (Clark, 2003, pp. 167–272).

The environmental alterations created by development projects have serious implications for the health of affected communities. Peoples' environments can be profoundly altered in two ways. Project construction can either completely change the surrounding environment, transforming a riverine into a lacustrine environment. Or environments can be destroyed, as in the case of Singrauli. Both have, for affected peoples' health, serious implications that may become central to their protests against displacement and resettlement by development projects. Depriving displaced peoples of their access to natural resources and assets has produced negative physical and psychological impacts on their health (Ault, 1989; Berry & Annis, 1974; Bodley, 1994; Chambers, 1970; Fahim, 1983; Kedia, 2009). People experience health risks simply by virtue of the stress and disorientation occasioned by the displacement and resettlement processes themselves, but also by exposure to degraded physical environments and unhealthy conditions in poorly planned and executed resettlement projects (Kedia 2002, 2009). In the case of hydroelectric dam projects, both the people who remain close to the flooded areas and those who are resettled experience significant challenges to their mental and physical health. In the case of those people who continue to reside in the project zone, changes in their local ecology and economy subject them to a broad array of insect-borne diseases. The waters of reservoirs formed by dams provide excellent breeding grounds for disease-bearing insects such as mosquitoes that carry malaria, encephalitis, and filariasis and the snails that are the hosts for schistosomiasis (World Commission on Dams, 2000). People who remain in the zones of mining and industrial projects are frequently subject to the risk of poisoning by exposure to mine tailings, chemical agents, and industrial effluents. Protesting against the wide variety of intensified exposures has become a high priority among communities affected but not displaced by development projects.

Health risks are also significantly increased for people who are resettled. When people are relocated, a frequent outcome is an increase in population in the resettlement area. Population densities may increase the transmission of communicable diseases, particularly those that are waterborne. Introducing populations into regions that are sparsely populated may also expose them to new diseases. The living conditions characterizing poorly planned and poorly implemented resettlement projects fairly routinely expose people to health risks of poor hygiene and unsafe or insufficient water supplies, as well as malnutrition due to inadequate economic planning. Resettled peoples also experience greater levels of stress in adjusting to new environments and economies, resulting in increased morbidity and mortality (Corrucini & Kaul, 1983). The stresses suffered by resettled peoples may result in increases in serious health problems such as diabetes, cardiovascular diseases, and high blood pressure (Ward & Prior, 1980). Although less well documented, an increased rate of serious psychosocial problems such as alcohol and drug abuse, spousal abuse, and suicide are frequently seen in populations experiencing rapid social change (Kedia, 2002, 2009).

Some forced resettlement actually takes place as the direct outcome of environmental impacts of projects, rather than as part of a planned or formal process. Projects, particularly in the extractive industries, tend to produce major alterations of the physical environment in the form of air and water pollution or actual destruction of land. While formal resettlement projects frequently do not accompany such activities, the resulting degradation from some mining projects renders the environment unfit for life, much less human habitation, and residents are uprooted less by external authority than by environmental conditions. In many instances these people become known as environmental refugees, although the term is much disputed (R. Black, 2001; Myers, 1997; Oliver-Smith, 2009a). As noted earlier, there is a very fine line between people who are uprooted by a development project that, for example, submerges their community under a reservoir, and people who are uprooted by a mining project that makes their environment uninhabitable. In both cases, development projects have rendered the environment of a community unusable and uninhabitable. Glossing one group of people as development refugees and the other as environmental refugees does little to mask the direct environmental impacts of development activities. In terms of impacts and outcomes, there is an equally fine line between the victims of an environmental disaster and those of a development project that destroys an environment. Most certainly, the distinction is insignificant for those affected, and both kinds of victims manifest their loss and outrage in very similar forms of resistance and protest.

Case Study: The Tambogrande Mine Project and Citizen Resistance

A wonderful property of the desert coastline of Peru emerges when irrigation becomes available.[†] Since the pre-Incaic era, during which it became the basis of early-state civilizations, irrigation has enabled the desert to flower. Prior to 1959 the San Lorenzo valley in the Department of Piura in northern Peru, where the district of Tambogrande is located, was sparsely populated and largely desert. In 1949 a collaboration between the Peruvian government and the World Bank, costing US$45 million, constructed an irrigation project that led to the establishment of a productive agricultural sector producing limes, mangoes, rice, carob, and other foods for local and national consumption as well as export. Paralleling the growth of the agricultural sector, the population of the town of Tambogrande grew to roughly 16,000 and that of the district to 70,000 people. The agricultural sector now directly or indirectly employs most of the economically active population. Agricultural producers obtain an estimated US$12.5 million for limes and US$83.5 million for mangoes. Export

[†] All information in this case study is drawn from S. Rousseau and Meloche (2002) except where otherwise indicated.

revenues for the national economy are estimated at nearly us$41 million for limes and us$106.5 million for mangoes.

In 1978 explorations by the French state-owned company BRGM revealed significant mineral ore deposits in the subsoil under and surrounding the town of Tambogrande. That same year the Peruvian government formally stipulated in order no. 22672 that the district of Tambogrande was a national reserve for mining development for the benefit of the country. Subsequently, mining concessions were acquired by Manhattan Minerals Corporation of Vancouver, Canada. Mining has long been one of the mainstays of the Peruvian economy and had grown significantly since large-scale privatization and an influx of foreign investment. In 2000 mining represented 47.5 percent of export revenues and employed between eighty thousand and ninety thousand people in large- and small-scale operations. The approval of mining exploration and operations, including related environmental regulations, is the responsibility of the Department of Energy and Mines in Peru. A mining concession gives a company the right to explore in a defined territory and to operate a mine, providing that certain conditions required by law, including the approval of an environmental impact assessment (EIA), are respected. An annual payment for the mineral rights, calculated on the basis of the size of the concession, is also required. The mining concession to Tambogrande stipulated that a new company, Empresa Minera Tambogrande, would operate the mine. Manhattan Minerals Corporation would own 75 percent of the new company, and Minero Peru, a state-owned company, would own the remaining 25 percent.

The project, estimated to cost us$240 million, would include an open-pit mine and affect an area of 750 hectares, requiring the relocation of approximately 8000 residents of the town of Tambogrande and the purchase of 540 hectares of agricultural land. Also included in the project would be an ore processing plant, a mine tailings pond, and the diversion of the Piura River. The project would also include a compensation program for the construction of residential buildings and investments in social and economic development for the displaced and the general region, including the postmining operations period. The mine would have a projected lifespan of roughly 3.5 years for gold and silver and 10 years more for the copper and zinc that lay beneath.

In Peru the only entity entitled to give or refuse access to the nation's subsoil is the national government. Legally, communities have no place in the decision. However, S. Rousseau and Meloche state that conversations between the deputy minister of mines and the president of the company revealed that "it was clear to us that the community's consent was a precondition to setting up the mine" (2002, p. 6). The company's socioeconomic policy further commits them to supporting the social, economic, and institutional development of the communities affected by the project. The company therefore undertook a public relations campaign that included a monthly news bulletin, weekly letters from the president of the company to citizens, information workshops, and company-paid trips for community leaders to visit other mines to demonstrate the compatibility between mining and agriculture. Six demonstration houses of the sort to be provided to those to be relocated were built. A company report states that a total of us$1,457,849 had been spent for roughly 50 socioeconomic projects, including literacy campaigns, well construction, a satellite dish, equipment for a local television station, and university preparatory courses. Roughly us$800,000 of that total went to local labor as wages for manual labor in the exploration work of the company. The company also asserted that consultations with residents of affected communities had been carried out in 1997, prior to the initial exploration and environmental assessment work period.

However, according to some members of the Tambogrande Municipal Council, the company had begun exploration even before any agreements had been reached. And in some instances, the company had signed agreements with specific landowners and community leaders without informing the municipal council, thus dividing the population, at least initially. In mid 1999 the company initiated discussions with the municipal council to undertake explorations in the urban zone, which the mayor authorized in November of that year. Roughly six months later, in mid 2000, the company began discussions with the municipal council about relocating all or part of the community. Although the final decision was that the number of homes to be relocated would be limited to roughly one third of the homes in Tambogrande, the period of uncertainty deeply disturbed the population.

While there had been a traditional antipathy to mining in the region since the 1970s, the exploratory and other activities of the company galvanized the local population into more active resistance. Opposition was based primarily on two issues: hostility to mining, which was felt to be incompatible with agriculture, and the mode and manner in which both the company and the Peruvian government operated, particularly with regard to the participation of the community in decisions that would affect its future.

The principal concern of the local population was that the mine would transform the region from an agricultural zone into a mining and industrial zone with all the social and environmental ills the people felt accompanied such a transformation. People were particularly concerned that environmental changes brought about by the mining operation, in addition to claiming both urban and agricultural land, would contaminate the water so vital to their thriving agricultural sector. Despite efforts by the company to demonstrate that agriculture and mining could coexist harmoniously in the same context, experts declared that the few harmonious contexts elsewhere in the world were too few and too recent to serve as a basis for any conclusions regarding long-term viability. Indeed, an evaluation of the preliminary EIA by a geologist funded by Oxfam America, the Mineral Policy Center, and the Environmental Mining Council of British Columbia tended to confirm those fears. Moreover, the geologist, Robert Moran, demonstrated that the mine's acid runoff combined with the El Nino–generated torrential rains that cyclically affect the region could produce an ecological disaster.

Local people further thought that the irregularities in the granting of mining concessions to Manhattan, the problematic timetable for local consultations, and the overall lack of local participation in such processes were evidence of complicity between the government and the company to transform their environment from agriculture to industry and mining. As a 25 percent shareholder in the company, the credibility of the state was held in some doubt when it came to defending local interests or the environment. The fears of environmental transformation and the discontent with the procedures of both the company and the state, specifically the state's failure to hold a serious debate in Tambogrande over whether to grant mining concessions and exploration rights to the Manhattan Minerals Corporation, led in 1999 to the formation of the Frente de Defensa del Valle de San Lorenzo y Tambogrande (Tambogrande Defense Front, or TDF).

The TDF organized a campaign of resistance to the proposed mine around a number of issues. They criticized the company for seeking authorization from individual community leaders rather than discussing the project in the villages of the district. They faulted the company for reneging on some of the promises of investment in the community, such as building a sports center, and for changing the substance of other commitments over time. And the TDF censured the company for lacking a clear and detailed resettlement plan. This lack of a plan provoked citizen anger instead of interest when they were presented with the model homes that had been constructed.

In the early months of 2001, the conflict between the community and the company sharpened. Faced with the concerns of so many citizens, the mayor reversed his position and collected the signatures of roughly 28,000 people in Tambogrande, approximately 75 percent of the registered voters, on a demand for the termination of mining activities in the region and the withdrawal of Manhattan Minerals Corporation. The community presented the petition to the Peruvian congress and several other public institutions, but no action was taken. In February 2001 the TDF organized a large demonstration of thousands of people to demand the withdrawal of Manhattan Minerals Corporation. The demonstrators confronted the 300 police officers protecting the company's facilities, and fifteen residents and 25 police officers were injured. Many demonstrators were also arrested. Later that night, unknown individuals vandalized the company's offices, destroying equipment and materials, and burned down the model houses. Damages reached US$600,000, and the TDF leaders were charged with the "intellectual responsibility" for the acts. In March a community leader, Godofredo Garcia Baca, who had spoken out strongly and publicly against the mine, was murdered, after which he was transformed into a symbolic martyr in the TDF's struggle against the company.

The Piuran press attacked the leaders of the TDF, defaming their reputations and mounting numerous accusations against them for their resistance activities. The leaders considered this form of character assassination as part of an effort to tie the TDF to terrorist organizations in the minds of a public still traumatized by the horrors of the Sendero Luminoso guerrilla war. Despite these efforts, many regional and national social and non-governmental organizations came to the aid of the TDF and the community with support for their critique of the project. Internationally, Oxfam Great Britain and Oxfam America provided financial support for the publication of Robert Moran's EIA, which detailed scientifically the risks the project would entail for the community. Posters, promotional material, advertising spots, public meetings, lobbying of opinion leaders regionally and nationally, and coordination with international support networks also sustained the effort.

The resistance movement culminated, however, with the launching of a municipal consultation (*consulta vecinal*), an initiative that both the mayor and the TDF supported. By municipal council order, the *consulta vecinal* was created as a mechanism for citizen participation in community development. The resolution of October 11, 2001, stated that there would be a secret ballot in which the citizens could respond negatively or affirmatively to the question "Do you agree with the development of mining activities in the urban, urban expansion, agricultural, and agricultural expansion zones in the district of Tambogrande?"

Although the national government opposed the municipal consultation on the grounds that it was not a legal mechanism provided for in the legislation on mining projects, the planning process continued and the municipal consultation was held on June 2, 2002. Oxfam Great Britain provided US$20,000 to hold the referendum.

Official results of the referendum revealed that with a participation rate of

Three villages face inundation by the Ximapan Dam in Mexico. All three villages are now underwater. (photograph by Ted Downing)

73.14%, the NO side won with 25,381 (93.95%) votes. The YES side received 347 votes (1.28%), and the rest (4.77%) consisted of blank or spoiled ballots. Peruvian government representatives asserted that the municipal consultation had no legal standing but conceded that such massive opposition to the mine could not be ignored. Some sectors of the national press continued to try to link the resistance to terrorism, including an accusation that Oxfam Great Britain had been infiltrated by terrorists. On the other hand, U.S. supporters of Oxfam America sent 7,000 emails urging Manhattan Minerals to respect the outcome of the vote (Oxfamamerica.org, 2003). In December 2003 the people of Tambogrande were informed that the government had decided to block the project on the basis of Manhattan Minerals' failure to meet the financial criteria required for opening the mine.

Dams and the "Taming of Nature"

Perhaps no other instance so epitomizes the subjugation of disorderly nature to human rationality as the "taming" of rivers by channeling and dam construction. The environmental consequences of large dam construction have been the focus of intense opposition campaigns by environmental groups for several decades. Dam construction stands accused of the destruction of entire environments, including flora, fauna, landscapes, river systems, water quality, and shorelines, as well as resultant mercury contamination, greenhouse gases, water quality deterioration, downriver hydrological change, reservoir sedimentation, transmission line impacts, quarries and borrow pits (Ledec, Quintero, & Mejia, 1997). In addition, other ecological impacts attributed to dam construction include increased seismicity, spread of waterborne disease, dam failure, water loss through evapotranspiration, and salinization. Furthermore, the environmental destruction created by development projects has deep spiritual repercussions for many peoples whose religions are based on a close relationship between the natural and supernatural worlds. Although the anti-dam movement essentially began as an environmental movement, it quickly found common cause with human rights activists who quite correctly realized that all the negative environmental and cultural impacts were experienced first and most directly by local people. Indeed, environmental issues have become one of the foremost elements in resistance campaigns launched by local people as well as by local, national, and international NGOs in DFDR resistance. With dam construction that displaces people, specific environmental issues emerge that enter powerfully into the discourse of resistance, both before displacement and after resettlement.

Case Study: The Tucurui Dam and Environmental Conflict

The Tucurui Dam, the largest of the tropics and fourth largest in the world, was part of an overall plan of the Brazilian government to build eighty dams and reduce national dependence on petroleum-generated power. Before the gates closed in 1984 and flooded 2,850 square kilometers of forest, including part of the Parakana Indian reservation, between 20,000 and 30,000 people had to be relocated. The Brazilian government and the administrating agency, ELETRONORTE, had a woefully inadequate resettlement policy that included only a minority of those relocated upstream from the dam and obligated many to fend for themselves in settlements upriver and along the Trans-Amazon Highway (Biery-Hamilton, 1987). Even those who were included in the resettlement scheme were inadequately compensated for their losses. Environmental impacts both upstream and downstream of the dam became the engines for significant protest and resistance that eventually empowered local people for future negotiations with the state (Scudder, 1996).

THE MOSQUITO PLAGUE

Upstream from the dam, an area close to the banks of the reservoir, known as the Parakana Glebe, suffered severe environmental impacts (Acselrad & da Silva, 2000). Many people displaced by the reservoir had been relocated to the Parakana Glebe. In effect, the filling of the dam had transformed the Glebe from a forest fluvial environment to a lacustrine ecosystem. The reservoir area closest to the Glebe had not been deforested prior to submersion, and when the reservoir was filled in early 1986, the decaying and floating vegetation provided an ideal spawning habitat for mosquitoes. The insects proliferated uncontrollably and soon became a major plague. They quickly spread from the lakeside to secondary breeding grounds on roads and to certain trees in the forest whose foliage collects considerable water. Initially, the resettled communities attempted to endure the conditions, going about their normal activities, but the infestation became . . .

unbearable. Nobody could work anymore, or even sleep . . . My wife went to the front of the house to swat the kids' bodies with clothes, but it didn't help. Then desperation came, we became really desperate. People abandoned their lots and went to look for some solution. The government should have helped people in that calamity (Interview with a union leader, February 1996, as cited in Acselrod & Da Silva, 2000, p. 5).

Faced with these conditions, the people began to organize and in 1987 founded the Committees of Expropriated People, aligned with the Tucurui Rural Workers Union. People visited the offices of ELETRONORTE, the principal dam constructor and operator, to protest and demand a solution to the plague. The government response was to initiate an intense campaign of insecticide spraying, which temporarily reduced the plague, but people felt that their health and the health of their animals was seriously affected as well. The impact of the mosquito plague was to alter the nature of the struggle of the displaced communities. The focus of protest and resistance was no longer only the losses occasioned by the displacement but now also included the unhealthy nature of the relocation environment, whose conditions severely impacted daily life and health. Indeed, as people experienced the new conditions, their belief that the lack of deforestation in the submerged area closest to them created the ideal breeding conditions for mosquitoes generally coincided with scientific assessments. However, scientific caution, based on a lack of field studies, in assigning direct causality enabled ELETRO- NORTE to challenge these conclusions and assign blame to the population itself. ELETRONORTE claimed that waste runoff from the communities themselves was creating conditions that allowed mosquitoes to proliferate, thereby setting up an environmental debate between the resettlement authority and the people. However, in 1991 evidence confirmed that mosquito larvae were present in the vegetation that emerged after the filling of the reservoir.

The lack of an effective policy to combat the plague, the problematic nature of the empirical information, and the severe impact on health and living conditions led the people to begin negotiations with land-tenure agencies, ministries, local governments, and politicians. The people also forcibly occupied the company's premises in Tucurui. When ELETRONORTE obtained an injunction evicting them from the premises, the protesters camped outside the main gate of the company compound and remained there in protest for four years. They undertook a number of direct actions as well, such as blocking SUCAM (the national public health organization) and ELETRONORTE vehicles as they tried to implement their ineffective insecticide operations. Although the mosquito plague was the main issue, the movement addressed several other problems that the population had been experiencing since the start of expropriation. Furthermore, the movement succeeded in gaining allies from communities in the broader region, from the Catholic and Lutheran churches and among NGOs who obtained information and provided publicity for the struggle. They also took their cause to Brasilia to confront the ministries, the national congress, and the president. In response to this pressure, the Brazilian government formed an interministerial committee to negotiate with the movement and ELETRONORTE for a solution to the problem. From these negotiations a new settlement project was established. Although the new settlement brought with it new sets of problems, primarily with competing landlords and their hired thugs, the movement had attained legitimacy and had succeeded in taking the political action necessary to alter the conditions into which the people had been forced.

DOWNSTREAM WATER POLLUTION

In addition to what the people upstream from the dam were experiencing, approximately 40,000 *caboclos* (peasants) who lived downstream on the hundreds of islands between the dam and the mouth of the river began to suffer serious ecological and economic impacts. In the course of research undertaken four years after the closing of the dam gates, Magee found that traditional subsistence strategies of riverine peasants were totally disrupted. As Magee notes, "If peasants above the dam suffered the loss of their land, peasants below the dam suffered the loss of their water" (1989, pp. 6–7). The water below the dam became seriously polluted by the decomposing trees in the flooded area that had not been cleared before the floodgates closed. In the four years since the dam began operation, the pollution of the water had caused a series of outbreaks of waterborne diseases ranging from serious vaginal infections in women to gastrointestinal ailments, particularly among children, to skin rashes in the general population. Island crops also suffered from the polluted water. Cacao and acai palm production were crippled. However, the most serious consequence of the dam was the destruction of the river's shrimp and fish populations, the very base of the local subsistence economy and an important source of exchange value as well (Magee, 1989).

Faced with the dam's continuing destruction of their resource base, the riverine *caboclos* were left with two options: migration and resettlement or resistance that, they hoped, would obligate the government both to recognize and compensate their losses and also to diminish the damaging impacts of the dam. In this effort, the Tucurui river peasants began to engage in new forms of political mobilization to defend their way of life. They acquired two extremely important allies: the Catholic Church and the Rural Workers Union. Both the Church and the union had been active in the struggle to protect the interests of people flooded out by the dam. When the Church became aware of the difficulties and privations suffered by downstream peasants, it began to work with them to organize and to represent their interests in negotiations with dam authorities. One result of these collaborations was that the peasants won control of the union, which had traditionally been controlled by local elites with strong ties to the state and national governments. At the top of the agenda of the new union leadership was the commencement of negotiations with ELETRONORTE and its consulting companies to establish responsibilities for the effects of the dam (Magee, 1989).

At the local level the Church and the Rural Workers Union played a crucial role in disseminating to all riverine peasants information on the struggle with ELETRONORTE. At the regional level they created a network of communication to transmit information over a large area of dispersed and isolated settlements. And at national levels they have functioned to articulate peasant concerns with a variety of organizations and institutions such as CRAB (Regional Commission of People Affected by Dams), which began organizing resistance to dam construction and operation at a national level (Magee, 1989) and eventually evolved into a national organization, the Movimento de Atingidos por Barragem (MAB), the Dam Victims Movement (see case study, Chapter 2). Any resistance movement that reaches national levels in a country as important as Brazil soon attracts international attention, thus projecting the struggle of the river peasants onto the world stage.

Due to their own efforts and the efforts of the Church and the union, the peasants impacted by the Tucurui Dam have become part of the larger community of Amazonian peasants and the new political identity the Brazilian peasantry is assuming. They have become aware that others, such as the rubber tappers and Indian groups, have suffered and have successfully organized to defend their interests. The Church is also encouraging some island communities to request outside funding from the Canadian government and the Dutch Catholic Church to address their problems of health care and nutrition (Magee, 1989). This strategy is important in two ways: first, the peasants are seeking solutions on their own, and second, they are appealing to entities beyond their national borders, not only internationalizing their struggle but expanding their own capacities and skills for communication and negotiation.

Undoubtedly, the assumption of a political identity and the acquisition of a voice by the Tocantins river peasants were facilitated by the political *abertura* (opening—democratization) in Brazil. Their political identity and voice developed because of their losses caused by the Tucurui Dam and because of their acquisition of significant allies who have represented them in negotiating with dam authorities and articulated them with broader contexts and information networks. In the process, the peasants have begun to acquire the political skills that will enable them to represent their own interests. However, as Magee (1989, p. 10) noted,

> it remains to be seen whether the Tocantins Islanders can muster the international support they may need to survive on the islands or whether they will join the ranks of the other disenfranchised groups competing for scarce land on the mainland.

The Tucurui experience is emblematic of the inferior environmental planning and implementation that has characterized many large dams around the world. These deficiencies with regard to the environment reveal environmental change as a moment of social struggle for land. That is, the new environment as created by the dam becomes the object of the protests and resistance of the affected populations.

Conservation-Based Dislocation and Resettlement

Although the integrationist or conservationist perspective toward nature occupied a position distinctly inferior to that of the dominant "command

and control" model for much of the modern era, the late twentieth century—
partly due to the extraordinary destruction and transformation of many natural features (air, water, soil, wetlands, forests) as well as entire environments—
has seen a resurgence of environmentally sensitive positions regarding the
society-nature relationship. This new conservationist trend holds serious implications for issues of displacement and resettlement (Oliver-Smith, 2009b).
For example, a position within tropical biology has emerged which holds that
human residence in tropical forests is not compatible with the conservation of
biological diversity (Schwartzman, Moreira, & Nepstad, 2000).

The construction of the categories of "wilderness," mentioned earlier as
playing a significant role in the application of utilitarian constructions of nature, were also key in the emergence of a conservationist perspective in the
United States. Central to these nineteenth-century constructions were essentially aesthetic images of a nature whose grandeur generally did not include
human beings. Since European Americans had virtually eradicated most game
and timber in the northeastern United States by the early nineteenth century,
they began to perceive the westward economic expansion as threatening the
natural splendor of western landscapes. Elite views on the proper use of nature, whether for hunting, aesthetics, or spirituality, generally felt that human
residence, particularly by Native Americans, diminished both the experience
and the setting they were striving for.

As settlers moved relentlessly westward, usurping vast areas of land and
driving off or resettling the original inhabitants, elites, emboldened as they
were by their theories of manifest destiny, also became concerned with pre-
serving some portion of these "pristine" environments (Igoe, 2004, p. 87).
There were additional concerns that the natural resources of the nation were
endangered. The use of the term "conservation," coined in 1903 by Gifford
Pinchot, Theodore Roosevelt's forestry chief, meant the careful husbanding
of resources for wise use by humans (Stewart, Drew, & Wexler, 1999). The
model that informed the formation of these protected areas was originally
enacted in the United States to create Yellowstone National Park. A national
park was considered to be a large area generally unaltered by human exploitation and occupation, whose flora, fauna, and geomorphology are of great
scientific, educational, or aesthetic value, all of which are the responsibility
of the highest national authority to conserve and safeguard. In the creation
of Yellowstone the claims of Indian residents of the area were simply erased,
and their local, culturally constructed relations with the natural world were
replaced by a set of formal codes and regulations administered by a distant
national government (Jacoby, 2000).

Thus, the national park emerged out of the aesthetic, sporting, and spiritual urges of urban European Americans and was the strategy devised to accomplish this process of preservation in the United States. The model was quickly adopted by other nations, both for their own territories and for their colonial possessions. Consequently, in the period between 1900 and 1950, roughly 600 protected areas were established around the world to conserve treasured environments (Ghimire, 1994). By 1995 there were almost 10,000 protected areas, encompassing roughly 5 percent of the earth's surface, and conservationists hoped to double that amount soon (Stevens, 1997). Indeed, by 1997, a scant two years later, there were more than 30,000, and by 2003 the number of protected areas had increased by more than 10 times the 1995 total to over 100,000, covering 17.1 million square kilometers, or 11.5 percent of the land surface of the globe (International Union for the Conservation of Nature/World Commission on Protected Areas, 2004). The United Nations list of protected areas establishes that by 2003 the number of protected areas stood at 102,567, covering 19,216,175 square kilometers. If this trend continues, the potential for more displacements is high.

In the United States and Western Europe the development boom in the 1950s in housing construction, road building, dam construction, swamp draining, and river channeling led to an increasing despoilment of the environment. In 1962 the biologist Rachel Carson published her startling *Silent Spring,* attacking the use of pesticides and detailing their impact on both wildlife and humans (Carson, 1962). The modern era of environmental awareness began when the aesthetic and spiritual motivations for conservation began to be complemented on the one hand by the public and scientific concerns about environmental contamination and on the other by discussion of the endangerment of the services of nature. The impacts of contamination on both humans and wildlife spurred the passing of protective legislation in many countries. In 1987 the World Commission on Environment and Development published *Our Common Future,* more widely known as the Brundtland Report, establishing sustainability as the model and discourse to mediate between economic and ecological concerns. Discourses focusing on the importance of biodiversity for both resilience and adaptation at the species and ecosystemic levels fueled efforts to set aside ever more parcels of land to protect both animals and plants.

In 1980, just prior to the publication of the Brundtland Report, the International Union for the Conservation of Nature published the *World Conservation Strategy,* in which they proposed an alternative to the national park model that advocated the incorporation of local people into the conservation process. The World Bank followed this initiative with a program called Integrated Conservation and Development Projects (ICDP), intended to integrate local people into and enable them to benefit economically from projects. This process has often been referred to as co-management. Although in the last several decades the majority of conservationists have worked with a model that includes participation of the people living within parks and other protected areas, actual practice has fluctuated between generally uneven local participation and conservation by administrative fiat backed up by force.

More recently, dissatisfaction with the outcomes of such projects has generated a more exclusionary strain within the conservation movement, recently dubbed the "protectionist paradigm." Based in part on a model of nature that repudiates integrationist perspectives, the new protectionist paradigm returns to the old oppositional perspective regarding humans and nature (Brechin, Wilshusen, Fortwangler, & West, 2002). The uneven results of ICDP strategies have convinced the authors of several recent influential publications to explicitly militate for the resumption of top-down conservation, requiring a radical transformation of nature, namely the removal of all human inhabitants from environments deemed endangered (Oates, 1999; Terborgh, 1999). Notwithstanding the well-documented fact that human beings have been integral parts and active shapers of "nature" for millennia, some conservationists called for the displacement and removal of long-resident populations from a wide variety of environments in which floral and/or faunal species are considered endangered (Redford & Sanderson, 2000). Referred to as "greenlining" or "ecological expropriation," this strategy entails the forced removal of people from their homelands, often without notice or consultation, producing yet another variety of environmental refugee (Albert, 1992; Geisler & de Sousa, 2001). While recognizing that low-impact rural dwellers inflict much less damage on environments than large-scale agents such as logging or mining enterprises, plantations, or extensive cattle ranchers, fully protected, people-free areas are, some insist, now necessary for adequate conservation (Redford & Sanderson, 2000).

Barring outright displacement, the "new protectionist paradigm" advocated radically restricting resource use practices employed by people resident in reserves and parks. Although criticized for misunderstanding the dynamics of local systems, not to mention their authoritarian tendencies (Dove, 1983; Guha, 1997; Peluso, 1993), new protectionists have called for radically limiting local usages and practices in protected areas. Such restrictions constitute a form of structural displacement in that while people have not been geographically moved, the norms and practices with which they have engaged the environment in the process of social reproduction become so altered as to effectively change their environment from one that is known to one that must be newly encountered with new norms and new practices if social reproduction is to continue. To be fair, many protectionists acknowledge the rights of people residing in areas to be protected, preferring to see them as allies rather than opponents in the struggle against the larger forces embedded in state and private interests that are destroying fragile areas. However, they also marked a clear distinction between their own interests and those of affected peoples. "They [forest peoples] may speak for their version of the forest, but they do not speak for the forest that we want to conserve" (Redford & Sanderson, 2000, p. 1363).

Some conservationists are actually more appropriately designated as "preservationist," seeking to maintain people- and use-free areas, but others can be understood as being concerned with conservation for purposes of "wise use," however that may be defined. While some might argue that conservation is the exact opposite of development in that it seeks to conserve rather than change, others may argue with equal validity that conservation is an enlightened form of sustainable development, particularly in light of the trend of valorizing resources and environments in terms of their contribution to the sustainability of natural cycles of renewability as well as their economic value. The realization that the unlimited exploitation of natural environments undermines the actual material source of value, basically destroying its own conditions of production and reproduction—referred to by J. O'Connor as the second contradiction of capitalism (1998)—has enlisted many ardent developers into the ranks of environmentalists. By the same token, the real and potential use value of plant and animal species is now appreciated as a source for new drugs, genetic banks for agricultural crops, and environmental services such as flood control, as well as non-use values of an aesthetic and recreational sort (Brechin et al., 2002). Sustainable development is a discourse intended to resolve the contradiction between nature and capital, moving capitalism into an ecological phase in which nature is valorized and therefore must be protected (Escobar, 1999). However, according to Escobar sustainable development discourses frequently lay the blame for environmental destruction not on capitalist development but on its victims, the urban poor, the rural swidden agriculturalists, the few remaining hunters-foragers, those often marginalized by development into fragile areas where they struggle to survive (1999).

Faced with these multilayered ideological and material threats to their residence and use of protected areas, local peoples have adopted a wide variety of resistance strategies to conservation projects. Often framing their resistance in terms of conservation as constituting their poverty, indigenous and traditional peoples have adopted multiple forms of political action, ranging from the everyday forms of resistance outlined by J. Scott (1985, 1990) to microlevel and informal politics to outright rebellion.

Case Study: The Montes Azules Biosphere Reserve and the Zapatista Rebellion

Roughly fifteen years ago in the Mexican state of Chiapas, the Zapatista rebellion, named after one of that nation's peasant revolutionary heroes, was launched to combat the abuse and neglect of that region by both local elites and the state itself.[‡] From their bases hidden in the Lacandon rain forest, the rebels emerged periodically to attack military and state targets, as well as to mount an extremely effective public information campaign designed to inform the world of the condition of Chiapas' indigenous peoples. In February 2001 the Zapatista leaders met with the newly elected president, Vicente Fox, to negotiate a peaceful settlement. However, one of the most difficult issues to resolve in the conflict was the fate of the Lacandon jungle and within it the Montes Azules Biosphere Reserve, which forms the core of the rain forest. The Lacandon jungle is the site of North America's last tropical rain-forest and home to an enormous diversity of plant and animal life, exceeded only by similar locations in Brazil and Indonesia. Montes Azules, established in 1978 as Mexico's first UNESCO biosphere reserve, contains more than half of the nation's bird species and 25 percent of its mammals, as well as many endangered species such as harpy eagles, tapirs, white tortoises, jaguars, and ocelots. It is Mexico's most important national park.

The forest is also the home of thousands of indigenous peasants whose cause was embraced by the Zapatista uprising. The focus of the tension between social justice for the people of Chiapas and the integrity of the environment are twenty-two "illegal" communities that emerged in the Montes Azules Biosphere Reserve during the seven-year rebellion. These communities are partly made up of peasants already marginalized by large landowners who control a majority of the land in Chiapas, peasants whose communal *ejido* lands on the borders of the reserve had proved insufficient to sustain their families. Other residents are refugees from the conflict itself, fleeing the abuses of the military and the right-wing paramilitary squads that engaged with the Zapatista combatants. However, the peasants are not the only invaders of the reserve. Only 30 years ago the Lacandon forest was relatively

[‡] Except where otherwise indicated, this case study is based on Wehner, 2000.

untouched and extended for 3.5 million acres. In the ensuing three decades the Mexican state opened the forest to immigration and exploitation of lumber and oil, shrinking the forest to its current 1.6 million acres, half of which are contained in the biosphere reserve.

For the Zapatistas and their allies, Montes Azules is a central issue in their struggle. One of their chief complaints is that the agrarian reform, the crowning achievement of the Mexican Revolution (1910–1917) omitted Chiapas. Rather than break up the large haciendas for redistribution to the peasantry, as was done in the rest of the country, in Chiapas the government resettled landless peasants from the fertile highlands into the jungle and promptly forgot them. In 1972, in a cynically manipulative move, the government relocated 6,000 of these mostly Tzeltal- and Chol-speaking Indians and ceded 1.6 million acres of the forest to 66 Lacandon Indian families, whom they soon convinced to accept a cash payment for large-scale exploitation of lumber, oil, and hydropower. Subsequently, in 1991, changes were effected in the agrarian reform law to permit Mexico's entry into the North American Free Trade Agreement (NAFTA), dooming any hopes the peasants had of receiving land distributions. It is hardly coincidental that the Zapatista rebellion began on January 1, 1994, the day that Mexico formally entered NAFTA.

Montes Azules officials offered the peasants a less than modest 12 acres per family, new homes, and agricultural extension services outside the reserve, but 22 of the 29 communities, or roughly 1000 persons, have refused resettlement. The town of Ricardo Flores Magón, in a public letter posted on the Internet, declared,

> We do not accept coordination, we are not going to permit relocation, and we do not accept the lie of the bad government. We have had 70 years of [the government's] economic programs, of seeing that they do not work, that they do not meet our needs, that others benefit from them, that they do not see our cultures, that after a while the support is withdrawn, in a few words, that they always fail. Our communities and our people are in resistance against the bad government (Wehner, 2000).

The local resistance movement and the government both acquired national and international allies in the dispute. On the government's side, international organizations such as Conservation International and the World Wildlife Fund supported efforts to remove the peasants from the reserve. They were fearful that, among other things, the swidden (slash and burn) agriculture of the peasants would prove devastating to the forest. The debate about swidden agriculture has fluctuated a great deal over time. In the nineteenth century it was seen as destructive of valuable commodities such as teak. Anthropologists have established that swidden systems as traditionally operated with vertical overlapping layers of different crop species, small settlements, and widely scattered gardens were actually minimally disruptive of the forest ecosystem (Bodley, 1994, p. 50). Today swidden agricultural systems seem to have fallen into disrepute again. In the Montes Azules reserve it is feared that the practice of swidden agriculture by the resisting peasants will result in large-scale deforestation as well as perhaps start large-scale forest fires. Fires have previously threatened the forest, and park officials are fearful of another series of fires that might completely consume the forest, although there are contesting claims that the previous fires were due to military campaigns against resisting villages (Bellinghausen, 2000). Certainly the increasing population of the marginalized, growing from 60,000 in 1960 to more than 400,000 currently, is contributing to these fears of environmental destruction, but Jose Ignacio March, Conservation International's director in Chiapas, stated that the number of people is less significant than the swidden system. "We can deforest the whole forest with the current productive systems, and everyone will still be in poverty" (Wehner, 2000).

Despite the Indians' deep distrust, the government, in collaboration with Conservation International, operates a number of programs in the forest that promote the cultivation of organic shade coffee, ornamental palm frond, and vanilla; support indigenous handicrafts; and encourage sustainable forestry and farming methods involving composting and crop rotation, eliminating the need to slash and burn. However, the industry that is considered to have the greatest potential for halting the destruction of the forest is ecotourism. The United States Agency for International Development commissioned Conservation International to develop a management strategy for the entire Lacandon region, but especially to protect the dozens of Mayan ruins, the indigenous cultures, and the great aesthetic value of the rain forest itself.

Opposing the government and the conservationist position are the human rights groups that have allied themselves with the peasants resisting resettlement. Such groups as Food First and the Mexico Solidarity Network in the United States maintain that until appropriate land reform measures are taken to assure marginalized peoples access to sufficient land, there will be no solution to the invasion of reserves, not only in Mexico, but in the rest of the world as well. The Zapatistas assert that the park authorities exaggerate the danger of fire as a pretext to forcibly remove the villages and also to allow the army access to sufficient terrain in the park to surround the rebel army. An official communiqué of the Zapatista rebellion contended, "But those who are today wrapping themselves in the green flag of saving the Montes Azules Biosphere are also strangely forgetting about the irresponsible and incoherent manner in which the reserve has been administered over the last thirty years." Indeed, such protectionist policies are even contradicted by the military's reforestation efforts that focused on nonnative, commercially exploitable species such as eucalyptus, cedar, and mahogany in monocropping schemes that ignore the complex diversity of the forest ecosystem. The continued oil exploitation and the Comision Federal de Electricidad's (CFE) planned construction of as many as 43 hydroelectric dams in the Lacandon forest region are also hard to reconcile as ecologically sustainable development (Osun, 1999).

Local people now frame the reserve and the resistance against it in larger contexts of the regional development initiative of the Inter-American Development Bank's Plan Puebla Panama.

> Today we are saying it quite clearly, the project to exterminate our indigenous communities through dislocation and relocation is a strategic part of the Plan Puebla-Panama (PPP) and of its economic interests, which are attempting to extend neoliberal policies and projects to the South and Southeast of Mexico and to all of Central America. In addition, in order for these policies to be imposed in our lands, the PPP is, at the same time, a counterinsurgency plan, because neoliberal interests find themselves thwarted by our indigenous communities and our different cultures, which understand land as mother, as a communal good that cannot be used for the benefit of just a few, because it cannot be destroyed or stolen in order to be made private and destroyed in order to take out its wealth. (Consejo Autonomo de Ricardo Flores Magón, 2002).

The resolution of the problem seems distant still as the government proposes relocation, and the Zapatistas and their allies are reluctant to discuss the issue. Despite great optimism for the talks held in March 2001 between the government and the Zapatista National Liberation Army, outcomes were disappointing as the bill for constitutional reforms of the law of indigenous rights and culture was considered a betrayal of the original agreement to approve the 1996 San Andres Accords backed by the Zapatistas. The National Indigenous Congress, in addition to the Zapatistas, planned organized protests over the law, which they alleged denies the rights of indigenous peoples. In Chiapas, thousands of indigenous people marched and demonstrated in protest over the congressional version of the law (Mexico Solidarity Network, 2001).

Conclusion

The issue of marginalized peoples and protected areas is one that most likely will continue to draw the attention of the conservation movement. Until more equitable forms of land distribution are developed, many protected areas will be seen as the solution to survival for those people marginalized by agribusiness. In turn, there will be attempts at forcibly relocating such communities because of their impact on the environment. Such people become double losers as they are sacrificed to the demands of both commercial agriculture and the conservation movement. Given the intensified efforts to partition off large expanses of land in protected areas, biodiversity conservation organizations must recognize that their methods must be altered and their approaches to local communities improved if future displacement and major human rights violations are to be avoided.

Both conservation biologists and anthropologists have recently intensified their efforts to address this need. Conservation biologist Kent Redford and anthropologist Michael Painter (2006) assert that indigenous peoples and nature must find common grounds for mutual assistance if both are to survive. Redford and Painter suggest that the collaboration between the Wildlife Conservation Society and the Capitania de Alto y Bajo Izozog, an organization of roughly 10,000 Guarani-speaking people in eastern Bolivia, constitutes an important example of successful cooperation between indigenous people and conservationists. Together these two organizations have developed the Gran Chaco National Park and Integrated Management Area. These researchers also contend that if the conflict between conservationists and indigenous peoples and their allies continues, the important decisions regarding both indigenous culture and nature will be made by parties seeking to further only personal, economic, and national power interests. Redford and Painter thus present a positive example that bodes well for the further development of productive collaborations. Most recently, Agrawal and Redford assert that without the consultation of people to be affected, there is no ethically satisfactory way to address the needs of people displaced by conservation projects. They have called for "a positive-historical" program of action for conservationists that would address more comprehensively the needs of the displaced, including reparations for past conservation forced displacements (Agrawal & Redford, 2006, p. 12). However, progress at the level of theory or even selected productive examples is under constant challenge by interests whose efforts result in the destruction of both natural and cultural diversity, destruction that is currently proceeding at alarming rates around the world.

CHAPTER FIVE

Challenging the Economics of Displacement

Evaluating Risks and Compensating Losses

Particularly in the developing world, where communities have been less dissolved into clusters of atomized economic actors, resistance to DFDR challenges the way states, multilaterals, and corporations do business. In many instances, resistance by communities subverts the individualistic economic model of the West. Economics, as constructed in the West, is purportedly about individual choice-making in the application of scarce means to prioritized ends. The market is the primary institution in which these choices are made, and money is the primary means through which they are carried out. However, for many communities, if they define economics as a separate domain at all, it is about provisioning households and communities on land and property that are valued in ways beyond the reach of market calculation. Since large development projects affect entire communities and often networks of communities, opposition frequently comes from communities, even those composed of groups with diverging interests, as well as individuals. In the developed world, displacement and resettlement are often accomplished at the individual level through the mechanism of eminent domain and the purchase of property at market value. However, resistance to this policy is increasingly organized at the community level even in the developed world, challenging the ways business is normally transacted by the state and corporations.

If the decisions to displace and resettle people are fundamentally political, the purposes of development projects that displace people are most often deemed to be economic. Despite the cultural and political forces and subtexts (see Chapters 6 and 7) that support their construction, large-scale development projects are ultimately justified on economic grounds. Similarly, in purely economic terms DFDR resistance involves a conflict between the needs of a local society and the purported needs of a regional or national one.

Infrastructure, facilities, services, and resources of various sorts are determined to be essential to the economic development process and deemed to override the rights and needs of people who occupy the terrain necessary for a project. Even in cases where the purported goal is conservation of a natural environment, the discourse of complementarity between good ecology and good economics created by the concept of sustainable development may provide an economic subtext to such projects. Furthermore, the discourse of biodiversity underscores the importance of conservation in economic terms by invoking the necessity of maintaining genetic diversity for the preservation of robustness and resilience of both environmentally and commercially valuable species. Also, secondary economic goals involving selected forms of resource exploitation are often revealed subsequent to reserve demarcation and displacement, as was shown in the Montes Azules case study in the previous chapter.

In Chapter 1, I made the point that the state and private capital often seek to relocate people on the basis of the efficient use of resources. That is, it is claimed that the state or private interests can exploit the resources of a place in a more economically efficient fashion than the original residents, producing more value for the society as a whole. The basis for this claim is both technological and organizational, but the underlying concept is that both features are thought to be more efficient in terms of the ratio of invested resources — capital and labor — to the amount of output or product.

The goal of efficiency is a basic concept of economics, and it is driving nations to strive to develop by increasing the scale of their enterprises. Efficiency is about the production of value. Resource use is considered to be efficient when the things produced are what people value most highly. In other words, resource use is considered efficient when more of a good cannot be produced without giving up another good that we value even more highly (M. Parkin, 2003, p. 102). This is just a way of saying that the production of value or a valued good is efficient when the process obliges us to forgo fewer other goods that we may also value. Economic efficiency occurs when valued goods are produced at least cost.

Closely related to the concept of efficiency is the notion of economies of scale. Dating back to Adam Smith's original discourses on the advantages of production brought about by the division of labor, economies of scale are present when the cost of production of a single unit of a good falls as the rate of output increases (M. Parkin, 2003, p. 207). Although there are numerous examples to the contrary, particularly in development projects, reducing the cost of production is frequently associated with the size of a production

Luxury lakeside apartment units occupy land previously owned by the indigenous Pehuenche people who were displaced by the Pangue Dam in Chile. (photograph by Ted Downing)

unit. That is, following Adam Smith's famous example of the manufacture of pins, rather than have a dozen small factories, each with its own workforce, technology, and management, producing the components of a product, it is deemed more efficient, in the sense of lowering the costs of inputs, to have one large factory in which all facets of the production process are under one roof, with one management structure, one workforce, and one technological infrastructure. This logic prevails, despite the frequency of diseconomies of scale in development projects and elsewhere.

As previously mentioned, the political and symbolic weight of the development process in national imaginations cannot be overemphasized. For many political and economic elites, such a process carrying such a high political and economic charge must command an equally charged physical manifestation. Although the tendency to produce large monuments to a society's (or a ruler's) greatness is ages old, contemporary nations have used the development process to produce their own temples to grandeur in the form of what have become known as "megaprojects." As the term suggests, megaprojects are mammoth development projects, and although the term is relatively new, they have been around for a long time. Certainly, one has to categorize the pyramids of Egypt and Mesoamerica, the Great Wall of China, and the great cathedrals of medieval Europe as megaprojects. They were gigantic for their time and would be considerable today. However, unlike their contemporary counterparts, they were primarily religious or defensive in nature. Today's megaprojects, while possessing similarly enormous symbolic power, address primarily economic purposes.

Predating globalization as a totalizing framework, the term "megaproject" was first used in the 1970s to characterize both the scale and the cost of the enormous energy development projects that were being constructed in many regions of the world (Altshuler & Luberoff, 2003). However, the scale suggested by the term fits well with the kind of totalizing ideology of triumphalism that characterizes much of the discourse surrounding globalization. Since it first emerged, the cultural power of the term has been made manifest in an increasing number of grandiose projects, ranging from the now nearly

People scavenged bricks and other construction materials from the rubble of buildings demolished for the construction of the Three Gorges Dam in China. (photograph by Ted Downing)

completed Three Gorges Dam in China to such enormous undertakings as the proposed expansion of the Panama Canal (Rosales, 2005, 2007) and the vast river-linking project in India (see Chapter 8). Various attempts have been made to frame a definition of "megaproject," many of them focusing on cost as the central variable, with examples ranging from US$250 million to US$1 billion (Altshuler & Luberoff, 2003; Capka, 2004). In addition to cost, the question of scale is also addressed and framed in language that suggests a kind of total domination and transformation of environments, subjugating nature's most enormous features and most powerful forces to human will and purposes (Gellert & Lynch, 2003). Others frame megaprojects as being transformative in their function as forces that carry out the logic of time-space compression of postmodernity and globalization, enabling faster communication and transportation among participants in the global marketplace (Flyvbjerg, Bruzelius, & Rothengatter, 2003, p. 2).

Megaprojects come in many guises and forms. They may take the form of infrastructure such as dams, airports, or tunnels. They are often linked to extractive industries such as mining, oil and gas production, or transport (pipelines). They appear as production complexes such as industrial parks, export processing zones, or the irrigation projects that are frequently developed along with dams. Huge complexes dedicated to consumption, such as stadiums, Olympic villages, theme parks, tourist installations, and real estate developments also can reach the scale of megaprojects (Gellert & Lynch, 2003).

The sheer scale of megaprojects today, in terms of both cost and impact, requires that they be framed by their proponents as promoters of development for all citizens of a nation, without regard for ethnic and class differences. They are often presented as producers of not only the obvious benefits of the project (electricity, water, transportation, etc.), but as generators of employment and income for the masses. The nationalistic agenda becomes clear when such projects are portrayed as the key element that will modernize whole national sectors, energizing regional and national economies and elevating the nation to full participation in international economic systems. Moreover, as the epitome of the application of rationality and science, megaprojects are interpreted as symbolic of the modern state and its efficient operation on behalf of all citizens (Ribeiro, 1987, pp. 9–12). Nonetheless, regardless of the scale and the political and cultural power expressed by a megaproject, it is ultimately judged, legitimately or spuriously, as economically justified in that it will produce benefits that outstrip its costs.

Case Study: The Expansion of the Panama Canal

Even by today's standards, the construction of the Panama Canal from 1904 to 1914 was a megaproject.* Over 65,000 people, 50,000 from the Caribbean region and 15,000 Europeans, worked on the canal. Nearly 25,000 of them died. The construction of the canal changed the ecology of Panama permanently. Almost 220 million cubic meters of land were excavated to create the 423-square-kilometer Gatun Lake, at one time the world's largest human-made lake. Thousands of hectares of forest were removed. Along the Pacific coast, islands were connected to the mainland, and on the Atlantic coast large jetties were constructed, converting the city of Colon from an island to a peninsula. Along the route of the canal, 21 communities were inundated, the thousands of residents arbitrarily displaced without consultation, fair compensation, or recourse (McCullough, 1977).

The canal, running 80 kilometers across the Isthmus, vastly reduced the time and distance that ships had to travel between the Atlantic and the Pacific oceans. A ship traveling between San Francisco and New York saves over 7,800 miles by passing through the canal instead of rounding Cape Horn at the southern end of South America. Almost 900,000 ships have used the canal since it was inaugurated nearly 100 years ago, averaging between 13,000 and 14,000 a year. Currently, 68 percent of all merchandise that is exported from or imported to U.S. ports passes through the canal, while 23 percent of China's shipping and 16 percent of Japan's go through the canal (Gualdoni, 2006). In the nine years since Panama took control of the canal, it has earned nearly one billion dollars, becoming a major resource for the economy of the nation. However, despite being a source of significant revenue for the nation, the benefits of the canal have not been widely distributed among the population. Many of the communities along the route do not have either electricity or potable water, their roads are poor, and national health and communication services are deficient in many regions.

In the more than ninety years of its existence, the canal has provoked further ecological changes, including increased population density along the route between Colon and Panama City, intensive cattle ranching, deforestation, and both water scarcity and pollution. High levels of sedimentation have reduced the capacity of Alajuela and Gatun lakes to store the water needed for the canal. The canal needs roughly 1.8 billion gallons of freshwater every day to effect the transit of the average of 36 ships a day that pass through

*Except where otherwise indicated, all information for this case study is based on Rosales, 2007.

its locks. Faced with increasing demands for freshwater from growing urban populations as well as the needs of the future expansion of the canal, the Panama Canal Authority has been seeking ways to increase the supply of water, particularly during periods of environmental scarcity such as El Niño. One method is to expand the canal watershed. In 1999 the Panamanian legislature hastily approved, without any consultation with the people to be affected, a law incorporating new lands into the canal watershed.

The imperative for expanded sources of water has been increased by recent changes in international maritime trade. The growth of Asian economies, particularly China's, has increased the volume of trade, stimulating shipbuilders to construct larger vessels that can carry greater amounts of cargo. However, many of these ships, some already in operation, are too large to pass through the canal. The Panama Canal Authority is now calling for an expansion of the canal to accommodate what are now known as Panamax vessels.

The plans to expand the dimensions of the canal and the concomitant expansion of the canal watershed led in turn to concrete plans for dams to be constructed to accumulate the greater volumes of water needed for both purposes, evoking considerable concern that communities in the areas affected would be uprooted. Small farmers in communities in the western part of the province of Colon began organizing meetings to discuss the problems. Soon, an organization called Coordinación Campesina Contra Embalses (CCCE), (Peasant Coordination Against Dams) was formed, bringing together peasant farmers from Colon, Cocle, and Panama provinces. The threats represented by these two linked initiatives of the Panama Canal Authority sharpened the discourse regarding the distribution of benefits from the canal that had been simmering in Panama for decades.

"They claim that if they don't enlarge the canal, it'll become obsolete. So what? The canal has been obsolete for small farmers like us since the very start, since we haven't received any benefits from it," said one farmer. CCCE leader Francisco Hernandez, in response to a question from a television interviewer, posed his own question. "I ask the viewers, how and when has the average citizen felt the benefits of the canal? When someone can answer that, or when a group of average working people tell us, 'We benefit from the canal,' then we can talk about the kind of sacrifice farmers would be willing to make."

Their opposition to the dams has brought the CCCE considerable scrutiny by Panamanian security forces, and many of its members have been interrogated. In 2001 security officials, in order to incriminate the CCCE, alleged that Zapatista guerrillas had entered the area. Since the canal is a vital national resource, the Panamanian government considers opposition to be a national security concern and closely monitors the activity of non-Panamanians working with the CCCE. In 2004 a Spanish citizen working for CARITAS was expelled from the country for this reason. However, the peasants of the CCCE have garnered the support of missionaries working in Colon province, the bishops of the dioceses of Panama, Colon, and Penonome, the national branch of CARITAS, and several worker and student organizations. The support of these organizations has enabled the CCCE and its members to be heard in many public venues, including radio stations, TV channels, public events, and the legislature. In these contexts they have made clear their position that they are not against development, but against injustice.

In addition to the increased scrutiny, the response of the government and the Panama Canal Authority has been somewhat opaque. Instead of dams, the master plan of the Panama Canal Authority included a series of holding pools that would run parallel to the locks and would recycle the water needed for ships to pass. Nevertheless, these official announcements were placed in doubt by the government's intense efforts, funded over the past two years by international sources, to survey and issue land titles in the region as a basis for a legal framework for expropriation. Canal authorities have also been conducting a public relations campaign both among the peasant communities and in the general population.

The ambiguity of the response by the government and the Panama Canal Authority has been the cause of no little discontent. First, the general secrecy regarding the information gathered in the surveys and other research was a source of considerable concern. Second, the publication of the studies only in English not only made them inaccessible to the general population but constituted a form of cultural insult as well. This concern has increased since the announcement of a referendum on the canal that was to be held before the end of 2006. Until recently, the government has provided little concrete information. The massive publicity campaign for the project has produced polls indicating that a majority of Panamanians are in favor of the canal expansion ("Panama's President Touts Canal," 2006). On April 24, 2006, the president of Panama formally presented the project to the nation, explicitly stating that the proposal did not include constructing any dams. In addition, he said that he would ask the legislature to rescind the law that expanded the watershed of the canal. Although it is dangerous to assume that the situation is entirely resolved, it appears that the peasant resistance movement played a key role in the reconsideration of the project (Rosales, 2007).

Regardless of the scale of the project—whether it is a megaproject like Three Gorges, the expansion of the Panama Canal, or only the removal of a poor neighborhood segment to make way for an expanded urban roadway—

Protestors mount the steps of the building housing the Panama Canal Authority (ACP) to protest their displacement by the widening of the canal. Their banner accuses the ACP of lying. (photograph by Renzo Rosales)

the economic criteria that are used to justify the undertaking impose a narrow and restrictive metric when we consider the impact on people to be displaced. As I have mentioned before, DFDR is a multidimensional, totalizing phenomenon, impacting virtually every aspect of the lives of the displaced. Thus, between a project that is justified on purely economic grounds and a community's multifaceted existence there is a fundamental analytical disjuncture. The data, rationale, and basis for projects are generally unidimensionally quantitative and economic. Economic planners and their models, methods, and tools cannot address the multidimensionality that is presented by DFDR. Characteristically, that which economics cannot address is dismissed as external to the problem, statistically insignificant, or unimportant. This idea of multidimensionality, so fundamental to any clear understanding of resettlement, much less human society in general, is therefore rarely factored into the planning process of projects that will displace people (Cernea, 1999, pp. 21, 23). Thus, the format in which the vast majority of DFDR-producing projects is conceived is almost inevitably inadequate from the perspective of the project-affected people and equally inevitably provides the rationale for resistance. Indeed, such is the hegemony of economics in development that the only option left to DFDR-affected people is protest and resistance (Cernea, 1999; Chambers, 1997).

Therefore, the rationale for projects is fundamentally economic, and the decisions to move ahead with projects are made by assessing economic gains over other considerations. Thus, even before the people to be displaced are aware of a project, the nature of the decisions that have been made and the plans that have been drawn up come from a perspective that in most cases has markedly different value orientations and rationalities from those of the people to be displaced. In many, if not the majority, of cases the bases on which these decisions and plans have been elaborated are derived from a set of value positions and perspectives that are almost inevitably going to provoke resistance. It is not just uprooting that sparks resistance. As Cernea (1999) notes, the disaster of resettlement is deeply embedded in both the rationale on which and the method by which the project is conceptualized and designed, making resistance virtually inevitable.

However, it is not only the value orientation or basis of those decisions and plans that evokes such immediate resistance. Recently, Cernea has severely criticized the form and method of the economic analyses that have been employed in resettlement projects as being responsible for the almost uninter-

Protestors against the project to widen the Panama Canal hold a poster that reads, "Clean Referendum Yes, Deception of the People No." (photograph by Renzo Rosales)

rupted string of failures around the world (1999, 2009). As Chambers wryly notes, "Economists tend to take a Pavlovian view of human nature which sees people as subject to reflexes which respond to economic incentives. The danger is that assuming that other people are economic maximizers makes economic maximizers of those who make the assumptions" (1997, p. 50). Thus, there is a failure to understand that the loss of jobs, the loss of livelihoods, is more than the loss of the means to make a living that can be replaced by another means. When a tourist project displaces a fishing village, the loss of livelihood is the loss of a way of life and a way of defining the self. Assuming simply that people who have spent their lives defined by a form of livelihood can easily shift to another is to reduce human life to mere labor power.

Moreover, much of the economic data on which such economic decisions are made can be seriously flawed by culture-bound elite notions about peasants, farmers, women, indigenous people, or other minorities or subgroups that may be threatened with resettlement. For example, assuming that rural dwellers are a single set of farmers with a uniform set of needs and requirements completely elides the class and ethnic distinctions that will generate important differences in economic and social resources, forms of tenure, amounts and kinds of land farmed, crop choices, credit access, and common resource access, all of which will determine the effect of resettlement as well as the intensity of resistance.

Cost-Benefit Analysis

Thus, many of the core disputes fueling resistance movements are economic in nature. They are disputes about property and legality, about price and value. In terms of property, the state holds a regulatory mechanism, the well-known power of eminent domain, that allows for the expropriation of private property that is required for the public interest. Under eminent domain, states are required, however, to compensate the owners of expropriated property at fair market value, which is presumed to be sufficient compensation for a rational actor in a market economy to be able to replace the expropriated land with a parcel of equal market value (Rose, 1994; Szablowski, 2002).

The proponents of the reigning models of development that emphasize large-scale transformations of the social and physical environments espouse values that elevate "the greatest good for the greatest number" over the rights of the less numerous and the less powerful. How the concept of "good" and how the numbers are arrived at are issues of some discussion. However, since most proponents of large-scale development—particularly nation-states and the multilateral agencies such as the World Bank and its companion regional development banks, as well as the private sector—are operating under primarily economically derived definitions of development, their approach to defining "good" is largely based on economic measures. In that approach they are generally consistent with a Western perspective that evolved in close relationship with the expansion of the market in social life. Indeed, part of that cultural perspective involves a close linking of the idea of economic quantification with rationality and science, allegedly allowing for precision and banishing the ambiguity that plagues decision-making through political discourse (Espeland, 1999). Thus, the concept of value embodied in the word "good" is fundamentally an economic one based on income and other quantifiable benefits.

The means by which such a position is derived is a calculus known as cost-benefit analysis (CBA), often hailed as a means of clarifying and rationalizing societal choices and minimizing social conflict. CBA itself has become the model from which a form of discourse emerges that purports to remove or replace other forms of discourse, such as politics, from debates about social and environmental projects. Originating from economics, CBA provides policy makers and politicians with a method for making decisions about social and environmental projects that is purportedly objective, fair, and democratic and whose decisions and outcomes are arrived at scientifically. The essence of CBA is expressed by its name. Basically, the analyst measures the costs and benefits associated with a project and then adds up the figures in each category to see which is larger (Adams, 1996, p. 2). If the value of the benefits outweighs the value of the costs, an objective basis for proceeding with a project has been provided the policy maker.

This formulation seems straightforward enough. But there are a number of issues that escape attention if we leave it at this level. In large-scale development projects there is an array of benefits to be perceived in the production of certain goods or services, say, electricity or transportation, and there is an array of costs, such as forgoing the production of other valued goods, that must be paid to produce the desired goods or services. What is often assumed in development planning is that the populations taking on the costs and enjoying the benefits of the production of the goods or services are one and the same, when in fact those who will enjoy the benefits are only forgoing some value while others may perceive very little value but assume enormous costs.

Nonetheless, in order to carry out this calculus, some prior operations become necessary because the costs and benefits of a project will be of various orders: some will be economic, some will be social, some will be environmental, and some will be cultural. In order to carry out a CBA, some common standard of measurement must be established for the appropriate calculation to yield the quantitative, objective result that will produce a decision unaffected by and essentially impermeable to political interference. That is, there has to be a single property possessed by all things, conditions, or states of affairs that is considered to be the source of their value (O'Neill, 1998, p. 98). This single property provides the strong commensuration that is required for a CBA.

> The only basic principle is that we should be willing to assign numerical values to costs and benefits, and arrive at decisions by adding them up and accepting those projects whose benefits exceed their costs. There is absolutely no need for money to be the numeraire [i.e. the unit of account] in such valuations. It could equally be bushels of corn, but money is convenient. (Layard & Glaister, 1994, as cited in Adams, 1996).

In effect, in this mode of discourse, money is considered to be a convenient means of representing the relative values that society places on different resources and practices. Thus, for a CBA to be carried out, the costs and benefits in all their diversity have to be expressed in some uniform, quantitative format, conveniently and preferably in money prices. Money values or prices are usually arrived at by the modified or unmodified intersection of supply and demand in a marketplace. Thus, the loss of land in a market society is considered to be compensated by the price that land would bring in the market if it were offered for sale. Using prices thus presents a problem for determining the value of costs and benefits from a project that are not the result of the intersection of supply and demand in a market.

Since CBA normally requires that everything be expressed in money value terms, a method must be devised to assess how people would monetarily value nonmarket items. Such a method is known as contingent valuation, and although, to be fair, its validity is still a much-debated issue among economists, it is integral to CBA (Bishop, Champ, & Mullarkey, 1995). In contingent valuation, people are asked how much they would be willing to pay (WTP) for the things the analyst is seeking to value, if they were for sale (Adams, 1996, p. 2). WTP works best when people are asked about benefits. However, in cases of DFDR, the question for people who are being impacted is more frequently one of costs. In the case of costs, the question revolves around how much money would a person be willing to pay to prevent losses or be willing to accept (WTA) as compensation for losses. These questions are not simply inversions of each other. They elicit manifestly different responses. On the one hand, asking a person how much they would be willing to pay to prevent a loss is constrained by that person's ability to pay. On the other hand, asking a person how much they would be willing to accept as compensation for a loss elicits what economists have characterized as "unrealistically high answers" (Adams, 1996). WTP is generally preferred, for reasons of sound economy.

> Consider the case of an environmental degradation in the form of a dam construction which will flood a valley. One old man who has lived in the valley for all his life will be forced to move if the dam is constructed. His equivalent variation, or the amount by which one should reduce his income in order to expose him to an equivalent worsening of welfare, is bounded upwards by his income (WTP). On the other hand, his compensating variation is not bounded upward and can be quite substantial. Although the two measures are radically different in this case, they both give valid measures of the welfare changes of the old man. The problem appears when we compare the welfare of this individual with the welfare of others, i.e. all those consumers of electricity who will gain by the construction of the dam. If we want to put special emphasis on the old man in the valley, we should choose to use the compensating variation (WTA), while if we want to treat him on an equal footing with the electricity consumer, we should use the equivalent variation. (Dasgupta & Maler, 1989, p. 232).

The goal of such an analysis is to provide a basis on which a set of benefits can be compared with a set of costs. Using dams as an example, benefits include such things as power generation, irrigation water, and/or flood control for estimated population groups. Costs normally include the cost of design and construction, perhaps mitigation of environmental impacts, and/or compensation for people who must be relocated from land to be inundated or otherwise affected. The method is intended to provide an objective, neutral, transparent basis for making decisions about the viability of projects and to inoculate them against the wrangling and influence of political interest groups. Martin O'Connor has described CBA as being driven by the political desire to escape politics (1999).

As Cernea points out, CBA justifies a project economically on the basis of benefits that are greater than costs in terms of total sums. However, CBA does not account for distribution of either costs or benefits. It cannot ask who pays the costs, suffers the losses, or reaps the benefits. Moreover, CBA establishes aggregate costs and benefits when it is individuals who incur the costs and absorb the losses (Cernea, 1999, p. 20). CBA also is inadequate for assessing costs that are real but difficult to quantify, such as the losses experienced in the breakdown of community or the loss of cultural or spiritual resources. Other critics of CBA (Adams, 1996; Espeland, 1998; O'Neill, 1999) contend that CBA distorts the values that people attach to both natural and cultural resources.

Natural Resource Valuation

The multiple costs and losses incurred by subsets of groups are often distinguished along class, ethnic, gender, or age lines. One of the main points of dispute in DFDR resistance is the appropriate means with which to measure or account for these costs and losses. The valuation of natural resources in terms of money, for example, is not problematical in societies that have an established principle of individual property in nature. In such societies many natural resources, including land, are customarily measured in terms of quantity or volume, valued in terms of money, and owned privately. However, the standard by which they are priced for compensation in DFDR is an issue of considerable debate. Particularly in the First World, the standard by which people removed for projects by eminent domain were compensated was basically market value. The market price was expected to reflect both the quantity and quality of resources lost and gained. However, a great deal of protest has emerged where this standard has been employed to compensate people for land, for example, because differences in value and quality of land lost and land in the region of resettlement may not be recognized in market transactions. Hence, many people engage in protest and resistance activities to militate for the use of replacement value as the standard for compensation for land. Thus, in many cases, money may be entirely acceptable as a means of compensation, but the standard by which the price of land is established may be very strongly contested.

However, property rights in these situations are rarely clear-cut. In many contexts in which DFDR has taken place, formal titles to land are more the exception than the rule. People with traditional forms of tenure embodied in ties between cultural identity and specific territories may have resided on and exploited land for generations without having formal titles, for a variety of reasons. Some may exist as renters or tenants. Others may informally occupy land belonging to others, as squatters. Moreover, they may also depend on resources that exist on land that is considered to be either government or common property. Thus, when people are displaced, the issues of whom to compensate and how to compensate are central in the demands resistance movements put forth. A frequent issue of contention between DFDR project authorities and resisters revolves around the requirements for compensation. Project authorities have often restricted compensation to holders of formal titles, thus sometimes condemning the majority of the displaced to total loss. Where the idea of individual ownership of property in nature is essentially alien, access to resources becomes the crucial element in compensation. The pressure resistance movements exert for the recognition of other forms of tenure and ownership has led in recent years to many projects in many regions modifying this position. However, even with efforts to compensate for lost communal holdings, pressures from the dominant society to conform to the legal forms of individually held land tenure are strong.

Loss of Access to Resources

Thus, from an economic standpoint the basic motivation for resistance lies squarely in the fact that resettlement projects consistently impoverish people, principally by taking their lands and other resources. While resistance may be seen superficially as a rejection of the loss of economic resources that only have to be enumerated for compensation, it is by no means a simple matter to ascertain where and in what aspect of their lives people lose resources and become materially impoverished so as to establish the economic bases for DFDR resistance. Indeed, a simplistic approach toward this issue is largely responsible for much of the economic injustice, impoverishment, and resistance that DFDR projects generate. For example, for women in India, whose lives tend to be more focused on natural resource use than on crops for market exchange, the loss of resources that may not be quantifiable in monetary terms will be actively resisted (Mehta, 2009, p. xvii). The loss of access to resources that are fundamental to the maintenance of life, whether in the rural or urban context, can provide the basis for mobilization of resistance. People generally are not compensated for assets less tangible than land, such as access to markets, communal property resources, and social networks (W. F. Fisher, 1995, p. 32). In urban contexts, resettled people frequently organize resistance movements over loss of access to employment. Slum clearance and urban renewal have frequently resettled people far from sources and sites of employment, and often even distant from regular transportation routes and facilities. The costs of transportation to work and the time involved are also seen as economic hardships that are cause for resistance by urban resettlers. And these hardships are very real. One study found that traveling to work from a housing project for the displaced took two hours a day and cost one third of the minimum salary in fares (Perlman, 1982, p. 233). Resettlement can distance both rural and urban people from essential access to the markets from which they derive all or part of their livelihoods or the basic material necessities of life. Furthermore, loss of access to markets also deprives people of access to the social, cultural, and political resources that tend to accumulate in markets. Such losses may be actively resisted because they impoverish people in diverse ways.

For many people, the arrival of large-scale development projects represents the intrusion of a set of economic institutions and practices with which they have had little experience. Often, the long-term outcome of such an intrusion is their increased integration into this institutional complex. The shift to a monetized economy from a use-value, reciprocity-based economy has rarely been smooth (B. Moore, 1966), but when such profound cultural change is coupled with the threat and/or trauma of resettlement, then social disarticulation, cultural disintegration, and resistance become likely.

Cultural Resources Valuation

Cultural resources prove to be particularly problematic for CBA. Cultural resources are increasingly being addressed by projects through the methods of CBA and contingent valuation, but for CBA to work, its requirements oblige a strategy that commodifies everything. Everything from fixed capital resources to cultural identity must be expressible in terms of a single common denominator, a money figure. In some instances the market has already effected the conversion that CBA purports to carry out in placing money values on non-market items. The commodification of local rituals for tourist consumption in many nations has accomplished surreptitiously what CBA attempts in contingent valuation, namely, to put a price tag on cultural heritage resources and inject them into the market (Garcia Canclini, 1993; Greenwood, 1977).

However, whereas the market seduces, often co-opting dismay and protest, CBA and contingent valuation are far more blunt. What is the consequence of asking someone what he or she would be willing to pay to prevent the inundation of ancestral burial grounds? The outrage that frequently results from such a query represents an intractable problem that increasingly confronts the discourse of CBA. The problem is known as constitutive incommensurability (O'Neill, 1999), which refers to an unresolvable plurality of values. That is, there are some objects, places, conditions, or states of affairs that resist being reduced to a single uniform measure. They are essentially constituted by particular kinds of shared understandings that are incompatible with market relations on moral or ethical grounds. The right to practice one's religion in the appropriate shrine, the right to speak one's own language, or the right to bury one's dead in and respect one's ancestors on sacred ground, as well as the loyalties of kinship, custom, and a way of life, are generally constituted by the refusal to treat them as commodities to be bought and sold (O'Neill, 1999). The suggestion that payment for the loss of such things would be appropriate is insulting, even morally repugnant. Such a construction challenges even the most well-meaning efforts at compensation. Appropriate forms and levels of compensation clearly cannot be arrived at by outsiders employing some ostensibly "objective" method such as CBA but only in consultation with the affected people (W. F. Fisher, 1995, p. 32). The issue brings up once again the whole question of how value is understood and how it differs from price. Some economists, as hard-nosed realists, might scoff at the difference as external to the problem, but it is very real to many people. The difference resides in the fact that price is constructed in the intersection of supply and demand in a market and value is a reflection of the importance of a thing for the role it plays in human relations.

The issue of compensation has been the subject of a discussion, if not to say a debate, since the 1930s. The core concept in this discussion of gains and losses in economic undertakings, although sometimes only in the background, was developed by Wilfredo Pareto. What has come to be known as a "Pareto improvement" occurs when at least one individual is better off as the result of a project and no individual is left worse off in terms of the status quo ante. Those who would lose from a project are thus protected by the Pareto improvement concept, for under such constraints, almost no project would be allowed, thus leading to virtually no policy and no action. However, the Pareto improvement turns out to be somewhat double-edged because under its guidelines, any redistribution from the rich to the poor would be prohibited (Kanbur, 2003, p. 28).

With the Pareto improvement as the grounding principle, the discussion about compensation started in the 1930s with a fairly simple CBA that left little room for interpersonal comparisons. A utilitarian objection to this formulation was based on the idea that a loss or gain of equal value has a different impact on a rich person than it does on a poor person. The question of weighting a poor person's loss relative to a rich person's loss was considered, particularly in light of the concern for equity. Some economists rejected the idea of weighting because they felt that the choice of weights fell outside the purview of science generally and of economics in particular. The difficulty of comparing losses and gains, particularly those experienced by individuals and those experienced by communities, was also discussed. Various other strategies, such as general taxation and transfers (compensation) to those who lose from a project, were advanced, but objections appeared regarding the question of distribution. That is, the benefits and losses of a project are rarely distributed at random, and therefore, there was no guarantee that the change would benefit everyone who was taxed. In its most contemporary form, the application of the compensation principle has returned to a CBA that employs weighted sums of gains and losses assessed along egalitarian lines (Kanbur, 2003, p. 30). Unfortunately, this application has not produced satisfactory results in practice, as the record of compensation in DFDR projects attests.

The dismal record of compensation has prompted some to call for steps over and above compensation. Kanbur calls for compensation plus a safety net. Cernea, similarly questioning the effectiveness of compensation, calls for a new economics of resettlement (2003, 2009). Rejecting CBA, he asserts that compensation is structurally incapable of redressing the losses experienced by the displaced and cannot restore incomes and livelihoods to where they would have been had the people not been uprooted. He furthermore contends that compensation does not address the time factor, in that the resettlement process interrupts a normal growth process that might have been underway in the affected communities before resettlement, thus placing them behind unaffected communities. He therefore calls for compensation and investment to address these issues. Affected peoples should be seen as investors in the sense that they have rendered up their lands for the project and are thus entitled to a return. Cernea sees investment funds as basically an advance on those returns (2003, p. 42, 2009). Whether calling for "safety nets" or "investment," Kanbur and Cernea fully recognize the inadequacy of compensation to address the losses of the displaced, and both call for additional support.

Reparations Issues

Recent work carried out for the World Commission on Dams (WCD) points to the overwhelming need for the payment of reparations to those people displaced by dam construction whose losses have never been appropriately compensated (Johnston, 2000, 2009). Both research and the voices of the displaced have urged that claims of past injustices be heard by national and international human rights commissions (McCully, 1999). The WCD has recommended reparations for uncompensated damages that have been experienced in both displacement and resettlement.

The issue of reparations raises some interesting questions that are located at the center of the contention over CBA and that may figure prominently in future forms of resistance to DFDR (Johnston, 2009). We have seen the response of people who are offered payment for cultural resources that will be lost in displacement. They are offended that anyone would suggest that they would surrender the burial grounds of their ancestors, their sacred forests, their holy river, or other such features for a compensatory payment (see the following chapter for further discussion). On the other hand, in those cases in which the damage has already been done—the sacred forest and the hallowed graveyard inundated, the holy river drowned—is a payment still inappropriate? Is it still placing a monetary metric on an element that has enormous cultural value that cannot be expressed in a price? Is it still morally repugnant to accept reparations in money form for losses that cannot be quantified? Can money payments ever come close to addressing, much less making good, the true nature of the loss? And if these questions are all answered in the negative, are reparations therefore as inadequate and unsatisfactory as compensation? Don't reparations simply unburden the offenders of their guilt by converting the loss into a form that can be addressed by a payment that then relieves those responsible of all further obligation? Do reparations simply complete the commodification process, putting a price tag on everything?

Reparations, however, come in many forms. Some distinguish between reparations and settlements. Reparations are intended as broad forms of redress that express atonement for actions or conditions of injustice and include a statement of apology. Settlements are more narrowly defined as payment transfers that express no concession of wrongdoing or apology (Boutte, 2002, p. 42; Brooks, 1999, p. 436). Reparation is defined as an action or process that repairs, makes amends for, or compensates damages. Legally, there are basically three forms of reparation: restitution, indemnity (or compensation), and satisfaction. Restitution is defined as a return of the offended state to its former condition. Such action might include restoration of a damaged ecosystem or of lost resources, such as water or fisheries, by removing dam structures. Indemnity, also referred to as compensation, involves the payment of money to the injured party for losses experienced by illegal acts, including property or opportunity lost (profit, for example). At the individual level, reparations or settlements are usually intended to be compensatory. At the community level, such transfers are designed to be rehabilitative (Brooks, 1999). For community losses, as opposed to individual losses, indemnity payments can be used to fund improved resettlement plans or develop projects that address community needs. Satisfaction addresses losses primarily in a nonmaterial format, such as offering a formal apology for losses sustained or disciplining the responsible individuals. In terms of development projects that violate human rights in DFDR, satisfaction might include public acknowledgements of wrongdoing and formal apologies to those who suffered as a result of the actions. Such demands for admission of culpability often figure as highly in the agendas of resistance movements as actual material transfers. However, satisfaction might also include damage awards for hardships experienced as outcomes of long-term effects of the original violation (Johnston, 2000).

Resistance and opposition movements have made payment of reparations to dam affected peoples a central issue in their campaigns. The 1994 Manibeli Declaration calls on the World Bank to establish a fund to provide reparations to the people displaced by Bank-funded dams. The fund would be managed by an independent, transparent, and accountable institution, and its tasks would include providing affected communities with training and assistance in the preparation of their claims. This demand was reiterated at the First International Meeting of Dam Affected Peoples in Curitiba, Brazil, in 1997. Dam reparations call for a variety of remedies, including monetary and such non-monetary measures as dam decommissioning, official recognition of injustices committed, and the restoration of ecosystems ("When the Rivers Run Dry," 2007). For example, in the late 1970s the World Bank helped fund the Chixoy Dam in collaboration with the government of Guatemala, which at the time was engaged in a counterinsurgency campaign that became a virtual genocidal war on the indigenous highland Mayan population. The Mayan village of Rio Negro, among others, refused to relocate to make way for the construction of the dam. In 1982 the Guatemalan army and paramilitary forces entered the villages and massacred approximately 400 people, mostly women and children. In effect, the DFDR resistance of Rio Negro provided the pretext for the military to continue its genocidal war against the indigenous population. Despite numerous construction-monitoring visits by World Bank personnel during the period, not much was known of the massacre until 1996, when human rights groups began to investigate. An internal investigation by the World Bank eventually cleared the Bank of any culpability or responsibility for the crimes. The World Bank considers the issue closed because most of the communities affected by the dam have now reached pre-dam (1976) standards of living. However, the survivors of the massacre and their allies are demanding reparations for the 25 years of deprivation and fear and for the murder of their families. The reparation demands include replacement land of equal quality and quantity, the construction of a monument to commemorate the 400 victims, and seeking out and initiating legal proceedings against those responsible for the massacre ("When the Rivers Run Dry," 2007; Johnston, 2005, 2009).

Brooks is working toward building what he calls "a theory of redress" that outlines four basic elements for successful reparations (1999, p. 7). In order to be successful a claim for redress of human injustice must be heard by legisla-

The banner reads, "When they built the Chixoy Dam, they did the Rio Negro massacre. Excuse me, but with the new and privatized hydroelectric projects, how many massacres will there be?" (photograph by Barbara Rose Johnston)

tors rather than judges. Judges are empowered only to enforce existing laws, and attempts at obtaining reparations frequently require new legislation. Second, successful achievement of reparations requires political pressure and the support of political leaders. The third aspect necessary for success is strong internal support by and among the victims themselves. And the fourth element is that the claim have merit, that is, that it be based on ample documentation of the commission of human injustice, the identity of victims as members of a distinct group, their continuing exposure to injustice, and the causal links between past injustice and current suffering.

Private Sector Approaches to Resettlement

As indicated previously, private sector policies and approaches to DFDR are in the vast majority of cases simply nonexistent. Some private sector interests, such as the Rio Tinto Corporation, have developed resettlement policies and attempt to work with the affected people to implement them. There are industries, mining in particular, that have attempted, through their influence with legislatures, to amend existing laws protecting indigenous peoples and the environment in order to resettle communities and gain access to land and resources (Rebbapragada & Kalluri, 2009, p 264). However, most private sector development relies on the market mechanism to assess adequate compensation for people displaced by its expansion.

In the developed world, the market mechanism is customarily employed to assess value and compensation in land transactions. The expansion of many private enterprises in urban areas, such as for hotel and tourist facilities, shopping malls, stadiums, and many other structures, is enabled by straightforward purchase of property and the departure of residents. As indicated earlier, the structure of the market mechanism, with its scenarios of choice and contracts freely entered into by autonomous and equal economic actors, provides the appearance of voluntary relocation by participants. Indeed, private sector–driven DFDR, which often involves large numbers of people, frequently passes unrecognized (Appa & Patel, 1996). However, the voluntary appearance is often deceptive. In some cases of urban renewal in cities in the developed world, resistance movements have developed to oppose dislocation by "gentrification," the process in which real estate interests and/or private individuals surreptitiously purchase properties in urban neighborhoods to upgrade, thereby raising property values and, by extension, taxes, and forcing long-term, lower-income residents to sell. Economic boom can also create the conditions for wholesale restructuring of neighborhoods. The explosion (and subsequent implosion) of the so-called dot-com economy in Northern California impacted property values in the entire region. New Internet companies flush with investor funds began locating offices in the traditionally residential Mission District of San Francisco, driving up property values and taxes and forcing many long-term residents to relocate. An antidisplacement movement was formed in late 2000, and rallies were held at which computers were smashed as symbols of resistance to dislocation. The subsequent implosion of the dot-com economy has reduced the pressure somewhat, but residents remain vigilant (Duncan, 2001). Similar movements have emerged in other urban neighborhoods in the United States and elsewhere. In New York City the symbolic importance of the neighborhoods encompassed by Harlem, a major site of African American cultural heritage, has attracted many people from middle and upper income brackets, some of them African Americans, to acquire and improve properties in that sector of the city (N. Smith, 1996). The gentrification by outsiders, albeit of the same ethnic or racial group, has sparked a resistance movement in which "dislocation free zones" have been declared in areas in Harlem (Jackson, 2001).

Recently, the issue of displacement by private sector development has come to revolve around the use of eminent domain by the public sector to expropriate land for subsequent sale to private interests. Civil authorities justify this strategy by claiming that private development of condominiums, sports complexes, shopping centers, Special Economic Zones (SEZS), Free Trade Zones (FTZS), etc., generate a larger tax base and more employment, thereby benefiting the public more than do middle and low income community real estate taxes. Although there are numerous instances, especially in the United States, in which public authorities have recently employed or attempted to employ eminent domain to expropriate land for private development, the case that has gained greatest attention is *Kelo v. New London* that came before the U.S. Supreme Court in 2005.

The city of New London, Connecticut, was declared a distressed municipality in 1990 and continued a downward spiral after the departure of a large federal installation in 1996. In January 1998 the pharmaceutical company Pfizer, Inc. announced plans to build a US$300 million research facility on land occupied by the former federal installation and private homeowners. The city council approved the plan, which eventually came to include developing a waterfront conference hotel, restaurants and shopping, a marina, a river walk, 80 new residences, and a state park, as well as Pfizer's research facility, all to be privately developed. However, several owners refused to sell and, as part of their resistance, brought suit in the New London Superior Court, asserting that the taking of their properties violated the "public use" restriction in the Fifth Amendment. After the denial of their petition, the owners, all of them residents, appealed and continued to pursue relief, eventually taking their case to the Supreme Court, where they were finally denied.

The fundamental question around which the case revolved was the interpretation of "public use." The Supreme Court held that while the Constitution prohibited the taking of land to confer benefit on a particular private party, economic development is traditionally a proper governmental function and therefore constitutes a valid public use, justifying the taking of the petitioners' land. The interpretation is based on a broader understanding of public use as "public purpose." While the city was not intending to open the condemned land to the general public, but rather to specific private interests, the public purpose of economic development would be served (Legal Information Institute—Cornell University). The Court's decision has led to some interesting political conflicts between traditional allies and some equally interesting alliances between old opponents. Libertarians see *Kelo v. New London* as an infringement on individual property rights, while many community activists hail the measure for supporting the broader general welfare.

This increasingly common phenomenon of the government and the private sector collaborating to appropriate land in the name of economic development is seen also in the developing world. In Tanzania in the 1980s, the government opened the economy to private investors through an Investment

Promotion Center in the president's office. Foreign investors were invited to submit to the center proposals for commercial farms, gemstone mines, private game reserves, and other kinds of projects. If the project was approved, the investor paid for a certificate that required the Ministry of Land, Natural Resources and Tourism to grant the investor a lease of land suited for the kind of enterprise proposed. The goal was to convert land from subsistence to more productive forms of use. Shrimp farms displaced fishing villages, gemstone mines and flower plantations displaced farmers, and seed farms and wildlife ranches displaced pastoralists. The government thus became the instrument of choice for private enterprise to displace rural Tanzanians from their traditional homelands in the name of private, usually foreign, investment and profit (Igoe, 2004, p. 107).

In rural contexts, particularly in the developing world, private sector expansion has often adopted informal and frequently violent methods of expulsion. In Brazil in the 1970s, the government-sponsored colonization by 13,000 families, along with the incursion of roughly 400,000 squatters from the impoverished northeast and other areas, of the Goias-Para-Maranhao nexus of the Amazon region produced conflicts with the cattle ranchers and land speculators who were expanding due to increasing land values. Despite legislated protection for the colonizers' and squatters' rights, the ranchers and speculators purchased land and began a period of land expulsions. The violence between the new economic interests and the squatters became so intense and widespread that in 1975 the Catholic Church established the Pastoral Land Commission to assist the squatters in these conflicts (Sanders, 1991, p. 5). Government responses to the violence included establishing military control of the region and a procedure to pursue and settle land claims. Although settlers were able to win some of these judgements, many were lost because of a lack of funds to hire lawyers. The area is now largely deforested and has converted to brush and pasture for cattle (Sanders, 1991, p. 5). Schmink has documented similar forms of expulsion in other regions of the Amazon (1992).

The expansion of the private sector tourist economy has led to the displacement of many traditional residents as well. Along the coasts of South Carolina and Georgia in the United States, the barrier islands had traditionally been home to African American populations who were only marginally integrated into mainstream economies and societies. They had established a diversified pattern of economic survival strategies based on hunting, gathering, fishing, small-scale agriculture, and occasional wage labor. Their economy enabled them to live on the margins of the dominant society, excluded from its economic growth but somewhat insulated perhaps from the daily, if not the structural, effects of its racial prejudices. Their economy focused primarily around social reproduction and did not produce much monetary income. In the late 1970s foreign capital, much of it based on increased petroleum earnings, began investing in tourism development on the islands, focusing on golf course and vacation-housing complexes. With investments, the taxable value of the land increased, straining the capacities of local people to meet these new cash obligations. With increasing taxes, local people found themselves forced to sell their land to developers or forfeit it to the county for unpaid taxes. They then moved to low-income housing and mobile-home communities on the mainland, far from familiar coastal environments, and entered the mainstream economy as maids, gardeners, and other low-paid labor, often commuting to the vacation communities on the islands they once inhabited ("The New Plantation," 1991).

Case Study: Tourism Development and Resistance in the Philippines

The rapid growth of commercial sport and tourism development has resulted in increasing demand for land on a global scale and has brought it into conflict with both the human and natural environment (Pleumarom, 1994). With this development, the environmental and human rights impacts of this growth have become the focus of considerable debate. At the center of this debate is the issue of golf course development. In the 1980s in the wake of the considerable economic growth, particularly in the new industrialized countries of Asia, golf became extremely popular. Investment in golf resorts expanded enormously. As with other sports today, golf is the central axis around which revolves a constellation of extremely lucrative development activities, including golfing clothes and equipment, golfing holidays, hotel chains, airlines, and real estate investment (Pleumarom, 1994). An average 18-hole golf course requires a minimum of 89 acres of land and consumes 6,500 cubic meters of water a day. A typical golf course uses land that approximately 40 peasant farmers could use to produce half a million kilos of rice a year, and its annual water consumption is enough to irrigate 65 hectares of farmlands (www .geocities.com/kmp_ph/strug/looc/looc.html). However, since most new golf development is taking place in the developing world, the courses are generally part of larger packages that involve luxury hotels, chalets, condominiums, marinas, and other recreational features, which can enlarge the total package by as much as a factor of ten (Ling & Ferrari, 1995, p. 8).

The golf craze has driven a demand for land that has affected indigenous peoples, farmers, and communities throughout Asia, as well as in Canada, the United States, the United Kingdom, and several other European countries. At the start of the 1980s Asia as a whole had only a few courses, but by the mid 1990s Thailand alone had 160 and Japan, already pressed for available land, had 2,000, although several hundred have stopped operating due to local resistance (Ling & Ferrari, 1995, p. 8). Resistance to golf course development took place first in Canada when the Mohawk Indians stopped the entry of developers by blocking the road into their land. The Canadian government responded with soldiers and tanks. Since that time, many other communities around the world have joined this struggle in defense of their lands and livelihoods.

The Hacienda Looc extends over 8,500 hectares in a coastal region of farming and fishing villages in the state of Batangas in the Philippines. The terrain is extremely varied, including coastal plains that local farmers plant in rice, corn, vegetables, and sugar cane. There is a sizeable portion of the land area in hills and mountains in which mangoes, bananas, jackfruits, star apples, and wild rice, as well as root crops like cassava and sweet potatoes, are grown. The coastal area gives access to the rich fishing grounds in the China Sea. This resource base has enabled the roughly 10,000 local farmers and fishers to live in relative self-sufficiency for the roughly four generations since the area was settled (Hacienda Looc: Struggle in the Philippines).

At one time Hacienda Looc was part of a large plantation owned successively by several elite families. One of the families used the land to pay off a loan from the Philippine National Bank (PNB) and the Development Bank of the Philippines (DBP). In 1973 the PNB transferred full ownership to the DBP. Under the Marcos regime roughly 1,300 hectares were distributed to 831 farmers under the land reform program. In 1987 the DBP transferred the entire hacienda to the Assets Privatization Trust (APT), the government agency charged with placing government assets for sale or lease to private interests. In the same year, under the Comprehensive Agrarian Reform Program of the Aquino government, a total of 5,218 hectares of the hacienda was organized into cooperatives. However, at the same time, the APT, in collaboration with USAID, was conducting a feasibility study for a land use plan to turn the hacienda into an agrotourism complex.

In 1993 APT put the remainder of the hacienda up for public bidding, bringing in a horde of land speculators offering to buy farmers out of even agrarian reform lands. Eventually the land was obtained by the Manila Southcoast Development Corporation (MSDC), which in 1995 entered into a joint venture with Fil-Estate Properties to develop 1,269 hectares into a world-class tourism and leisure complex called Harbortown Golf and Country Club. The deed of the sale states that MSDC purchased the entire 8,650.7778 hectares, in contrast to the bidding terms that stated that only the 3,248.24 hectares not covered by the land reform were to be sold. Raising the question of collusion and fraud, the deed contains a crucial and highly questionable clause that allows MSDC to circumvent the land reform law and expand its ownership, ultimately acquiring the whole hacienda for the price it paid for only 3,432 hectares. Both national and local governmental authorities supported the project. Indeed, the owners and boards of directors of both MSDC and Fil-Estate are deeply intertwined with key figures in Philippine national and international politics. It is widely thought that the reason Fil-Estate has become the nation's leading developer is its close political ties with the presidency. According to its prospectus, the club will have four golf courses, a 120-room luxury hotel, vacation chalets, and a yacht marina. The project will cover roughly 1,270 hectares of land currently held by farmers in 13 collective cooperatives. The first phase of the project is underway (Hacienda Looc: Struggle in the Philippines), and Tiger Woods was brought in for a celebrity golf clinic and to publicize the project in 1998 (Schradie & DeVries, 2000).

In 1996 the residents of the villages of Hacienda Looc founded an organization called Umalpas-Ka (Break Free) to fight the evictions that they were facing. They hired sympathetic lawyers to represent their interests against MSDC and Fil-Estate. Their legal counsel wanted to bar Tiger Woods from entering the country, but a peasant farmer said, "I learned the news that Tiger Woods is coming to the Philippines, but it would be better if he came to Hacienda Looc to find out for himself how the people strongly oppose the golf course" (Schradie & DeVries, 2000). Local residents and their attorneys have filed a series of law suits accusing local officials of taking property on behalf of Fil-Estate fraudulently, having peasants sign blank documents, and producing contracts with dead people (Schradie & DeVries, 2000). They publicized the issue, exposing the military's participation and holding rallies and media projects to protest the militarization of the region. When bulldozers began contouring the hills for the golf courses, women from Umalpas-Ka climbed the hillsides and formed a human barricade to protect the land, forcing a standoff with the Philippine national police, the military, and Fil-Estate security forces (Schradie & DeVries, 2000).

However, their resistance provoked serious attempts at suppression. Certain local authorities invested in the project maintain security forces that have been used to intimidate the members of Umalpas-Ka. Fil-Estate and MSDC also maintain a force of 134 security guards, deployed as combat units throughout the two central villages of Calayo and Papaya. The security, it is maintained, is necessary to safeguard construction equipment, but their stations throughout the area suggest that Fil-Estate is more concerned with control over the populations. Two farmers associated with Umalpas-Ka were shot to death without provocation by members of the Fil-Estate and MSDC security forces, who were arrested and later released (Hacienda Looc: Struggle in the Philippines).

Members of Umalpas-Ka believe that the two peasants were killed because they were opposed to the project. The killings mobilized the participation of the New People's Army (NPA), the Philippine guerrilla force that was instrumental in the defeat of the Chico Dam project. Carl Roger, an NPA leader, stated their position: "If they will continue these unnecessary killings, the NPA will be forced to launch a military operation against anybody responsible for these killings" (Schradie & DeVries, 2000). Thus far, the NPA has not intervened in Hacienda Looc, but their statement of support was a turning point in the villagers' resistance to the project, reducing the harassment from the government and Fil-Estate. The peasants of Hacienda Looc have also acquired the assistance of several NGOs working in the region.

In the face of resistance from the peasants of Hacienda Looc, Fil-Estate and MSDC have initiated a dual campaign of repression and co-optation. Project authorities have undertaken a census of the communities in order to award titles to home lots to residents who have been living there for generations. To offset the assistance of NGOs, Fil-Estate has created its own NGO to generate employment projects for the communities. They have also attempted to buy off the leaders of Umalpas-Ka, offering the chairman two million pesos for one hectare of his land if he will support the project (Hacienda Looc: Struggle in the Philippines). Attempts were also made to form a joint venture between farmers and MSDC–Fil-Estate in which control of the land remains with the corporations and the farmers become workers on the enterprise and earn dividends on their shares in the land. Such an arrangement would put to rest any questions about the illicit maneuvers between the corporations and the agrarian reform in the acquisition of the land. In 2000, rumors of a property glut in the Philippines shook the confidence of investors in tourist resorts, and Hacienda Looc has yet to see its first golf course (Hacienda Looc: Struggle in the Philippines). However, then-recently indicted president Joseph Estrada refused to return the lands to the people, and they were still on alert against the incursions of Fil-Estate bulldozers. And the NPA was also still watching events and conditions carefully under the new Macapagal-Arroyo administration (Schradie & DeVries, 2000). Although the maps and plans outlined in promotional brochures still display golf courses and marinas for Hacienda Looc, the villages were still there in 2007 (Godrej, 2007).

Conclusion

In the final analysis, as has been consistently pointed out, in the eyes of their proponents the justification for projects such as the ones discussed in this chapter ultimately rests on their economic success. That is, projects are justified by the more efficient use of resources and the capacity of the project to generate more benefits than costs. As we have seen, the calculations on which these judgements are frequently based leave a good deal to be desired, both in the way benefits are estimated and the way costs, particularly to affected peoples, are assessed. To assess the costs to local people, metrics of dubious appropriateness are applied to measure things that may ultimately be resistant to quantification. Reducing the realms of identity, belief, and tradition to the domain of money may not only be impossible, it may be considered an assault on culture. The distribution of costs and benefits is also frequently based on elite notions of who the affected peoples are rather than any clear understanding of their basic identities and lives.

Moreover, the actual economic justification for projects, their economic viability, has been called into serious question. The CBAs, the financial, environmental, and social statements that are drawn up as the bases for project justification, are not well known for containing "honest numbers." The projects are just as infamous for a lack of good governance, transparency, and participation (by affected peoples) in political and administrative decision-making (Flyvbjerg et al., 2003, p. 5). Even the efforts to compensate the displaced are impaired by project administrative mismanagement. The distortion and manipulation of project management frequently results in undercounting affected peoples, inappropriate valuation and undervaluation of assets, inability to measure nonphysical losses, undercompensation through late disbursement, nonrecognition of asset appreciation, undercompensation through lost consumer surplus, and the siphoning off of compensation funds by corrupt officials (Cernea, 2003, p. 41). Many of these projects, and particularly the larger ones, the megaprojects, also end up performing very poorly in terms of economic gains. Plagued by cost overruns and revenues that fail to reach projections, such projects not only wreak havoc on peoples and environments but often end up being obstacles to rather than vehicles for economic growth (Flyvbjerg et al., 2003). Particularly in the developing world, such projects are often financed by huge loans that are based on unrealistic assessments of project benefits. When those benefits fail to materialize, the developing nation is left ever deeper in debt and without the projected revenues to pay off the loans. Ultimately, all the environmental destruction, the losses and pain of the displaced, and the inept and underfunded resettlement of thousands of people are justified by assessments of the economic viability of projects that are manifestly false and impossible to realize once the project is completed.

CHAPTER SIX

The Lake of Memory

Cultural Discourses of Resistance

Memories are harder to erase than houses, people, countries. They are there,
like a flowing plasma or a deep subterranean lake. We row around on this lake.
Search for its shores, chart our own positions.
URSULA REUTER CHRISTIANSEN, 1986, FROM THE BOOK OF HER FILM
THE EXECUTIONER (1971), AS CITED IN *URC HC*, (2001)

There is a barely hidden cultural politics in many development projects that seeks to further a general expansion of the control of the state over local territories and people (J. Scott, 1998). In extending its physical control over territory, the state also strives to impose a process of standardization and simplification over inhabitants, including common measurement, language, codification, and mapping. In reducing local cultural, social, and economic complexity to a format dictated by the state, control and rationalization of local systems in accordance with state priorities can be achieved. Nation-building involves the creation of a comprehensible unity out of an incomprehensible diversity (Anderson, 1983). The outcome of this process has become known as legibility (J. Scott, 1998).

In many nations the not so covert goal of development is precisely that of reducing diversity and the imposition of uniform standards, not only of measurement and practice but of language and culture as well. The frequently covert secondary goal of these nations' large infrastructural development projects is the assimilation and absorption, if not the outright eradication, of tribal peoples or peasantries, constituted of local identities, into a mainstream of agricultural bourgeoisie and workers of national identities (C. Smith, 1996). Indeed, completely eliding the entire issue of choice or rights, we can recall from Chapter 3 Vidyut Joshi's query as to why anyone should oppose when a culture based on a lower level of technology and quality of life gives way

A temple in the Narmada Valley in Western India awaits inundation from the reservoir created by the Sardar Sarovar Dam. (photograph by Dana Clark)

to a culture with a superior technology and higher quality of life. He called this development (1991, p. 68, as cited in W. F. Fisher, 1995, p. 33). It's also what we call social Darwinism, that ideological relic of nineteenth-century imperialism.

While the reasons people resist DFDR are often assumed to be economic in nature, the concerns that people express in resistance movements are generally more complex, embracing economic, social, and, particularly, cultural issues. Indeed, project planners frequently err in supposing that people have only economic motives in mind when they undertake resistance to DFDR. While violation of economic rights has proven to be a powerful driver of resistance, a great deal of the moral content of resistance discourse derives its power from explicitly cultural issues pertaining to the rights to persist as cultural entities, to identity, to spiritual links to land and the environment, to loyalty to the dead, to both mythological and historical ancestors.

On the other hand, in their campaigns to raise funds and resist certain forms of development, many NGOs have tended to romanticize the bonds to the land held by many indigenous and peasant groups facing DFDR, when the actual concerns of the affected groups may be focused more on just compensation (Aryal, 1995). It is reductionist to attribute resistance solely to economics or for that matter, to purely cultural concerns. Human motivations in general are complex, and positions and actions in resistance to DFDR are adopted out of many interwoven concerns, challenges, and changing conditions rather than one overriding issue.

That notwithstanding, cultural issues play major roles in the constructing of discourses of resistance to DFDR. Actually, development projects provide contexts in which cultural issues become highlighted and especially significant in resistance. There is a great deal at stake socioculturally and sociopsychologically in resettlement. What does it mean from a sociocultural standpoint to be dislocated and resettled? How do we develop a language to speak of what is experienced socioculturally and sociopsychologically in DFDR? What is the impact on individual and cultural identity and integrity? Why has separation from a place so frequently resulted in cultural disintegration?

Place Attachment

There are two core concepts in resistance to DFDR. One is power and the other is place. One expression of political power is the ability to move people and things about the landscape in any way you see fit. The loss of a home territory constitutes not only the loss of a specific dwelling, but also the loss of a home ground — in some cases, the very ontological grounding of a culture. Place attachment refers to the bonding of people to places. Brown and Perkins offer the following definition of "place attachment":

> Place attachment involves positively experienced bonds, sometimes occurring without awareness, that are developed over time from the behavioral, affective and cognitive ties between individuals and/or groups and their socio-physical environment. These bonds provide a framework for both individual and communal aspects of identity and have both stabilizing and dynamic features (1992, p. 284).

Place, then, is much more than mere context for cultural and social action and behavior. It is itself socially constructed and contested in practice. In effect, although the relationship with place is often only partially expressed or cognized, it is created through the actions of specific individuals and groups invested, physically and symbolically, in the environment. Consequently, places themselves acquire multiple meanings, expressive of physical, emotional, and experiential realities.

Thus, place-attachment processes involve the behavioral, cognitive, and emotional embeddedness of individuals in the relationship between their sociocultural and physical environments, providing a form of ontological stability. Altman and Low (1992) assert that place attachment is an integrating concept that incorporates affect and emotion, knowledge and belief, behaviors and actions—and the interplay of all these aspects—in reference to a place. A place may become the matrix in which a repository of life experiences is embedded, thereby becoming, in some sense, inseparable from the feelings associated with it. The nature of the attachment may involve biological processes of evolutionary and physiological adaptations to a particular environment, in other words, the ecological fit between a local population and a place. Such adaptations involve not only biological processes associated with subsistence and shelter, but develop as well through the culturally mediated meanings emerging out of the interaction of technology and environment.

Attachment to place may transcend the unique experiences of individuals and come to involve the constellation of social relations, and the cultural values that inform them, of entire groups or communities. Places come to signify relationships between people and may take on greater importance in the strength of those bonds than in the places' physical qualities. Both as the context of these relations and as a physical environment, place plays an important role in the formation, maintenance, and preservation of individual, group, and cultural identities. The feelings, memories, ideas, values, and meanings associated with everyday life in some setting become a dimension of a person's or group's identity. From a sociocultural perspective, place attachment is based on the historical depth of a group's experience in a particular setting. To paraphrase Munn (1990, as cited in Rodman, 1992), a place in the world is not given but lived.

Places are essential to the encoding and contextualization of time and history and become identified with the genealogy and continuity of families and groups through history. Economic ties of individual or collective ownership, inheritance, or other forms of appropriation are fundamental to many place attachments. Other cultural factors—such as the intimate connections between environment and religion, cosmology and world view, especially as enacted through rituals and celebratory cultural events, as narrated in folklore, or as expressed in place names—play significant roles in the relationship of a society to its land base and general environment. Ultimately, such ties lie at the core of both individual and collective constructions of reality. In effect, the ties between people and place lie at the ontological ground of culture itself. As Rodman notes, "Place then is both context and content, enacted and material. It is the lived world in physical form" (1992, p. 650). One's place, along with one's body, is thus the most basic physical dimension of existence.

Places are not simply containers of behavior; they are constructed, representative, and embodied by people.

Moreover, a sense of place plays an important role in individual and collective identity formation, in the way time and history are encoded and contextualized, and in interpersonal, community, and intercultural relations (Altman & Low, 1992; Escobar, 2000; Rodman, 1992). "Geographical experience begins in places, reaches out to others through spaces, and creates landscapes or regions for human existence" (Tilley, 1994, p. 15). Resistance to resettlement reveals how important a sense of place is in the creation of an "environment of trust" in which space, kin relations, local communities, cosmology, and tradition are linked (Giddens, 1990, p. 102, as cited in Rodman, 1992, p. 648). Removal from one of the most basic physical dimensions of life can be a form of removal from life. The disruption in individual or community identity and stability in place, resulting from resettlement in a strange landscape, can baffle and silence people in the same way a strange language can (Basso, 1988, as cited in Rodman, 1992, p. 647). Culture loses its ontological grounding and people must struggle to construct a life world that can clearly articulate their continuity and identity as a people again.

The case of the Hopi Partitioned Lands (HPL) in northeastern Arizona offers an example of the cultural significance of land. The proposed relocation of 240 Navajo families from this land has given rise to a resistance movement that gives full voice to the centrality of ties to land in Navajo culture and identity. The origin of the dispute can be traced to the somewhat arbitrary and capricious 1882 presidential declaration creating a Hopi reservation in an area where many Navajo people lived. The actual wording of the declaration is vague enough to allow for interpretations that, by turns, permit or prohibit actual occupation of the land by other Indian groups. Within a short time, conflicts over the land began. In 1970 the U.S. Supreme Court issued a writ calling for the establishment of a Joint Use Area divided into Hopi Partitioned Land and Navajo Partitioned Land, requiring a painful relocation process for approximately one hundred Hopis and ten thousand Navajos (Davidheiser, n.d.).

The Navajos are a natural resource community, raising crops and livestock on their land in the Four Corners area. There are powerful symbolic, religious, social, and personal features tying the Navajo families to their homesites and natural environment. One intimate connection the resisters have with their land is the biological linkage that is forged by burying the umbilical cords and placentas of their newborns near their homesites. One young resister expressed the bond in these terms: "Well, this is where I was born and this is where my umbilical cord is, and according to Navajo culture wherever your umbilical cord is buried, you are going to be attached to that area, you are going to be attached to that land." The Navajo believe that they originated in the area between the four sacred mountains that are near their reservation, and many of their religious beliefs and rituals are linked to specific locations within the region. Many sites, such as springs and mountains, are sacred, and the resisters visit them to hold ceremonies and make offerings. The land holds further ties for the resisters by being the burial ground of the ancestors. The Navajo bury their dead near their homesites and, as one woman put it, "I feel they are a part of me" (Davidheiser, n.d., pp. 2–4).

However, the psychological and sociocultural centrality of place as physical space needs to be further tested cross-culturally. Liisa Malkki cautions against the application of what she refers to as a Western "sedentarist metaphysic" that "incarcerates the native" in an ecological or territorial identity and assumes that the rooting of peoples is "not only normal, it is also perceived as a moral and spiritual need" (1992, pp. 30–31). Her work in Tanzania reveals that Hutu refugees imagined the true Hutu nation as a deterritorialized moral community formed by the refugee community while, on the other hand, the land expanse called Burundi was merely a state (1992, p. 35). Malkki's point is well taken. There is a long history of people leaving home regions and successfully adapting to entirely new environs. As Hansen's work with Angolan refugees in Zambia also demonstrates, a far greater sense of dislocation occurred among refugees who were settled in camps than among those who self-settled among co-ethnics in villages. In effect, the people who fled across the border but settled with co-ethnics never felt themselves to be refugees (Hansen, 1993). Brown and Perkins also present the view that human experience may be seen as separable from context. Following a rational choice approach, people may be presented as disengaged and objective observers of settings who carry out rational economic analyses of places, specify the costs and benefits of those places, and are willing to move from one place to another according to the perception of advantage (1992, p. 283). As well as place, then, the separation or fragmentation of community that frequently accompanies uprooting may be the primary source of socially based stress and suffering. Hansen's and Malkki's work shows that communities that can maintain their cultural identity and social fabric are more resilient in the face of dislocation.

Notwithstanding the examples provided by Malkki and Hansen, land and place in the sociocultural systems of many peoples around the world lie at the core of their identity and society, and they articulate these priorities clearly in resistance. It becomes clear in many cases that removing people from their known environments separates them from the material and cultural resource base upon which they have depended for life as individuals and as communities. Clearly there is a human need for "environments of trust," however they may be defined, and that need is fundamental for the sense of order and predictability implied by culture. Threats of removal from these physical and symbolic environments have generally elicited some form of resistance. The narratives of resistance to displacement, particularly by indigenous peoples, consistently reference the centrality of place in their culture and life ways.

Identity and Resistance

Although always at risk in uprooting, the durability and flexibility of cultural identity throughout the extensive migratory history of humanity is impressive. The frequency with which cultural identities have been sustained, reinvented, and mobilized after migration to new environments is testament to the adaptability of human beings to change. However, the modern era has also seen the demise of hundreds, if not thousands, of ethnolinguistic groups who have virtually disappeared through disease, exploitation, and assimilation into dominant cultural groups. This is particularly the case for indigenous and minority cultural groups that are small in numbers and frequently isolated spatially. When contact in the form of private or public economic expansion into their territories has taken place, the result has frequently been cultural extinction. The loss of this incredible cultural diversity and the wide spectrum of knowledge it represented, particularly over the last five hundred years, may yet have telling evolutionary impacts for the future of humanity. For some of these endangered groups, local efforts, combined with the efforts of allies in the indigenous rights, human rights, and environmental movements, have led to new political stances, often in response to development projects that include DFDR (Bilharz, 1998; Blaser, Feit, & McRae, 2004; Gray 1998; Salisbury, 1989; Schkilnyk, 1985; Turner, 1991a, 1991b; Waldram, 1980).

In the conflict of resistance, particularly for small, relatively isolated groups, more precise and politicized definitions of cultural identity are often worked out, and conceptions of the community in broader national and global contexts may be developed. For many small peasant or indigenous societies, traditional worldviews construct a sense of identity that is almost coterminous with the sense of being human. With the increasing presence of the state, such small societies often lack an awareness of the political meaning of their own culture in the larger context in which they are becoming subsumed (Turner, 1991a). This lack of awareness, particularly of their minority status and its implications for their subordinate position within the larger society, can lead to an erosion of identity and cultural collapse when confronted with dominant group power and exploitation (Henry, 1964).

Development projects that include DFDR carry with them the potential for a virtually total undermining of local identity. Resettlement imposes forces and conditions on people that may completely transform their lives, evoking profound changes in productive activities, social organization and interaction, leadership and political structure, and world view and ideology. Resettlement may mean that people may be relocated in a new place where they may have little firsthand knowledge and experience. Uprooting people from the environments in which the vast majority of their meaningful activities have taken place separates them from the context on which much of their understanding of life and their sense of identity are based.

Resettlement not only relocates a people in space; it also remakes them. When a community is relocated, it is not reproduced whole in a new site. In most cases the community is reconfigured in specific ways. As mentioned earlier, most development projects, especially those that occasion the large-scale resettlement of rural populations, directly or indirectly further two fundamental processes: the expansion of the state and integration into regional and national market systems. Neither of these processes of inclusion is particularly simple or straightforward, but in most instances they both initiate a restructuring of social, economic, and political relationships to more closely resemble those of the larger society. In many respects, the process of resettlement, insofar as it is oriented by development goals, is designed to change local cultures. In that sense, resettlement will not necessarily destroy "local cultures," but it will appropriate them and restructure them around values and goals that often originate from far beyond the local context. Such a process of development must involve the reduction of local cultures, societies, and economies from all their variegated expressions to a narrow set of institutions and activities that make them compatible with the purposes of the larger society (Garcia Canclini, 1993).

Cultural issues are important to most if not all groups facing displacement, but they are particularly significant to indigenous peoples. Although there is no universally accepted definition of "indigenous peoples," they are usually distinguished from national populations by the possession of certain cultural features, most notably language and religion. Other features may include distinctive forms of livelihood, clothing, house type, and settlement patterns, among other elements. In some nations indigenous peoples may be designated by state authorities as ethnic minorities, tribal groups, or minority nationalities. Moreover, indigenous peoples are crucially linked through ancestral ties and long-term residence and use to specific lands and resources. Indeed, the association with a specific territory, both through current use and ancient tradition, comes to form a key element in the formation of cultural identity of indigenous peoples. The World Bank has in fact codified the relationship between land and indigenous people, recognizing that "the identities and cultures of Indigenous Peoples are inextricably linked to the lands on which they live and the resources on which they depend. These distinct circumstances expose Indigenous Peoples to different types of risk and levels of impacts from development projects, including loss of identity, culture and customary livelihoods, as well as exposure to disease" (World Bank, 2005). Notwithstanding this position, the World Bank has recently weakened the safeguards in its policy on indigenous peoples (see Chapter 8).

The fact that most DFDR projects impact the poor, minority groups, and indigenous peoples so deeply explains the centrality of cultural identity in resistance. Indeed, the determination of indigenous identity has become an increasingly contested feature of the national and international politics of development. With the emergence of human rights and indigenous peoples' rights movements, international covenants and conventions, and national legislation over the past quarter century, possessing indigenous identity may afford individuals and communities certain rights to protection. The state will frequently attempt to deny that certain affected populations are of indigenous identity or culture because the special status and rights accorded indigenous peoples through their primordial ties to land and resources present significant obstacles to developers. The contested nature of indigenous identity in contemporary contexts was amply demonstrated at the United Nations Permanent Forum on Indigenous Issues in 2005 when the representative from Bangladesh spoke eloquently of that nation's support of all the international conventions safeguarding the rights of indigenous peoples but stipulated quite firmly that Bangladesh had no indigenous peoples. She asserted that the Chakma people of the Chittagong Hills region, who were displaced by the Kaptai Dam and have been engaged in almost forty years of conflict with the state, were not in fact indigenous, but were an ethnic minority and relatively recent immigrants to the area, having come there within the last two hundred years.

One problem that emerges, given the multiple assaults on indigenous life that have been underway in many areas for centuries, is that indigenous identity may have been suppressed or hidden for survival purposes. Today, however, in the changing climate of international and national human rights legislation, indigenous peoples are reclaiming their identities publicly. This reclamation process, in effect the right to define one's own identity, should be recognized as an important effect of the global expansion and acceptance of human rights policies (Bolaños, 2008). Given the frequently contested relationships between the state and indigenous peoples, reliance on the nation-state's framework for identification of indigenous peoples may be of doubtful utility. Within the context of a nation and its development projects, the final determination of indigenous identity must lie with the people themselves.

In most respects, nonetheless, the cultural politics of development projects are ultimately assimilationist in both effect and intention. M. Bartolome and Barabas, in fact, frame this intention in terms of "ethnocide" (1973). Referring specifically to a program of regional development in the Papaloapan basin of southern Mexico that involved the construction of two large dams, the Miguel Aleman and the Cerro de Oro, Bartolome and Barabas assert that the 20,000 Mazatec and as many Chinantec Indians were subjected, through the displacement experience, to an intentional and systematic process of ethnocide. Nor was this process in any way covert or surreptitious. Both the Papaloapan Commission and the Instituto Nacional Indigenista openly declared these intentions.

> The removal of the natives and their resettlement in a new environment does not represent a simple change of residence, but rather the beginnings of a change in their psychology, in their emotional lives and even in their customs . . . They are in a process of change from a tribal life to today's civilized life . . ." (Commission of the Papaloapan, 1958, p. 37, as cited in M. Bartolome & Barabas, 1973, p. 8).

The director of the Instituto Nacional Indigenista echoed these thoughts in several publications, which, according to Bartolome and Barabas, were circulated throughout all the institute offices as expressions of official policy.

> The purpose is still integration and in no way to develop in them [Mexico's Indian population] an ethnic consciousness that separates them from the rest of the nation (Aguirre Beltran, 1972, p. 3, as cited in Bartolome & Barabas, 1973, p. 16).

In another context, Aguirre Beltran, one of Mexico's most distinguished anthropologists, continued

> The indigenous societies—rural and isolated within their self-sufficient economy and technological backwardness—try to conserve modes of life which they consider acceptable, but which constitute an obstacle to the integration of a common nationality and nation (1973a, p. 223, as cited in Bartolome & Barabas, 1973, p. 16).

Facing this threat to their lives and cultures, the indigenous people responded to the dams and the displacement through an incipient messianic movement. The elders of the Chinantec community ordered their shamans to use their companion spirits to kill the president of Mexico. These efforts were thwarted, the shamans said, by the president's own companion spirits, and the resultant sense of futility led to the formation of a messianic movement based on the Virgin of Guadalupe, who appeared on a hill near the construction site to announce her opposition to the dam and to ask that the president and the priests of the municipality come to speak with her. A cult developed around this apparition, focused on certain pieces of wood that were found at the site. The site has become a pilgrimage destination for the Chinantecs, and the pieces of wood are now carried in large processions as holy relics. At roughly the same time, the devil also appeared at the Cerro de Oro Dam site, asking the engineers to leave. He also demanded that the president of Mexico appear to account for what had happened. In addition, popular belief had it that the devil's appearance coincided with the deaths of several engineers who were working on the dam. It is interesting that both the Virgin of Guadalupe, Mexico's patroness, and the devil appear in opposition to the dam. In Latin American ideology the Virgin is traditionally a beneficent figure, and the devil often appears to mediate the tensions between traditional cultures and modern society, providing a means of explanation for the injustices encountered, as well as protection from harm if he is properly propitiated (Nash, 1979; Taussig, 1980).

Finally, in another context Aguirre Beltran clearly expresses the lack of tolerance of the dominant society for alternative cultural models, as well as the cultural politics and complementarity between development projects and nation-building.

If the regional and parochial populations [the Indians] of Mexico do not share in a national consciousness, the changes which they experience as the inevitable consequence of their contact with modern culture could bring them . . . to the organization of a pan Indian movement that could lead them to the formation of a second nationality. As such an event is contrary to goals of national formation, the education for integration carried out among the Indian population should complement the education of the dominant population (Aguirre Beltran, 1973b, p. 259, as cited in Bartolome & Barabas, 1973, p. 17).

It is clear that an opposition between traditional indigenous culture and modern society is being constructed, juxtaposing self-sufficiency against national integration. That opposition, according to the dominant model, constitutes an obstacle to the creation of a modern nation. It is instructive to consider these statements in light of current indigenous movements in Latin America, in particular those in Ecuador and Bolivia, in which pan-Indian movements have succeeded in gaining for themselves not only important but also decisive roles in national politics, including the presidency of Bolivia, in nations where they constitute the majority of the population. While the cited passages were published more than thirty years ago, many state agendas today, while not as transparent, are very similar, public statements to the contrary notwithstanding.

On the other hand, development projects can also, in an inadvertent and oppositional process, provide a context for developing forms of social consciousness that are more appropriate to the minority position of small communities within an interethnic social system. In effect, development projects can catalyze a shift in cultural consciousness from an ahistorical and acultural sense of identity to that of an ethnic group with a culture and identity to protect in confrontation with a national society (Waldram, 1980). The struggle to resist the Ralco Dam on the Bio Bio River in Chile has reunited Mapuche Indians, who have come back to the region to reconnect with their communities. People who had hidden their indigenous identity began to reclaim their cultural heritage with pride (Evans, 2001, p. 6).

Although many small societies face total assimilation and cultural disappearance, others have begun to foreground their minority status and have constructed it in terms of active defense of cultural identity and concerted political action. One such group is the Kayapo of the village of Gorotire in the Brazilian Amazon (Turner, 1991a). Although initial contact occurred in 1938, the Kayapo, in adjusting to their new situation with regard to the Brazilians, had not conceptualized their new condition as an ethnic minority within the larger Brazilian society. Their sense of their own culture and identity continued to be based on certain institutions, such as the extended family household, the men's house, the age set system, and naming and initiation rites of passage, that were key in the reproduction of traditional social relations.

However, in the 1980s, with the onslaught of a number of activities undertaken by the state and its citizens in their territory, the Kayapo had to adjust certain features of their worldview to see themselves as an ethnic group among many other indigenous peoples in common encounter with Brazilian society. In their confrontation with both public and private economic development initiatives, the Kayapo have come to define their very survival in terms of successful resistance to the destruction of their natural environment by the Brazilians. Development aggression against their culture and environment began in the 1980s, when gold mines were illegally opened in their territory and radioactive waste was dumped on their borders. The Kayapo met these assaults with skillful manipulation of Brazilian fears of savage Indians, resulting in a successful recapture of the gold mines. A sit-in at the presidential palace in full regalia halted the radioactive dumping.

Perhaps the greatest triumph among many has been the leading role the Kayapo of Gorotire played in the great intertribal rally at Altamira. Held to protest the project to construct five large dams in the Xingu River Valley, the rally contributed to the eventual delay of a World Bank loan that would have made the project financially possible. Subsequently, through an international campaign led by the Kayapo with the assistance of international allies, including media figures like the rock star Sting, they achieved the demarcation of a large new reserve for Kayapo communities, which had formerly lacked duly constituted territory. Basically, in their resistance to the incursions of Brazilian society, the Kayapo have made their culture a political issue. Moreover, they have found that their culture is important to others and have discovered the importance of having control over how their culture is represented to others. They recognize that control over the power of representation is a means of conferring value and meaning on themselves in the eyes of the larger world. The great rally at Altamira to protest the Xingu River dam project was organized by the Kayapo as a demonstration of their culture and the political solidarity between all Kayapo and their allies. The Kayapo encampment at the rally was designed as a model Kayapo village, with traditional houses, artifacts, and family groupings, all of which were avidly viewed by the hundreds of journalists, photographers, and videographers in attendance. The Kayapo astutely reasoned that the more national and international witnesses they had, the less likely the Brazilian state would be to undertake any violent retaliations for the demonstration, in which the Kayapo very forcefully demonstrated their resistance to the project and their scorn for the Brazilian authorities (Turner, 1991a; for further discussion, see Chapter 7).

The protest was part of a successful effort to cancel the project. However, dam projects, like vampires, are hard to kill permanently. In the 1990s ELETRONORTE undertook new planning for a single dam on the Xingu, called Belo Monte, that allegedly would do less harm to the environment and impact fewer people. The Kayapo and other indigenous groups in the region, as well as their national and international allies, were not convinced. Subsequent research has shown that the dam's viability is dependent on the construction of other dams and a huge reservoir upstream to keep adequate levels of water flowing to Belo Monte for electrical generation year round. In April 2008 a Brazilian federal judge issued a restraining order suspending feasibility studies for the dam because the contracts had not been awarded competitively (Switkes, 2008a).

The next month, a five-day meeting of more than 800 people from 26 ethnic groups, the largest gathering of indigenous peoples of the Amazon in nearly 20 years, was held to affirm their resistance to the construction of the dam. The Kayapo played a central role, again displaying their ceremonial body paint and feather adornments, foregrounding their culture through dances and chants at the beginning of each day, as did many of the other attending groups. As at the Altamira meeting, there were threats and physical confrontations between Kayapo individuals and ELETRONORTE representatives, including the minor wounding of an official on the arm by a machete-wielding Kayapo. A declaration called the Xingu Forever Alive Letter issued at the end of the meeting affirmed their opposition to all dams on the Xingu and stated, "Our culture, our spirituality, and our survival are deeply rooted in the Xingu, and we depend on it for our existence . . . We who have protected our Xingu River demand respect" (Switkes, 2008b, p. 15).

Development projects, particularly those that involve resettlement, can inadvertently catalyze a shift in cultural and political consciousness among small subordinated groups, bringing about a process of political socialization that enables them to articulate more clearly for themselves and for others their interests and identities in the defense of their culture. Although the damage they inflict can threaten the existence of subaltern groups, development projects, even those that fail economically, can, given a degree of accountability, sharpen local identities through the oppositional process and resistance and further political development. As such, development projects can inadvertently produce positive outcomes when they stimulate the development of civil organizations that are able to resist excesses of the state in its efforts to transform local systems (C. Smith, 1996, p. 47).

Cultural Heritage Resources

Cultural heritage refers to the historical memory of a community, to that which links people to others throughout time. Cultural heritage is constituted in objects, resources, and practices that locate a people in the universe, giving them a sense of identity through time. Places where events of historical or sacred importance have occurred; objects such as shrines, cemeteries, or ancient ruins that express local identity; resources such as rivers, springs, lakes, and forests that not only provide material sustenance but also express or nurture the spiritual life of the community; speaking one's native tongue and practicing one's religion—all these things constitute elements of cultural heritage. For example, in Brazil, the Catholic Church and CRAB (see case study) developed a powerful discourse about the losses that the people would experience if they were displaced by dams. The threat to homes, churches, and cemeteries was deeply felt and nourished the spirit to defend these community institutions (Rothman & Oliver, 1999, p. 49). Consequently, it is not just "place" in the sense of geography that is significant, but the relationship between people and place as encoded in objects, socially constructed places, and historically derived cultural practices.

Previous discussion of cost-benefit analysis (CBA) emphasized the need to establish a discourse of commensurabilities among the various losses and gains for that approach to be applied. The discourse of people who are the objects of the policy and discourse of CBA, namely, those who must respond to questions about Willingness to Pay and Willingness to Accept for losses and those who must be relocated by projects, may respond to distinctly different cultural values. If CBA arrives at its conclusions through an objective calculation based on a constructed commensuration of values across a wide spectrum of costs and benefits, the cultural models or values that energize the discourse of those impacted come from different sources.

> You tell us to take compensation. What is the state compensating us for? For our land, for our fields, for the trees along our fields? But we don't live only by this. Are you going to compensate us for our forest? . . . Or are you going to compensate us for our great river—for her fish, her water, for vegetables that grow along her banks, for the joy of living beside her? What is the price of this? How are you compensating us for fields either?—we didn't buy this land; our forefathers cleared it and settled here. What price this land? Our gods, the support of those who are our kin—what price do you have for these? Our Adivasi [tribal] life—what price do you put on it? (Mahalia, 1994, as quoted in O'Neill, 1998).

This is part of a letter written to the chief minister of the state government of Gujarat by a tribal person from the Narmada Valley in Western India who was being displaced by the construction of the Sardar Sarovar Dam. The issue of compensation is clearly of concern to this individual, but he or she is incredulous that the government could conceive that compensation could begin to address their losses. Such things as "our forest . . . our great river . . . the joy of living beside her . . . this land . . . Our gods, the support of . . . our kin . . . Our Adivasi life" cannot be thought of as having determinable prices. This person is plainly arguing from a premise completely different from those of her audience, one which clearly differentiates between a set of values in which price is seen as a neutral measuring rod and a set of values that are based in the socially constructed relationship between a community and its environment. The suggestion that people, in exchange for a price, will be willing to abandon a cultural heritage to which they are committed corrupts the relationships that are the bedrock of a culture (O'Neill, 1998, p. 99). Indeed, clearly what is at stake for this individual is not a bundle of material resources that can be valued in a market, but a set of relationships that link a people to each other, to their environment, and to their way of life. Their value cannot be expressed monetarily. The existence of "spheres of exchange," in which categories of goods are incommensurable and separated by moral boundaries that prohibit transactions among them, is widely documented in many cultures (Bohannan, 1959).

Some of the major points of contention voiced in the discourse of the displaced revolve around issues of property. Compensation suggests that environmental goods can be subsumed into a liberal conception of property rights, with rights of exclusivity and alienability. In this understanding, land is a commodity that can be exchanged in the market. Threatened with relocation by the proposed construction of a dam, a Yavapai Indian from Arizona suggested that

> Indian people view the land as a gift from God, that they're only temporary and that God gave them the use of the land to live on . . . to take care of the earth . . . They don't really own the land. There's no one big title and a deed and stuff, and they pay off the land and they say, 'This is mine. Nobody else can take it.' An Indian doesn't view the land that way . . . The Indian knows that his land and life is intertwined, that they are one unit. Without the land, the Indian cannot survive and without the Indian, the land cannot be land, because the land needs to be taken care of to survive life. (Espeland, 1998, p. 201).

The land is sacred and basic to the core of Yavapai identity. In effect, Yavapai land and Yavapai identity are mutually constitutive. To separate one from the other is to destroy both humanity and nature. Moreover, for uncontacted indigenous groups who lack an awareness of their subordinate status within a larger society, displacement from territory can lead to an erosion of identity and to cultural collapse when confronted with dominant-group power and exploitation (Henry, 1964).

Essentially, land is an incommensurable entity, and it is morally repugnant to commoditize it. The suggestion that money could express its value or compensate them for its loss is to distort the relationship they have with the land. As another Yavapai individual put it, "Land is like diamonds, money is like ice" (Mariella, 1989). Land and money are being compared to two things that are similar in appearance but different in substance. And it should be noted that land is being compared to diamonds not in terms of monetary worth but in that diamonds have lasting qualities—they endure. To paraphrase the well-known commercial, diamonds and land are forever. Ice and money melt.

Clearly the necessity for strong commensuration in CBA and its equally strong rejection by dam-impacted people, particularly regarding cultural heritage resources, present a thorny problem. But it is a problem of politics, not economics. Economics cannot resolve issues of value. It can only resolve issues of price. And in many instances prices do not reflect peoples' values. In dam projects the attempt—in order to set compensation levels—to use contingent valuation to reflect in monetary terms the value people place on cultural heritage resources settles nothing. Indeed, the attempt simply sharpens political dispute.

Time, Cultural Memory, and Uprooting

The events and processes associated with DFDR, much like wars and natural disasters, have a way of cleaving time into "before" and "after" periods. A major challenge for the uprooted is to formulate a sense of meaning for their loss and to integrate it into some context consistent with the values and beliefs of their culture—bridging "time before" and "time after." Meaning can be imposed on suffering if it serves some purpose and if that purpose and the experience of suffering are recognized as significant by others (Bode, 1989; Lifton, 1967; Oliver-Smith, 1992). Resistance to uprooting, whatever the cause, provides individuals and communities a means of reaffirming both personal and cultural identity by demanding recognition of their losses and a means to reassert control over lives that have been disempowered. It has been suggested that the process of individual and cultural recovery and reempowerment is encoded in the reconstruction and repossession of objects of cultural significance (D. Parkin, 1999).

Case Study: Displacement, Loss, and Cultural Resistance in Yongjing County of Northwest China

The development strategies of the People's Republic of China since 1949 have included construction of large hydroelectric projects, resulting in the displacement of 10.2 million people (Human Rights Watch/Asia, 1995, p. 10).* Estimates of resettled people associated with the current megaproject, Three Gorges Dam, will add between 1.2 and 1.6 million to that total. In the early period the vast majority of these people were resettled involuntarily, resulting in major economic losses that were largely concealed by a government policy that glorified the benefits of large dams. The case of Yongjing County in Northwest China fits clearly into this pattern. A major government plan to build 46 dams on the Yellow River included Yongjing. The dams were intended to control flooding, provide irrigation, and produce 110 billion kilowatt hours of electricity per year. Three of those dams were constructed in Yongjing province, the last being completed in 1975. A total of 101 villages were affected, and 43,829 people were displaced after 7,900 hectares of farmland were submerged.

The original plan for the region was to resettle people in remote areas, but the affected villages protested. Government officials realized that resettling people in distant regions would be too costly and consented to relocating people in the local area, but on lands that were of lesser quality and with less access to water. When villagers realized that resettlement entailed serious declines in welfare, they protested again, but they were quickly silenced. Those who complained were ejected from the Communist Party, and one leader was sent to a labor camp. All overt resistance was suppressed during the "big manhunt of 1958," which lasted from mid August to mid September. Resistance to resettlement became equated with resistance to the Great Leap Forward, and 855 people, including landlords, leaders of dissent groups, and organizers of religious societies, were preemptively arrested. Public executions of 21 people took place, effectively ending overt resistance. The county government employed the militia to evict the villagers. The terror of the big manhunt of 1958 suppressed resistance for several decades.

The peasants who were resettled lost their homes, ancestral tombs and religious monuments, their lands, and their spiritual and economic well-being. Even after post-Mao economic reforms began to improve the economic lives of people in rural China, the resettled peasants of Yongjing continued in

---

*Except where otherwise indicated, all information for this case study is based on Jing, 1999.

poverty because they had been resettled on inferior land and had received no compensation for their losses. However, after the dissolution of collective farming and the arrival of greater local autonomy and personal freedom in Yongjing, low levels of protest and resistance to the state began to emerge. Groups of people refused to pay taxes or interest on loans they had received from state-run banks. To voice their complaints with the Communist authorities, the peasants, ironically, employed the Communist practice of the "recalling bitterness tradition" that was used to generate hostility toward the old pre-Communist system.

In 1981 a memorial movement was formed, commemorating the losses and persecution the people suffered in the displacement and resettlement and transforming those events into a force for collective recovery. The memorial movement aimed to force the authorities to acknowledge the people's losses and suffering and to demand reparations. The movement employed three basic forms of collective action: the staging of public, frequently ritualized protests to evoke the grievances suppressed in the past; the circulation and submission of petitions insisting on more adequate compensation for the loss of the means of agricultural production; and the documentation and reconstruction of lost temples and tombs of the families of the displaced. The kinship and lineage system frequently provided the organizational basis for the development of resistance networks that carried out these strategies of collective action.

The staged protests often consisted of carefully orchestrated narratives of suffering. The protests emphasized and compressed two separate events—the dismantling of homes and the flooding of villages—into one sudden, unexpected assault. These cataclysmic narratives were designed to rewrite the official history of the period of resettlement, obliging the authorities to recognize that the people had sacrificed a great deal in the name of national development and that the state had both failed to acknowledge their pain and loss and to fulfill the promises made to them. Further, they rejected the bureaucratic label *shuiku yimin* (reservoir relocatees) applied to them by the government, employing (but altering through tonal change) the local term *kumin* (reservoir people), to mean "embittered" or "embittered people."

The movement addressed the material losses through petitions to the government for economic reparations. Even twenty years after the resettlement, villagers were still so poor that they were dependent on emergency food rations. The villagers organized sit-ins at government offices and submitted 322 petitions for financial restitution. One of the organizers of the sit-ins was arrested, and a group of young men retaliated by taking the chief administrator and party secretary of the township hostage. Two hundred protesters

marched to the county seat and demanded the exchange of the sit-in orga-
nizer for the hostage, to which the authorities acceded. Although the government refused to pay reparations, it did provide low-interest loans and free
irrigation equipment in an effort to address the need to alleviate poverty.

The recovery of religious tradition and identity as elements of a search for
transcendental meaning in the trauma of political persecution and loss was
accomplished through two strategies: the creation of memorial texts and new
genealogical records and the reconstruction of village temples. The displacement had destroyed 100 village temples and 44,000 family tombs. Temple
reconstruction and, later, reconstructed temples became focal points of un-
official, sometimes secret, networks of religious association. The rebuilding of
mosques was equally impressive. In Yongjing, 63 mosques were rebuilt for a
population of only 20,000 Muslims. Plaques with written references critical
of Maoist policy on resettlement appeared on temples. Texts were written
memorializing the importance of deities' statues to community. Memorializing texts were part of monastery reconstruction, which was a project that provided people of one village, for example, now actually split into four different
settlements, with a means of commemorating their lost village.

History and memory became the means by which community members
obliged authorities to recognize their losses and injuries and to redress them
in forms of reparations and reconstruction. As material losses were recognized
and validated, people themselves were validated and social reconstitution was
enabled. It was not only land and buildings that were repossessed. It was
one's history and identity as a community as well. Protest and resistance, even
twenty-five years after the displacement and resettlement process, enabled
people to create a politics of identity and to undertake processes of recovery
that were founded on fidelity to local cultural tradition.

The Yongjing case indicates that the social reconstruction of memory and
the assertion of relevance of that memory through resistance play crucial roles
in recovery after displacement. In Yongjing, individual memories of suffering
that had been suppressed by the government were transformed into a collective consciousness of rights that provided a moral justification for resistance
and protest against old and new grievances. However, the movement was
careful not to embrace open rebellion. Even in the newly opened political
spaces in China, villagers were realistic about what they could achieve. They
negotiated, made compromises, altered tactics, and awaited new opportunities for political action. Their main goal was to hold government to its word.
They argued that the government had reneged on its promise to compensate
the losses the people suffered in the name of national development. Their
movement combined invoking rights of public expression, the "speaking bit-

terness" tactics, and open but controlled confrontation with government authorities for recognition of their losses.

The memorial movement also publicly undermined the notion of people's indebtedness to the party. By commemorating the experiences of resettlement, hunger, and political persecution in demonstrations, petition drives, temple reconstruction, and records of the destruction of family tombs, the villagers were able to reconstruct the official doctrine of popular indebtedness to the party by demonstrating that the party was indebted to them. The path chosen by the villagers of Yongjing is increasingly seen elsewhere in China as village religious life and organization are emerging as an alternative base of power and authority precisely because they are closely linked to the reemergence of kinship organizations, temple associations, and village autonomy.

Part of the impact of DFDR is measurable in terms of resources and income lost, and the failure to recognize and compensate those losses is seen as causal in generating resistance. However, such losses and the failure to recognize them may have profound effects that undermine the ontological ground of culture itself. Victims must struggle with the reconstruction not only of material circumstances but of their culture itself. Material compensation or reimbursement may be insufficient to enable people to reconstruct culture and life way after resettlement. Central to the ontological basis of many cultures are the notions of time and place. People are linked to places by residence in time as well as space. Long histories in a place in which family and community roots are deeply embedded tie generations to each other in a "community of memory." It is through such communities of memory that people come to know themselves "as members of a people, as inheritors of a history and a culture that we must nurture through memory and hope" (Bellah, Madsen, Sullivan, Swidler, & Tipton, 1985, p. 138). Lack of understanding or acknowledgement of the symbolic importance of place and time by relocation authorities limits the probabilities of successful transition among resettled peoples, but as the Yongjing case and others (e.g., Bilharz, 1998; Conuel, 1981; Gray, 1996, p. 102; Greene, 1985; Jeffrey, 2000) illustrate, the power of memory as a mobilizing force for resistance and protest remains strong long after resettlement.

Languages of Resistance

The languages of protest and resistance to DFDR develop a wide array of themes, images, and symbols. Since resistance movements themselves exist on a multiplicity of levels and encounter development projects that are articulated with local and global interest groups as well, the discourses must be equally multivocal. Moreover, their discursive styles must fit the particular context, idiom, and problem area they are addressing. The broad discursive styles associated with two domains, human rights and science, play key roles in the campaigns of resistance movements. For instance, if one is arguing that construction of a dam increases the seismic potential of an area, a scientific discourse and style based in geology and seismology and emphasizing canons of objectivity and evidence are appropriate. If one is arguing that DFDR is a violation of spiritual rights, another form of discourse and style based on values and cultural heritage and appealing to emotion and sensibility is called for. Weeks has recently argued that both these discursive strategies may be characterized as "Jeremiad discourses" (1999, p. 20). Taken from the name of the prophet Jeremiah, who chastised the Jews for breaking their covenant with God, Jeremiad discourses criticize the listener (or reader) for a particular failure, evoke appropriate sentiments or actions, indicate the way to redemption, and resolve the tension between seeming opposites. Further, Jeremiad discourses rely on two strategies: evocative and implementational. Evocative strategies elicit emotions, using poetic and metaphoric language. Implementational strategies offer guides to action as opposed to sentiment (Weeks, 1999, p. 20). DFDR resisters rely on both strategies to draw support for their cause and to reject and refute the arguments of developers.

Since the discourse of developers relies heavily on a scientific approach and discursive style, resisters are extremely careful about the accuracy of both their data and the facts on which their arguments are based. NGOs have developed their own cadres of scientific experts, who often volunteer their services, from a diverse array of scientific fields to generate both data and perspectives to confront the arguments displayed by developers and their funders. The critiques that NGOs and networks have developed to refute the positions held by governments, private developers, and their funders minutely dissect both the adequacy of the databases and the theoretical perspectives of their opponents. Consistently calling attention to the lack of adequate research, the faulty methodology, the shoddiness of data collection, and the inconsistency and incompleteness of studies, NGOs assume a position of scientific rigor that contrasts with the politically compromised, biased, and inferior science of the developers. McCully's critique of *The World Bank's Experience with Large Dams,* which was written by the Operations Evaluation Department (OED) of the Bank and was an instrumental factor in the eventual creation of the World Commission on Dams, exemplifies this discursive style.

The OED review does not assess the actual performance of the projects it covers, is based on flawed methodology and inadequate data, and displays a systematic bias in favour of large dam building. Its conclusions must be rejected as untenable . . . The extremely poor quality of the OED review strongly indicates that OED is not a suitable body to entrust with the task of undertaking a comprehensive, unbiased and competent review of World Bank lending for large dams—and also casts doubt on the competence and independence of the work of OED on other areas (McCully, 1997, p. 2).

The themes developed by local people and their allies in the area of human rights, based on fundamental concepts of sacrifice and justice, question the morality of development projects that displace people. The pronouncements and publications of resisters, whether local people in a march on government offices, NGOs in their publications to enlist support, or a network appeal protesting the arrest of an activist, generally reflect the themes of sacrifice and justice. The listener or reader is called upon to recognize the sacrifices that people are forced to make in the name of development and the injustice inflicted by inadequate compensation and nonexistent or faulty resettlement. The dishonesty and hypocrisy of governments that call upon the poorest to sacrifice for the benefit of the richest are themes that commonly appear in both the spoken and written discourse of resisters.

Selections from an IRN mail campaign against the San Roque Dam reflect both the issues and the emotional and metaphoric discursive style:

A social and economic crisis is brewing . . . 186 families have already been moved to the Camanggaan resettlement site. Many have sunk into despair as the reality of their new lives finally hits them. They have no land to grow food or graze animals and are forced to live in small concrete houses. Most are still waiting for the small amount of compensation promised to them . . . Promises of livelihood projects have not been honored . . . From the beginning, people affected by the San Roque Dam have been lied to and shut out of the planning process . . . 'Like cows in a corral' San Roque oustees battle to survive . . . Take action to stop this social and economic disaster! Sign and mail the attached postcards today! (Cordillera Peoples' Alliance/International Rivers Network, 2001).

A leaflet (translated here by the author) distributed at a CRAB rally organized against the Tucurui Dam denounces the actions of the project authorities in simple yet powerful poetic style:

On the first day they came, they spoke to us of progress . . .
They measured our lands and we said nothing . . .
On the second day they came, they invaded our houses . . .

They expelled our children and we said nothing . . .
On the third day the water covered everything . . .
And because we said nothing we will never be able to do anything . . .
Are we going to let this happen again? (Comissao Regional dos Atingidos
de Barragens, 1988).

In addition to clearly expressing their sense of violation and outrage, the peasants displaced by the Tucurui Dam are describing a peculiarly one-sided conversation in which some people speak of progress and others say nothing. Part
of the reason that the conversation is so one-sided is that at the core it is a
conversation about value, and the peasants, in citing what they have lost, are
saying that their values mean nothing to the government. That is why they
would not have been heard and why they did not speak. They vow to speak in
the future and never to go unheard again. The similarity of the CRAB leaflet to
the famous Martin Niemoller (attributed) poem[†] about the dangers of political apathy under the Nazi regime suggests the growing identification felt by
local people and their allies with history and broader human rights struggles
around the world.

Another key theme in the human rights discourse involves an evocation of
fidelity to a cultural heritage. Abandoning one's land means separation from
and the loss of the right to express one's identity and practice one's religion.
Accepting resettlement is equated with betraying one's ancestors and everything that one stands for.

This is where we were born and where we grew up . . . The roots of our
grandparents are here. The land that is ours, the culture, the wisdom, the
native earth—all this is sacred. (Nicolasa Quintreman, quoted in Evans,
2001, p. 6).

Persecution, determination, martyrdom, and finality are also themes that run
through the human rights discourse. People consistently affirm their intentions to perish either by drowning in reservoirs or at the hands of oppressive

---

[†] First they came for the Socialists, and I did not speak out
      Because I was not a Socialist.
Then they came for the Trade Unionists, and I did not speak out
      Because I was not a Trade Unionist.
Then they came for the Jews, and I did not speak out
      Because I was not a Jew.
Then they came for me—and there was no one left to speak for me.
(United States Holocaust Memorial Museum, Washington D.C.)

authorities before they abandon their homes. In project after project, from dams to pipelines to golf courses, martyrdom is a consistent theme evoked by the people to be resettled. In Manibeli, the first village in Maharashtra that faced submergence from the Sardar Sarovar Dam in 1991, fifty families who had rejected resettlement, activists, and people from other affected villages awaited *Jal samadhi* (to drown in the reservoir's rising waters) in defiance of the government's decision to continue construction (Parasuraman, 1999, p. 244). Hunger strikes by both members and leaders of the Narmada Bachao Andolan represent another form of this discourse of martyrdom and finality.

Conclusion

In the final analysis, development projects and resettlement conflicts are at some level conflicts between two forms of knowledge, two forms of understanding reality, and, to a certain extent, two kinds of culture. One of the central features of modernity has been the separation of expert and lay knowledge, essentially a gulf between science and narrative (Kroll-Smith & Floyd, 1997). Although it is clear that all peoples engage in both forms of knowledge, the contrast is useful here to illustrate the nature of the conflict over cultural heritage resources in dam projects. On the one hand, the discourse of developers finds its source of truth in the abstract, scientific knowledge of the CBA experts and is based on what they consider to be tangible and measurable proofs. This knowledge adheres to meticulously followed paradigms and protocols that define both the parameters of what is to be studied and how it is to be studied. Kuhn has pointed out how the reliance on paradigms can blind their practitioners to important issues that do not fit the conceptual and instrumental tools that the paradigm supplies (1970, p. 37).

On the other hand, lay or local knowledge is narrative and historical in character, dealing with human experience of the world as lived. Lay knowledge is both embedded in and part of cultural heritage. It is contextual and local, resting on the assumption that knowing something cannot be separated from daily experience. Rather than relying on strictly defined paradigms and protocols, local knowledge is eclectic, deriving its truth from the biographical, from that which is learned from a variety of sources of teaching and experience. Local knowledge sustains community by being produced through the narrative of continuity between one's past and one's present (Kroll-Smith & Floyd, 1997).

Although modernity has rejected the value of situated experience and enshrined science as the arbiter of reality, the conflict over cultural heritage resources in dam projects reveals that the rejection of local knowledge is far from universal. In dam projects the tension between the two forms of knowledge is manifest. CBA is presented as objective, quantitative, data-based "science" as opposed to "narrative," or lived experience, as the basis for knowledge. However, it need not be a simple case of either-or. Indeed, the importance of cultural heritage resources in dam projects impresses with the necessity of finding a way to valorize other forms of knowledge and other decision-making models or means. Certainly, an economic analysis of how much a dam project is going to cost is necessary for a decision about construction, but that economic analysis has to be assessed along with other forms of knowledge, such as the social analysis, the cultural analysis, and the environmental analysis, all expressed in their own idioms. Economic analysis has a place, but it is only one place among many. It is not at the top of the hierarchy of values nor of a hierarchy of knowledges. Nor is it first among equals. It is one factor of many that must be taken into account in assessing the viability of projects. Different forms of information must make up the knowledge base upon which decisions are made because different kinds of value are at stake. Value heterogeneity requires knowledge heterogeneity (Espelund, 1999).

Such heterogeneity of value and knowledge obliges political dialogue and debate rather than mathematical ratios and a retreat from politics into an economics of grotesque prices. Here I return to my original point. If the conversation about large development projects is fundamentally a political debate, the relative political power of the different value positions must be recognized and compensated for. If different forms of knowledge are to be valorized, then the holders of each kind of knowledge must be empowered as well for their voices to be heard. However, as things stand currently, the words of a Chinantec elder displaced by the Cerro de Oro Dam in Mexico speak volumes for the defenders of local cultural heritage resources: "The government sent us the deluge because we didn't know how to speak the language of the government" (Bartolome & Barabas, 1990, p. 83).

CHAPTER SEVEN

Confronting Goliath

The Politics of DFDR *Resistance*

In the final analysis, all the disputes between the state, private interests, and people threatened with displacement by development projects—disputes over economic issues, environmental problems, cultural violations, and social conflicts—end up being contested in the domain of the political. However, the vast majority of cases of involuntary migration and resettlement are sociocultural and/or economic processes that are inflicted upon people as the intended or unintended outcomes of particular economic courses of action and goals. In this sense, while the actual resettlement project may be defined in social or, more commonly, economic terms, the phenomenon of resettlement is fundamentally a political one, involving the use of power by one party to relocate another. These power relations are conditioned by the climate of the various political contexts in which they are engaged. As was discussed in Chapter 2, DFDR resistance involves a form of "fractal" politics in which all the different participants—as allies, opponents, or mediators—interact across various scales of space and time (Little, 1999). The interactions among the transnationally allied activities of GROS, NGOS, social movements, lawyers, courts, corporations, and multilateral organizations both affect and are affected by global and national politics dealing with normative issues of human rights and the environment (W. F. Fisher, 2009; Oliver-Smith, 1996, p. 96).

A study by Khagram (2004) of transnational struggles for power and water, focusing especially on the Sardar Sarovar Project to dam the Narmada River in Western India, suggests that the transnational politics of NGOS directly or indirectly helps to form new arrays of norms that are propagated globally through conferences and other international events and publications. International organizations and international epistemic communities also contribute to global norms by codifying, validating, and conferring authority upon norms as adopted in formal institutions and practices. The more a state is connected into the global network of states that accept and validate these norms pertaining to human rights and the environment, as well as the international actors and organizations that contribute to their creation, the likelier it is that those norms will inform the institutions of that state. The assimilation of global norms by states can produce new political spaces for NGOs, GROs, and social movements to further their goals by holding states accountable for conformity with their own normative principles and rules. On the other hand, states and their institutions and practices may be resistant to changes even after formal acceptance of international regimes of norms and principles. State institutions and practices are also embedded in local structures and are susceptible to pressure from domestic actors, such as dominant classes and class coalitions, social mobilization of particular local interest groups, or the interests of political elites (Khagram, 2004, pp. 20–27). In other words, it is local authorities that enforce, however differentially, national regulations and laws.

Thus, states may respond both to internationally accepted norms and principles pertaining to human rights, the environment, and the rights of indigenous peoples and to domestic institutions and practices that may not necessarily share the same philosophical, political, or social values as the state. Nonetheless, Khagram suggests that a political climate that permits organized and sustained social mobilization in the context of democratic institutions is critical to the formation and success of both local and transnational collective action that furthers the acceptance of global norms in the political economy of development in the Third World. Khagram further asserts that local and transnational resistance to large-scale development projects will have the least success in states with authoritarian regimes and local actors with little or no capacity or political space to organize (2004, p. 21).

A number of basic conditions common to democratic regimes seem to be essential to the efforts of GROs, NGOs, and social movements seeking to halt DFDR. The free flow of information both nationally and internationally is absolutely essential for NGOs and their lobbying efforts for changing environmental and development policies (Khagram, 2004, p. 22). Under democratic regimes, NGOs, GROs, and social movements are freer to gather and to make information public in the attempt to alter public opinion. They are more able to lobby government and bureaucratic actors regarding their positions on development issues. Since leaders in a democracy are generally more responsive to public opinion, the existence of a free press, including other forms of media such as radio, television, and the Internet, has proven to be crucial for the acquisition and dissemination of information by NGOs and GROs working in DFDR resistance. In a democratic regime in which political parties vie for the votes of the electorate, DFDR resisters can take advantage of the competition among parties to further their agendas, particularly those regarding forms of alternative sustainable development, as well as other social justice issues that relate to DFDR, such as gender, indigenous rights, or the environment (Khagram, 2004, p. 24). However, by the same token, when resisters come from the traditionally marginalized groups in a society, their lack of political power may make them less appealing, as constituents, to politicians (Bilharz, 1998).

In regard to dams, Khagram argues persuasively that transnational NGOs that are allied with grassroots organizations and social movements have changed the terms of debate and now significantly affect both policy and practice in the political economy of development in the Third World. Moreover, these changes have been enabled by the expansion and institutionalization of norms and principles regarding human rights, the environment, and indigenous peoples. The continuing success of these coalitions in changing development policies and practices is contingent on the existence of democratic regimes in which they are able to mobilize grassroots organizations and support (Khagram, 1999, p. 44). However, recent retrenchment to authoritarian methods, even in ostensibly democratic regimes, suggests that powerful interests both inside and outside of government may limit, often forcibly, the capacity of grassroots organizations to mobilize for change both locally and at the policy level. Recent events in Mexico, India, and Thailand suggest that democratic institutions may be insufficient protection for DFDR resisters (Robinson, personal communication, June 6, 2007).

Negotiation Between Unequals

Barring immediate, outright, and open conflict between people facing DFDR and the state and project authorities, most resistance at some point involves dialogue and negotiation among the various parties over such points as alternative sites, resource valuation methods, compensation levels and quality, timetables, and benefits eligibility, to name only a few key issues. DFDR resistance movements face considerable difficulty in their discussions with state or corporate authorities due to the great imbalances of power that are usually built into the structure of the national political economy and sociocultural context (Davidheiser, 2000). While there is little explicit analysis of DFDR negotiations specifically, the literature on negotiations and conflict resolution provides some useful perspectives for understanding the problems resisters face when they encounter state or corporate representatives across the table. Since they are frequently the poor or the marginalized, most people facing resettlement have little power or influence in national or even regional contexts. Often members of minority groups or the poor who live at the margins of national societies, they lack the economic, social, and political capital necessary to affect decisions beyond the local level. Even where those threatened with resettlement are not minorities or the poor, as in the case of the Nimad plains upper peasantry in the Sardar Sarovar Project (Dwivedi, 1999), they enter negotiations with project authorities at a clear disadvantage, although by virtue of their status, their position may get a better hearing than that of the landless or the tribal peoples. The cultural gaps among the parties entering into negotiations—especially situations in which the lower-status participants are not familiar with the cultures, values, norms, or conventions of ordinary behavior regarding issues of conflict and communication—can reduce the possibility of fair and just outcomes.

The James Bay Cree, for example, contend that the negotiation of the James Bay and Northern Quebec Agreement of 1975 took place under the pressure of the ongoing destruction of their lands and the refusal by the courts and the Canadian government to recognize their aboriginal and constitutional rights. To substantiate their contention, they cite articles in the agreement, insisted upon by Hydro-Quebec at the time of negotiations, stating that the Cree forfeit their right to raise sociological impacts on their people as arguments against future hydroelectric projects in their territory (Colchester, 1999, p. 35).

The James Bay and Northern Quebec Agreement has been described as "a forced purchase." According to the Canadian Royal Commission on Aboriginal Problems and Alternatives,

> it would be most difficult to avoid the conclusion that the Aboriginal parties
> . . . were repeatedly subjected to inappropriate, unlawful coercion and duress
> . . . These actions were incompatible with the fiduciary obligations of both
> governments and substantially affected the fundamental terms of the "agreement" reached (as cited in Colchester, 1999, p. 35).

However, the situation of the James Bay Cree presents more than a case of unequal power in development negotiations. Fighting since 1971, through legal action in federal courts, to preserve a way of life based on traditional hunting, fishing, and trapping, the James Bay Cree ultimately were able to renegotiate power and roles and won financial compensation, the protection of key rights, and retention of control over a portion of their territory (Ettenger, 1998, p. 51). The Cree have been able to achieve participation as owners with rights to project benefits in a water/energy development project. Although this outcome is far from unanimously accepted by Cree communities, the benefit-sharing component of the contract between the Cree and Hydro-Quebec creates a significant precedent, one that is being promoted currently as part of the solution to the consistent impoverishment resulting from re-settlement (Cernea, 2009; Ettenger, 1998; Feit, 2004).

The balance of power and the relative power status of the participants is a crucial variable in negotiations, seriously affecting the possibility of establishing fair and equitable interactions and outcomes among them (Bercovitch & Houston, 1996). One of the leading authorities on alternative dispute resolutions, Laura Nader considers overcoming the power differential virtually impossible and counsels that weak parties seek recourse in formal legal systems rather than modes of negotiation to achieve just and equitable solutions (1994, 1997). However, such options may also be of limited use since many marginalized groups have customarily been ignored or discriminated against by formal legal systems (Little, 1999). Power disparities may actually reduce the likelihood of undertaking negotiations in the first place since there is little to be gained by the stronger party in compromises that substantively address the interests and needs of all participants (Ott, 1972). Bercovitch and Houston's review of research demonstrates that power imbalances correlate highly with lower rates of success in negotiations (1996).

There has been some discussion of factors that can offset power imbalances. R. Fisher and Ury (1981) have argued that "principled negotiation" employing "objective criteria" to present one's position and arrive at group decisions can reduce the role of "raw power." Despite the difficulty of establishing truly "objective criteria," much less principled negotiation free of self-interest, if some criteria can actually be agreed upon, they can support the position of the weaker party by bestowing the symbolic power of legitimacy when the criteria are met and can increase the possibility of successful outcomes by establishing some clear measures for making decisions (Davidheiser, 2000). The chance of successful negotiations for weaker parties can also be improved if decision-making is relegated from a central bureaucracy to regional or local institutions, thus possibly reducing the social distance between local communities and the state representatives (Penzich, Thomas, & Wohlgenant, 1994).

Another way to address power imbalances in negotiations is the formation of alliances (Penzich et al., 1994). Allies help to offset disparities in power, particularly if they hold a higher social and political status. Especially today the acquisition of allies from national and international contexts contributes greatly to strengthening the negotiating position of local communities. Such allies provide a variety of significant resources, including negotiating experience, material resources, and, perhaps most importantly, information. People impacted by DFDR frequently are forced to operate in novel contexts with a serious lack of adequate information, placing them at a severe disadvantage in negotiating positive outcomes with project authorities (Dwivedi, 1998). It is extremely difficult to further one's interests in negotiations with incomplete or faulty information on the situation at hand or on one's opponent. A lack of knowledge of the state and its agencies is a serious disadvantage in such negotiations since weaker parties are unable to take advantage of internal factions, potential alliances, or opportunities for cooperation (Davidheiser, 2000). Alliances with national and international NGOs have enabled local-level resisters to acquire enough knowledge and, while not total parity, enough leverage in these novel circumstances to engage the planners, administrators, and funders of development projects in debate and negotiations. From these interactions, some development agents have realized, albeit reluctantly, that they cannot ignore the rights of those affected by their projects. For example, ELETROSUL in Brazil (see case study) admitted after the fact that had they sat down to discuss the project with protesters, outcomes would probably have been more positive for both parties in the long run (McDonald, 1993, p. 99).

DFDR resistance may start as a spontaneous, ad hoc response to the unexpected presence, at the local level, of development project advance personnel. This ad hoc kind of resistance, expressed in the form of passive obstruction or active harassment of project personnel and their activities, may last for considerable lengths of time. Indeed, local communities may gain some leverage in negotiations through threats or actual subversive activity. If the state or corporate interests refuse to negotiate, and local communities feel that the dominant power structure does not serve their interests, they may see no alternative to violent or peaceful disruptive action at any point in the negotiation process. Generally, with greater and more constant project presence and action, resistance tends to become more formalized, eventually establishing features that are associated with local or grassroots organizations or social movements. The potential of external allies supporting these nascent organizations to offset the great disparities in power in negotiations between local communities and the national or corporate forces that seek to relocate them offers resisters some opportunity for gain in such contexts.

Scales of Interaction and Conflict

When resistance movements develop, they tend to generate contacts and linkages with social actors that operate at four levels: the local community, the project, the national political context, and the international or global context.

Initial contacts, whatever their character, eventually may generate contacts and relationships with social actors in the three other levels: the project that requires relocation, the national political economic context, and international political economy and political culture. These four levels, community, project, national, and international, all contain or possess different features that are separate—and at times internally contradictory or opposing—but interacting also. That is, contradictions and inconsistencies are found both within levels and between them. In addition, actions are not confined to one level; that is, they can occur simultaneously on multiple levels. In some contexts the project may provide a means through which local interests articulate with national institutions perhaps for the first time (Oliver-Smith, 2006).

The organizational capacity of a movement to operate effectively at both the local and national levels will prove important as the movement develops (McAdam, McCarthy, & Zald, 1988, p. 697). However, it is important to maintain the distinction between internal and external actors in a local case of DFDR. If the focus becomes too trained on external actors and their resources, it becomes easy to see local movements only as the outcome of external resources (Rothman & Oliver, 1999, p. 43). Local activists are generally anything but passive recipients of external aid. The relationship between internal and external actors is reciprocal, composed of exchanges of resources, influence, information, and validation.

The Local Scale of Action

The majority of resistance movements emerge in response to a specific project in a specific local context. That local context may vary in size, from one community or even one part of a community to a very large region such as the Narmada Valley in Western India, which occupies parts of three states (see case study). In many cases, the first news that people may receive of a project consists of the appearance of surveyors or other advance personnel. The initial reaction of local people is usually disbelief. They simply do not believe that anyone could seriously contemplate uprooting them. (Scudder & Colson, 1982, pp 271–272; Wali, 1989, p. 74). Their incredulity may be an index of their lack of acquaintance with the state. As the state expands its influence and as interaction with local people becomes more frequent, it is probable that their incredulity will decrease. However, there are indications that many people are still quite surprised and that levels of disbelief remain high for considerable periods of time, even after project intentions have been officially made public (Aguirre, personal communication, November 30, 2000).

First encounters between local communities and a project may take place upon the arrival of surveyors or other early reconnaissance teams who signal the beginning of a project. Confrontations of varying intensity may result from these encounters, ranging from puzzled reactions to physical assaults. Communities, as their first quasi-organized response to these encounters once they are aware of the nature of the mission, have been known to uproot survey markers after dark or destroy campsites when engineers and surveyors are in the field. However, in most cases responses by local people are quite reasoned and frequently take the form of a request for dialogue and information. The response of project personnel to these requests is often so abrupt or evasive that resistance can move quickly to more activist stances. However, in some cases the idea of displacement and resettlement is so unbelievable and so unimaginable to local people that even the appearance of survey teams has often not been sufficient to provoke communities into action. As occurs with so many of the state's promises and projects, they simply do not believe that displacement and resettlement will happen.

However, the idea of displacement and resettlement, once the implications are fully realized, may constitute such a threat to both physical survival and cultural identity that it mobilizes communities rapidly. Resisting resettlement often stimulates people to engage in innovative forms of behavior, producing changes in social relations and organization as well as creating or changing the nature of linkages with external individuals and organizations. When the decision to resist is taken and formalized, such action often evolves into the formation of grassroots organizations, in many instances initiating efforts and attracting new participants that may eventually produce changes in the way the local community interacts with power structures at various levels in the hierarchy of state institutions (Ghai & Vivian, 1992). Furthermore, the speed and intensity with which electronic communications now link areas remote from each other can establish contact between groups with similar goals in other regions of the world, creating networks of resistance movements that share information and other resources. Joining networks can improve the resource base and strategic potential of local resistance movements. For example, the experience of people resettled by the Itaipu Dam greatly influenced the development of resistance by communities facing resettlement by the Santo Capanema project in Brazil (L. Bartolome, 1992, p. 10). Similar networking and sharing of experiences by resettled people with those threatened with resettlement resulted in the formation in Brazil of the Regional Commission of People Affected by Dams (CRAB) and eventually the nationwide organization, National Movement of People Affected by Dams (MAB), composed of many regionally and culturally diverse local populations facing resettlement (Rothman & Oliver, 1999) (see case study). MAB's broad national power base enables it to negotiate effectively with the Brazilian power company ELETROBRAS and its regional subcontracting affiliates (L. Bartolome, 1992; Serra, 1993). MAB is also affiliated with numerous other organizations, including the Landless Movement (Movimento sem Terra, or MST), in the broader struggle to change development models and processes. Thus, changes initiated by the decision to resist often link local communities into regional and national networks that provide them important resources for furthering their struggles.

Local culture may frame resistance in highly traditional, even conservative, terms, but the resistance still may change the ways a community interacts with outsiders, including project personnel. People may reorient their central cultural symbols to construct interpretations of the threat of resettlement in very traditional forms. The Chinantecs and Mazatecs of Mexico recontextualized the threat of resettlement in mythological symbols, generating a resistance movement expressed largely in messianic terms (M. Bartolome & Barabas, 1990, pp. 76–77). The messianic resistance movement revitalized local culture, producing an activist posture toward regional and national authorities. The "incipient messianic movement accomplished what politicians, engineers, businessmen, and false mediators have tried to prevent: the unity of the Chinantec people" (M. Bartolome & Barabas, 1973, p. 15). Local unity in opposition to the state suggests both an alteration of traditional relationships and pressure to adjust relations on both sides of the conflict. However, the internal changes in communities set in motion by the decision, organization, and actions of resistance do not inevitably bring about changes in policy or the establishing of new public goals at any but the local level. Indeed, depending on the reigning political climate, mobilization for resistance at the local level may provoke a hardening of some policies at the regional or state level.

Regional levels of social and institutional development in local contexts also affect the action and organization of DFDR resistance movements. Local leadership structure and organization and linkages to similar structures at the regional level are important. The degree to which local structures are articulated with state structures, procedures, and goals will affect how DFDR resistance relates to external resources, as well as their choice of strategies and tactics. For example, resisters aware of or affiliated with a national union may elect to establish a local chapter of that organization to tap into a larger resource pool for their struggle (Wali, 1989, p. 85). Local DFDR resistance movements, however, risk becoming pawns of local and regional political parties if they tie their fortunes too closely to them (Baviskar, 1992).

Since resistance in many instances in effect constitutes a challenge to the state, the politics of state-local relations in all their complexity come to the fore. This sort of challenge constitutes "news" and attracts the attention of the power structure as well as the media (and, I might add, the academic community) quickly. When brought into broader public contexts, displacement and resettlement of this type become the forcing ground for basic policy questions regarding development and the extension of state hegemony over territory and population, as well as questions of majority-minority relations, state versus local determination, national development priorities, and human rights issues.

Local and National Leadership

Although there has been relatively little discussion of resistance leadership, it appears that the established leaders of the community, if they favor resistance, are usually chosen to lead local movements. However, if they prove unsatisfactory or unequal to the task, new leadership may emerge in the context of the conflict. For example, in response to the unfair negotiations with Hydro-Quebec, the James Bay Cree voted out three chiefs who were enthusiastic advocates of continuing discussions of Hydro-Quebec proposals and replaced them with three who were opposed (Colchester, 1999, p. 37). In many instances, the government or the project may devote considerable resources to co-opting of local leaders, offering them special rewards for their acceptance of the project (Parasuraman, 1999). The enhanced contact with others brought about by resistance, combined with more precise definitions of community or ethnic identity, may lead to more sophisticated understanding by local power holders of the operation of state-level organizations, particularly those power-holders whose authority is based on ethnicity, class, gender, or religion, as opposed to those leaders whose power is derived from the state.

Indeed, leadership success at the local level has led to important leadership roles in national and even international contexts. Kayapo leaders, for example, are drawn from both traditional authorities and the younger members of communities with greater experience of the outside world who have been particularly astute in their understanding and use of local, national, and international sources of power for resisting the Tucurui Dam and other Brazilian government and private initiatives affecting their land (W. H. Fisher, 1994). Kayapo leadership has become knowledgeable about and has taken advantage of the relatively progressive statutes in the 1988 Brazilian constitution that enable them to seek legal counsel and take legal action independent

of the Brazilian Indian Foundation (Posey, 1996, p. 125). In 1988 two Kayapo
leaders, Paiakan and Kube-i, who had worked closely with a multidisciplinary
research project in their region, traveled to the United States where they informed several academic and political gatherings, including four executive directors of the World Bank and representatives of the U.S. State Department,
of violations of World Bank resettlement guidelines by the Altamira-Xingu
Complex (Posey, 1996, p. 126).

The leadership of other grassroots resistance organizations has generally
arisen from within the ranks of the membership. For example, the leadership of CRAB in southern Brazil largely came from the ranks of the farmers
facing DFDR. So successful were some of these local leaders that they have
subsequently assumed positions of responsibility in MAB (see case study) and
in the evolution of the struggle at international levels ("Activists Put IRN on
the Map," 1988). As has been mentioned, the role of "Gramscian organic
intellectuals" has been key in movement leadership. Antonio Gramsci, the
pre–World War II Italian Marxist theorist, emphasized the importance of
culture and ideology in the struggle against capitalism. He distinguished between traditional intellectuals, who constituted part of the ruling elites, and
those individuals who emerge "organically" from local communities, perhaps
leaving for economic or educational purposes but retaining their strong ties
and identification with their homelands. If such organic intellectuals elect
to return to their communities and take up local causes, they may assume
important leadership roles in the struggle to resist displacement (Rothman
& Oliver, 1999). In one case, a trained anthropologist who is also a member
of one of the Nahuatl communities that were threatened with DFDR by the
San Juan Tetelcingo Dam became a spokesperson, activist, and analyst of that
resistance movement (Celestino, 1999). While leadership of grassroots resistance movements may originate in the community, many such movements
have profited by the presence of involved outsiders, such as physicians, public
administrators, merchants, and others who are knowledgeable about the affected communities. These individuals adopt the struggle as their own, invest
their own personal and economic resources, and advocate extremely effectively
in defense of the peoples' rights. Often these individuals have little experience
in either advocacy or protest but are simply moved, out of a sense of morality
and conscience, to respond to the threat of DFDR facing the people. Such
individuals become invaluable to protest and resistance movements because of
their personal contacts and knowledge of the larger administrative and political system. For example, the Yavapai Indians received great assistance from a
local neighbor, a Mexican American, in their struggle with the U. S. Bureau
of Reclamation over the construction of Orme Dam. Mrs. Caroline Butler

helped the Yavapai in correcting public officials' and newspaper misstatements about the Yavapai's acceptance of the dam project. She also explained to them that they had alternatives to selling their land to the government. Throughout the resistance, Mrs. Butler was a constant source of advice and information regarding governmental and bureaucratic procedures, and she was able as well to contact government officials at all levels to urge them to consider the tribe's perspective. She also was key in resolving internal dissension and helping the Yavapai to reach community decisions in the struggle (Khera & Mariella, 1982, p. 171).

Women in Participation and Leadership

Women have played important roles in organizational leadership and in spearheading movement activities. The profound disruption that DFDR signifies for women's lives has led them into major forms of participation in resistance movements at numerous levels. Often called upon to assume the high moral ground and to question the morality of development, women have been in the forefront of voices condemning DFDR. The women of the Yavapai tribe in the southwestern United States, facing DFDR because of dam construction, effectively questioned the morality of a government that would disregard the basic rights of a community that had lost many men in World War II and the Korean and Vietnam wars.

As spokespersons for particular movements, women have been eloquent orators, often dramatically making their points in debate with project authorities. The participation of Tuira, a Kayapo woman who denounced as a liar Jose Lopes (a director of ELETRONORTE) and waved a machete in his face at the great protest meeting at Altamira, left an indelible impression on the assembled crowd, including 200 journalists and 200 NGO representatives ("More Dams in the Works for Brazil," 1989, pp. 3, 7). According to one published version, Tuira, speaking in Kayapó, told Lopes, "You are a liar—We do not need electricity. Electricity is not going to give us our food. We need our rivers to flow freely: our future depends on it. We need our jungles for hunting and gathering. We do not need your dam" ("A Knife in the Water," 2008).

Women have also taken leadership roles in local-level resistance movements. The resistance of the Pehuenche against the construction of the Ralco Dam on the Bio Bio River in Chile has been led by a contingent of five women who head the organization Mapu Domuche Newen (Women with the Strength of the Earth) (Evans, 2001, p. 6). As both leaders and participants, women have taken important roles in specific resistance actions. In the case of the protest against DFDR from the Yacyreta Dam in Argentina, women are represented as one of a number of affected constituent groups. The Inter-Neighborhood Commission was composed of six gender-specific occupational groups representing the interests of the marginalized urban poor before the Entidad Binacional Yacyreta (EBY, The Yacyreta Binational Entity), local authorities, and specialists from the MDBs funding the dam (Rapp, 2000). In the struggle against the Maheshwar Dam on the Narmada River in India, women have been major participants in resistance actions. They have lain down on the access roads, in relays lasting months, to prevent construction materials from arriving at the dam site, despite the fact that their husbands thought such behavior was indecent (R. Black, 2001, p. 16). The women of Hacienda Looc formed a human chain to block bulldozers that were sent to level the hills surrounding their community for a golf course that would have displaced thousands of villagers (see case study). The Seneca women who participated and took leadership roles in fighting the Kinzua Dam relocation gained the necessary experience with local and national administrative systems to prepare them to subsequently take more active leadership roles in local, state, and national politics (Bilharz, 1998, p. 131). Women who battled to save their neighborhood from redevelopment in Chicago in the 1960s began a trend in which a whole new generation of women moved into leadership roles in community organizations (Squires, Bennett, McCourt, & Nyden, 1987, p. 135).

Without question, the most notable leader of a recent resistance movement is a woman. Medha Patkar, the charismatic leader of the Narmada Bachao Andolan, took a major role, along with the well-known champion of India's tribal peoples, Baba Amte, not only in the development of that organization but in the transnational anti-dam movement and the evolution of the discourse on sustainable development as well. Trained in the physical sciences, with graduate study in the social sciences, Medha Patkar was a member of the faculty at the prestigious Tata Institute of Social Sciences before becoming involved in 1985 in organizing the Sardar Sarovar Project–affected villages in the state of Maharashtra. Resentful about being required to move even before any resettlement plans were outlined, the people, with Patkar's assistance, organized the Narmada Dharnkarsta Samiti (Parasuraman, 1999, p. 237). In addition to her earlier work in helping to organize the affected peoples of the Narmada Valley and in founding the Narmada Bachao Andolan (Save the Narmada Movement), she has also assumed the role of spokesperson and leader of the movement, while Baba Amte, the long-respected social activist who died in February 2008 at the age of 93, was venerated as the spiritual leader of the struggle.

Patkar has launched marches, hunger strikes, drowning team vigils, and law suits, arguing tirelessly for the restoration of both rights and resources to the project-affected peoples. She has militated for the withdrawal of international funding for the Sardar Sarovar Project. She has also endured arrests and detainments at the hands of outraged authorities and had to go into hiding at one point when authorities attempted to interrupt one of the drowning team vigils. She has testified before numerous inquiries, including a U.S. congressional committee, on the failures of the project to inform the people, on their failure to plan adequately for resettlement, and on the overall lack of sustainability of projects. Patkar also became a commissioner when the World Commission on Dams was formed, and in the commission's final report she claimed the right to make a final comment in which she continued to challenge the reigning model of development as leading to the marginalization of the majority despite any precautions that might be recommended by the commission (World Commission on Dams, 2000, pp. 321–322). Even though she herself has not been threatened with displacement and resettlement, she has shown her commitment to the struggle in so many ways, including her promise to drown in the rising reservoir if the dam was completed to its planned height, that she has come to symbolize resistance to DFDR around the world.

Despite the leadership of Patkar and other women in the NBA's struggle to halt the Sardar Sarovar Project, women's issues have not been foregrounded in the movement's efforts. The central issue of the plains farmers' resistance to DFDR remains land marginalization. Cash compensation for land loss goes to male rather than female family members. In the three states in which people have been affected, land is given primarily to males, particularly in Gujarat and Madhya Pradesh, the exception being Maharashtra where, in certain circumstances, land may be granted to women. These provisions tend to concentrate resources and decision-making power in men's hands. According to Dwivedi, this focus on largely male concerns overlooks the impact on women. Women, while certainly invested in land issues, in fact may have greater concerns about social disarticulation, given their greater dependence on kinship and neighborhood networks. However, in mobilizing women against the dam, the NBA has not chosen to politically construct women's perceptions of risk as a strategic resistance factor (Dwivedi, 1999, p. 57, p. 57 footnote).

The active roles taken by many women in DFDR resistance movement organization, leadership, and action is both the result of and a contributing factor to increasing changes in the status and roles of women in societies all over the world. The struggle against DFDR in many contexts becomes part of a larger struggle of women against the everyday injustices and exploitations of patriarchy that marginalize and impoverish them (Palit, 2009). Much NGO activity has focused on empowering women and improving the economic conditions of women and children within their societies. Out of this general movement the participation of women, particularly as voices calling on the conscience of the developers to consider the impact of projects on the least powerful sectors of society, has been one of many social changes that DFDR resistance has both gained from and furthered. However, leadership and participation in resistance movements have also placed women at considerable risk. As will be discussed further in Chapter 8, which highlights the risks and results of resistance, women have been subjected to beatings, imprisonment, and rape, targeted specifically by security forces for their leadership and participation in resistance movements and activities.

The Project Scale of Action

The quality of the resettlement project itself may play a major role in the decision to accept or resist DFDR (Chambers, 1970). DFDR projects are really about reconstructing communities after they have been materially destroyed and socially traumatized to varying degrees. Reconstructing community is an idea that needs to be approached with a certain humility and some realism about the limits of our capacities. Such humility and realism have not characterized the planners of DFDR projects to any major extent to date.

Under normal circumstances, communities do not construct themselves; they evolve. Even purposive communities, self-organized around a common ideology and possessing a high degree of homogeneity, do not have an impressive record of success or longevity. Reconstructing a community means attempting to replace through administrative routine an evolutionary process in which social, cultural, economic, and environmental interactions, arrived at through trial and error and deep experiential knowledge, develop, enabling a population to achieve a mutually sustaining social coherence and material sustenance over time. The systems that develop are not perfect, are often far from egalitarian, and do not conform to some imagined standard of efficiency. However, when people are faced with the risks and uncertainties of DFDR, these imperfect but working arrangements have the enhanced appeal of the known and the predictable.

The kind of community that sustains individual and group life, never perfectly, is not a finely tuned mechanism or a well-balanced organism, but rather a complex, interactive, ongoing process composed of innumerable variables that are subject to the conscious and unconscious motives of its members. The idea that such a process could be the outcome of planning is ambitious to say the least. Many DFDR resisters maintain that adequate and just resettlement is impossible from the outset, leaving total opposition to the project as the only strategic option. Other resisters do admit the possibility of adequate and just resettlement and commit themselves to achieving that goal. One of the best outcomes that might be imagined for DFDR projects is to work out a system in which people can materially sustain themselves while they themselves begin the process of social reconstruction. However, if the level of impoverishment experienced by most resettled peoples is any indicator, even adequate systems of material reproduction are beyond either the will or the capabilities of most contemporary policy-makers and planners (Oliver-Smith, 2005b). Projects almost inevitably have generated high levels of impoverishment, dissatisfaction, and often resistance, even after resettlement has taken place.

When national resettlement policy is inferior or nonexistent, DFDR resistance at the project level may become a means to improve policies at a national level. The support of international allies will be crucial in such cases (Cernea, 1993, p. 32). In a sense, the project constitutes the projection of state ambitions into the local context, restructuring it toward government priorities and goals. Moreover, people facing DFDR projects often consider the project an expression of what their government thinks of them. The poor, the marginalized, and ethnic minorities harbor few allusions about their place in the scheme of things, but DFDR projects and the often disparaging attitudes of personnel toward the people to be resettled simply confirm to them the disdain in which they are held. An Adivasi villager protests the way the tribal peoples are being treated by the Sardar Sarovar Project:

> We cannot be treated like monkeys on trees, who will simply climb up to a high plane when the water rises. We demand land—for all the families. It is no use talking in the middle of nowhere in these mountains. We will not be heard. We must organize, get out of these mountains and let the outside world know that we are also human beings and we must also get our due before you flood our lands, our homes (Patel & Mehta, 1995, p. 385).

After resettlement due to the Bargi Dam on the Narmada River, Mrs. Ram Dai, an Adivasi woman who now lives in a slum, spoke of the way she feels the authorities see her:

> Why didn't they just poison us? Then we wouldn't have to live in this shit-hole and the government could have survived alone with its precious dam all to itself (Roy, 1999).

Although difficult to assess exactly, it is not far-fetched to attribute a significant proportion of DFDR resistance to the appallingly bad baseline research, planning, and implementation of most resettlement projects. Much of this social and environmental research has been purely pro forma, designed to validate decisions already taken at the political level and allow the project to proceed. Even where the research is sound, if design or implementation are faulty, as they frequently are, resistance will probably result, as will a confrontation with the state that may ultimately contest its assumption of the right to shape local priorities. In other cases, when local interests so dictate, the goal of resistance is more limited in scope, seeking to improve the terms and conditions of the project rather than altering policies at the national level. Here DFDR resistance rejects a bad resettlement project and produces strategies of negotiation to improve the terms and conditions of resettlement, such as better replacement land, increased compensation for losses, or increased housing allowances. However, resistance to specific projects can prove to be important to more than improving only those projects. Where policy-makers are sensitive, DFDR protest and resistance can lead to the improvement of poor policy. There is little question that protest over and resistance to specific projects is responsible for the increased attention to the deficiencies in resettlement policy by national authorities and has lead to the adoption of guidelines for resettlement projects at the World Bank and other multilateral organizations (Cernea, 1993; Gibson, 1993; Guggenheim, 1993; Morse & Berger, 1992; Serra, 1993). However, resistance movements that produce policy and project improvements differ from conflicts that emerge during consultation with relocatees during implementation. For example, resistance to government plans to resettle communities for the Aguamilpa and Zimapan projects in Mexico did change national policies, partly because of international pressure, and created the conditions in which participatory planning of resettlement could develop. The participation of community members produced unforeseen problems and conflicts that, in confronting them, stimulated improvements in the planning and implementation processes (Guggenheim, 1993).

Projects that do not provide relocatees with important roles in design and implementation, roles that can increase their understanding of and control over the process, tend either to reduce people to mere dependent pawns or to ignite resistance. Vague or poorly organized resettlement plans that are not sensitive to local economic, social, political, and cultural patterns will further fuel negative responses and resistance. Despite any authentic quality a resettlement plan may contain, bad implementation in DFDR clearly provokes resistance (Serra, 1993). Sound policy and good planning are rare, but where they have occurred together, they have often been undermined by poor implementation. In such a context DFDR resistance serves as a fund of important information for a specific project and for resettlement policy in general. The record of broken promises, unfulfilled plans, destructive environmental impacts, inadequate or inappropriate compensation, inferior replacement land, or cultural violations in settlement or residential patterns constitutes a tragic litany of error and corruption that has produced profound misery and justifiable anger and resistance (Wali, 1989; Serra, 1993). Staunch resistance to DFDR will result after resettlement is underway if schemes oblige people to radically alter culturally important aspects of their lives. In the final analysis, resettlement projects must be designed and communicated well, affording resettlees some control over and understanding of their circumstances if there is to be any hope of effectively reducing the impacts of DFDR (Cernea, 1988, p. 15). Resettlement projects have generally been poorly and inappropriately designed and implemented, traits that have been responsible, in part, for the frequency and intensity of resistance. In fact, some argue very convincingly that positive, productive resettlement schemes are extremely difficult to achieve, even under the best of circumstances, and inevitably promote cultural disintegration (Chernela, 1988, p. 20). The record of resettlement projects offers little to contradict that argument and tends to vindicate the protests and resistance of resettlees.

The National Scale of Action

The national scale of action involves the two major institutions that develop projects that require DFDR: the state and the private sector. In confronting each of these institutions, DFDR resistance movements that are project-specific or locally specific have been known to evolve into national entities themselves. In cases where the state initiates the project and seeks political support and financing, it generally contracts with the private sector for actual construction. In the case of large infrastructural projects that require resettlement, the corporations that undertake construction may be either national or multinational. In either case, they are large enterprises and must be so to handle the tasks assigned them. And some of them, particularly those involved in dam building, figure among the world's most powerful economic interests. As such, they have an important stake in seeing the continuation of policies that require such projects and may be relatively insensitive to arguments to the contrary.

When the state initiates, finances, and constructs development projects

producing DFDR, resistance movements very often come into contact with
state institutions for the first time. Their first reactions may be somewhat
tentative since the state has historically been absent or an infrequent presence
in local affairs in more remote areas. In less remote regions the presence of
the state is more constant. In urban areas, informants report that pressure
to relocate, from both the state and the private sector, can be fairly constant
for slum dwellers. Moreover, ethnic or class differences between state/project
personnel and local people often complicate the situation in resettlement
contexts (M. Bartolome & Barabas, 1990; Colson, 1971; Oliver-Smith, 1991;
Wali, 1989; Zaman, 1982). In some cases a secondary and somewhat covert
goal of resettlement is actually the control and integration of ethnic minorities; here, resistance will be expressed in terms of defense of ethnicity as well
as territory (Zaman, 1982).

However, it is important to recognize that the state is not a monolithic
structure. It is composed of different agencies, departments, and ministries
that may have competing agendas. Similarly, the personnel of those state
entities are not always of a uniform class and ethnic origin. Some state officials may have ties to affected regions and be sympathetic to the concerns of
resisters. DFDR resistance may find that there are alliances both with sympathetic individuals and supportive entities to be made within the apparatus of
the state. For example, state governments in Brazil supported the resistance
to dams to be constructed by ELETROSUL, and in India the Environmental
Ministry Working Group sided with the NBA against the states of Maharashtra, Gujarat, and Madhya Pradesh.

The degree to which a nation allows freedom of expression and other political rights, such as that of assembly, conditions the possibility and kind of
political space for DFDR resistance (L. Bartolome, 1992; Magee, 1989; Robinson, 1992). In the 1960s Brazil had a repressive military regime that provided
little opportunity for resistance during the construction of the Sobradinho
and Itaipu projects. In the late 1970s and 1980s the Brazilian political system "opened," and with the return to electoral politics strong national-level
resistance movements were created and captured sufficient political power to
negotiate with relocation authorities alternatives to or cancellations of projects
requiring DFDR (L. Bartolome, 1992, p. 21; W. H. Fisher, 1994). DFDR resistance in Brazil by MAB negotiated a reconsideration of national resettlement
policy, developing new environmental initiatives and new relationships between the power sector and affected populations. The resistance movement
both locally and nationally provided one of several pressures on the Brazilian
power sector requiring more rigorous environmental scrutiny. International
funding agencies, national and international environmental and human rights

NGOs, and academics also pushed the power sector for more stringent requirements on resettlement and environmental issues. Brazilian DFDR resistance movements with national and international allies have broadened their agenda to include a critique of overall development policy, urging more sustainable alternatives (W. H. Fisher, 1994; Rothman & Oliver, 1999; Turner, 1991b). The goal of all these interest groups was the recognition of previously unperceived sociocultural, socioeconomic, and environmental costs experienced by populations impacted by projects. The new plan provides for better information on projects, as well as formal representation of all interest groups (Serra, 1993, pp. 68–71). Adequate implementation of this plan has not been as forthcoming as hoped. The NBA in India also expanded its goals to include critiques of the lack of sustainability in urban culture and, in the process, has called into question the entire nature of the development process in that nation (Bandyopadhyay, 1992, p. 276).

DFDR resistance generally is part of a broad national front of human rights and environmental movements that exert pressure for change in civil and political rights policies. However, in India the intolerance exhibited by the Bharatiya Janata Party, the Hindu fundamentalist party in power until recently, may have had a dampening effect on what these changes could achieve. The climate of Hindu nationalism fomented by such interests may signal a period of diminished governmental effort on behalf of non-Hindu tribal peoples displaced by the Sardar Sarovar Project. Expressions to the effect that the disappearance of "inferior" cultures is an expected outcome of the development process are not uncommon (W. F. Fisher, 1995).

DFDR resistance movements among different groups facing resettlement in Mexico have openly confronted the national government and the Comision Federal de Electricidad with questions regarding inhumane policies toward indigenous peoples. Although Mexico has relocated thousands of people, primarily for dam construction and many of them of indigenous cultures, recent victories by the resistance movement of the Nahuatl people in achieving the cancellation of the San Juan Tetelcingo Dam may signal a change in this practice. Particularly significant in this context was the importance of the media campaign undertaken by the Nahuatl communities threatened with DFDR. These DFDR resistance movements in various locations in Mexico are part of an array of pressures for more transparency, greater governmental accountability, and increased governmental responsiveness that have resulted in what can only be described as an epochal change in national politics—the defeat of the Partido Revolucionario Institucionalizado (PRI) that ruled for more than 70 years. On the other hand, confrontations between resisters and authorities over the construction of La Parota Dam in the state of Guerrero indicated a hardening of the government's attitude toward civil society. Many felt that the government had adopted a hardened attitude towards protest because then-president Vicente Fox had capitulated to the protests of peasant farmers over the expansion of the Mexico City airport. Although the government has recently cancelled construction of the dam, many are still fearful that the government is turning away from policies that addressed the concerns of dam-affected people toward more authoritarian positions and forceful suppression of protest. Out of these and other protests two associations have formed: the Mexican Movement of Dam Affected Peoples and for the Defense of Rivers (MAPDER),and the Latin American Network Against Dams and for Rivers, their Communities and Water (REDLAR).

Print Media

One cannot overstate the importance of the media to movements resisting DFDR; the media documents and publicizes both the processes through which much displacement and resettlement are carried out and the impacts on the lives of people. Accurate and timely information is essential to the struggles of people to resist DFDR, allowing them to formulate appropriate strategies and tactics. But communicating the challenges they face and the conditions they suffer to others is just as important for the long-term success of their campaigns. In this effort, the role played by the print and visual media is indispensable, as the case of the San Juan Tetelcingo Dam struggle illustrates.

Case Study: San Juan Tetelcingo

In the late 1980s, as part of its overall hydropower development strategy, the Federal Electricity Commission (Comision Federal de Electricidad, or CFE) of Mexico, initiated plans to build a large dam on the Balsas River near the village of San Juan Tetelcingo in the state of Guerrero. The dam was projected to produce 1,300 gigawatt-hours of electricity annually for the central region of the nation. In addition, it was hoped that the new dam would catch some of the silt that was filling the reservoir of the Caracol Dam downstream, as it was projected that Caracol would be rendered useless in 20 years (D. C. Scott, 1990, p. 3). The CFE estimated that between 18,000 and 20,000 people would have to be relocated because their lands would be flooded by the 100-kilometer-long reservoir the dam would create.

The estimates of the CFE were criticized by both local officials and anthropologists working in the region. Catherine Good, an anthropologist from the Universidad Ibero-Americana in Mexico City, estimated that somewhere between 30,000 and 32,000 people would be directly affected and another 15,000 would be indirectly affected by the loss of farmland and the disruption of family, religious, and economic ties (D. C. Scott, 1990, p. 3). Moreover, the society to be relocated was unique. The 22 villages that would have to be relocated were Nahuatl, an ethnolinguistic group resident in the region since AD 1250, before both the Aztecs and the Spanish arrived. The Nahuatl people, unlike many other indigenous groups in Mexico today, were economically successful as farmers, artisans, and merchants, selling their bark paintings, wooden masks, and clay crafts to tourists. They were also successful at maintaining their language and culture while interacting with the outside world. In addition to the losses the Nahuatls would endure from the dam, the reservoir would also inundate important archeological sites, among them Copalillo, an Olmec site dating to 1400 BC. The Olmecs are considered to be the "mother civilization" of pre-Columbian America (Crossley, 1986, p. 1).

People in the region first learned of the CFE plans for a dam near San Juan Tetelcingo in August 1990. The municipal president of Copalillo lodged a protest with the government, referring to the fact that the project would mean the disappearance of 30 indigenous communities (Rodriguez, 1990a, p. 1). On October 21, 1990, the communities formed and ratified the constitution of the Consejo de Pueblos Nahuas del Alto Balsas (CPNAB, or the Nahuatl Villages Council of the Upper Balsas River) to mobilize their population to resist the construction of the dam. They began their resistance movement with a march of more than a thousand people from 22 communities to the Guerrero state capital Chilpancingo, parading through the streets at the center of town and arriving finally at the steps of the Palace of Government, where they pledged to stay until their demands were heard by the authorities (Rodriguez, 1990b, p. 1). One member of the CPNAB said, "It is a lie that the energy (from this dam) will serve Mexico. It will be exported to the United States, and they have already given money up front in exchange for the entombment and disappearance of our towns" (Cervantes Gomez, 1990). The government committed itself to creating a commission to review the project, and the demonstration was terminated. On that same day the CPNAB also sent a letter to the International Labour Organization (ILO), informing them of the problem of the dam (Garcia, 1999). A short time later, just before Christmas, the Nahuatl people organized an "informational roadblock" on the highway between Mexico City and the tourist resort of Acapulco, stopping cars to hand out fliers, briefly discuss the dam, and accept donations for their struggle. The cars were only briefly stopped, and there was no conflict or disturbance (Rodriguez, 1990a, p. 1).

The past experiences of other resettled communities was important in the way CPNAB approached the dam. One CPNAB representative said, "If they resettle us, we are aware that we won't be able to recover again. Even though they say that this [project] is in the name of development and progress, we know that we will lose that which is absolutely fundamental, our lands. Even though they tell us that with the Mexico City–Acapulco superhighway modernization would come, that we would have hospitals, tourist centers where we could sell our folk art, we tell them not to come to us with fairy tales because these same promises we heard when they built the Cerro de Oro dam and they told the Chinantecos the same thing and now in practice, there are no roads, no development, no nothing" (Leal, 1991, p. 23; see also M. Bartolome & Barabas, 1973, 1990).

Forms of resistance included 20 marches on state and federal capitals, 12 information campaigns, letters to the press rejecting government claims of adequate resettlement plans, hunger strikes, a complaint to Mexico's National Commission on Human Rights, the elaboration of a series of plans for alternative projects, an academic forum at the Universidad Ibero-Americana, attendance of representatives at the Earth Summit in Rio de Janeiro, meetings with state officials, letters to the president, and numerous CPNAB meetings and declarations of unceasing resistance to the dam project. The CPNAB quickly acquired allies from the academic and other professional communities and among the press corps. This group was soon formalized with the creation of a Committee of Support. Eventually the group was composed of lawyers, environmentalists, social scientists, agronomists, and journalists of both national and foreign origin. The division of labor was clearly demarcated: CPNAB would work on mobilizing the Nahuatl grass roots and organizing local activities, and the Committee of Support would work on political issues, press coverage, and the logistics of expanding the political struggle beyond regional borders (Garcia, 1999, p. 1).

The Committee of Support worked on two principal fronts: the academic community and the media. They organized forums and symposia in universities and other institutes of higher education as well as at the National Museum of Anthropology, focusing on the problem of dams and resettlement. In collaboration with the press corps they began a photographic archive of the struggle. They wrote and translated documents relating to the struggle and distributed them to the ILO, the World Bank, and the Inter-American Development Bank. The struggle of the Nahuatl peoples of the Alto Balsas is perhaps most distinguished from other indigenous struggles by the press campaign that the CPNAB and the Committee of Support launched. Thanks to their efforts, the entire struggle over the roughly 28 months between the first protest in August 1990 and the cancellation of the dam in December 1992 was carefully documented in 49 articles in 15 newspapers and journals, two of them foreign (Garcia, 1999). The campaign took major advantage of the fact that the struggle of the Nahuatl peoples of the Alto Balsas coincided with the much-disputed and -discussed celebration of the 500th anniversary of the "discovery" of America. Indeed, much of their discourse was couched in terms of their continuity with 500 years of indigenous resistance to cultural annihilation. Importantly, the vast majority of the coverage of their struggle in national newspapers was on the cultural pages of the papers, with only occasional appearances in political sections. (The local newspapers tended to cover the struggle on the political pages.) The struggle, as depicted in the national media, was framed in terms of indigenous cultural survival. The success of the media campaign was categorical. Not one local, national, or international newspaper wrote unfavorably of the struggle, despite the efforts of the government to influence coverage in its favor. The positive coverage of the struggle by the newspapers influenced favorably the postures adopted by politicians running in the 1992 elections, although the CPNAB went to considerable lengths to avoid any identification with particular political parties (Garcia, 1999).

The CPNAB has not disappeared with the success of the resistance movement and the cancellation of the plan to build the San Juan Tetelcingo Dam. They have continued to press forward with the alternative projects of sustainable development that they proposed in 1990 in lieu of the dam. They have also become part of the worldwide struggle against dams. However, their victory over the dam may have come with a political price. Despite their continuing efforts to obtain support for their communities, they have been left without government assistance, despite the fact that their jurisdiction is included in a federal program of aid to marginalized zones (Garcia, 2000).

Video and Film

Other resistance movements have also made great use of the media in struggles against DFDR. In Brazil the Kayapo became acquainted with visual media when the anthropologist Terry Turner, during his long-term fieldwork with the Kayapo, made a number of ethnographic films for the BBC in the 1970s (1991a). Turner continued this work with two films in the Disappearing

World series with Granada Films in the 1980s. Thus, representational media (photography, audio recording, film, and video) became important means through which Kayapo culture was portrayed to the outside world in the 1970s and 1980s. The Kayapo themselves also became aware of the importance of the power of representation in the political culture of their relations with the outside world. Through being portrayed as a significant culture in the representational media to others, they felt validated and confirmed in their own eyes as well. They further understood that if they had some control over how they were represented, their own power in dealing with the outside world would be greatly enhanced. Thus, Kayapo individuals have become skilled videographers of their own culture and of their interactions with Brazilians. The Kayapo planned that the great intertribal meeting at Altamira to protest the dam on the Xingu River would be optimally represented by film, video, and television. In addition to the hordes of media representatives from the outside world, Kayapo videographers also filmed the proceedings of the meeting at Altamira. The purpose was not only to make an independent record of the meeting itself, but also to demonstrate, as Turner says, that "the Kayapo are not dependent on the outside society for control over the representation of themselves and their actions, but possess to a full and equal extent the means of control over the image, with all that implies for the ability to define the meaning and value of acts and events in the area of inter-ethnic interaction" (1991a, p. 307). Whether made by the people themselves or by others, film and video in particular have become important tools in the campaigns against DFDR around the world for their power to depict the destruction visited upon people and their efforts to resist both projects and displacement and to disseminate those images and facts widely. Films and videos documenting DFDR struggles and disasters have been made in Mexico (Robinson, n.d.), the Philippines (Schradie & DeVries, 2000), India (Singh Foundation, n.d.), and Brazil (Switkes & Aguirre, 1991), to name but a few examples, and several have been made that address multiple national situations (Phinney, n.d.).

Information Technology

Information technology, which greatly facilitates the dissemination of both the printed word and still and moving images, has become an essential feature of DFDR resistance. The increasing access of wider publics to the Internet has made the websites of NGOs, social movements, and GROs, as well as the networks formed among them and their constituents, a key feature of the struggles of those resisting DFDR. Websites offer visitors prepared infor-

The headband on this Kayapo protestor reads, "Kayapo Against the Dam."
(photograph by Glenn Switkes)

The Kayapo group at the center of the crowd formed the core of protestors at a recent meeting to combat the Belo Monte Dam and protect the Xingu River. (photograph by Glenn Switkes)

mation and visual packages about DFDR struggles in specific countries (e.g., India, Thailand), around specific development forms (e.g., dams, pipelines, conservation, private industrial development), or involving specific institutions (e.g., the World Bank, the Inter-American Development Bank). Visitors can find out how to contribute support for these struggles, influence policy, send letters to appropriate authorities, order more information, and offer their own ideas through bulletin boards (Weeks, 1999 p. 20).

Moreover, the Internet becomes not only a medium for the communication of information, but also a means for participation. One of the most significant aspects of information technology for "electronic politics" or cyberactivism is the speed with which it transmits information and consequently the speed and level of organization of the response that the information elicits globally. The capacity for activists to learn of developments around the world has been vastly increased, as has the speed with which they can respond to them. Events in the Brazilian Amazon or the Narmada Valley that take place today do not have to wait for tomorrow's local newspaper or the following day's national newspaper. Events can be learned of and responded to on a global level sometimes within hours. For example, events in the protest against the Pak Mun Dam in Thailand in late 2000 were communicated through the website of the NGO Friends of the People, and subsequently through the HelpAsia and IRN email list managers, to people all over the world connected to those sites and email list managers, all within hours of their occurrence. Indeed, such is the speed with which information is now disseminated that central governments are sometimes among the last to learn of events and are forced into a reactive posture by national and international DFDR allies who have learned of events and processes and developed initiatives to counter them long before government has even become aware of what has transpired. Often the initiatives developed by these allies take the form of "cascades," a term borrowed from the study of chaos and complexity that refers to a single event in a large and seemingly random series that occurs at the right time and place in such a way as to cause open and turbulent systems to change form (Kumar, 1996, p. 20 footnote). In network activity, a cascade denotes a strategy in which an action taken by one member of a network is rapidly communicated through the Internet to all others, who reproduce it, initiating a virtual wave of events and messages that can overwhelm the policy process (Kumar, 1996, p. 20). The linkages among websites and email list managers representing many different interests enable a single individual or group to connect with and inform many thousands of people around the world with one message.

The campaign to respond to the World Bank's proposed changes in resettlement guidelines serves as a good example (see case study, Chapter 2). The cascade undertaken by the network organized by the Center for International Environmental Law and the IRN effectively forced the World Bank to reexamine the changes it had proposed in resettlement policy. The Internet campaign mobilized by a relatively small number of individuals and institutions produced thousands of letters and messages from people and institutions expressing concern to the Bank. As a result of this cascade, then-president James Wolfensohn and vice-president Ian Johnson publicly stated that the Bank was completely committed to its safeguard policies and would not weaken them. However, the victory was short lived, as ultimately the board of directors approved the revisions.

Authoritarian regimes with diminished freedoms of speech and the press generally reduce the amount of political space available for presenting resisters' causes to the public (Khagram, 1999). National and regional authorities, usually appointed by the executive or, at best, by rubber-stamp legislatures, tend also to be less responsive to constituents' interests, particularly if those interests run counter to national agendas. Furthermore, the tendency of authoritarian regimes to use relatively unrestrained force also reduces the strategic options of DFDR resistance groups. In the case of the Philippines under the authoritarian Marcos regime, resisters felt it was necessary to use violent methods and to ally themselves with a guerrilla movement because of the unresponsiveness and oppressive tactics of the government when local peoples protested the planned construction of a series of dams on the Chico River (Drucker, 1985; Hilhorst, 2000).

Case Study: Chico Dam Resistance in the Philippines

In 1973, partially as a result of increased world oil prices, the Philippine government proposed to build four dams (Chico I, II, III, and IV) on the Chico River, the longest river in the Gran Cordillera mountain range.* A World Bank–financed feasibility study recommended that construction be scheduled to begin with Chico II in Sadanga Province in 1978. As has often been the case, the people to be affected by the dam learned of the project only when teams of surveyors entered their region. It was not long before the people understood the implications of the dam for their future and, given a tradition of local village-based resistance to intrusions, their initial response was to tear down the surveyors' camps. The government sent a military escort in to establish another camp. The military forces abused local people in an effort to intimidate them. The people were further disturbed by damage done to crops and fruit trees by the surveying teams.

Attempting to avoid further direct conflict, the villagers sought the intervention of the president, sending six petitions in 1974 that requested the withdrawal of the project on the basis of the destructive impact it would have on local people. Indeed, the early petitions expressed only local-level concerns, some even supporting the dam as long as it was built in the area of another village. The petitions were personally delivered by commissions of village elders, financed by the village, to Malacañang Palace, but none succeeded in actually meeting with the president. In response to the first delegation, President Marcos wrote a letter in which he characterized their arguments as sentimental and advised them to "sacrifice themselves for the sake of the nation."

The failure of their early efforts led to more coordinated strategies to resist the dam project, which were assisted by predominantly church-based outsiders. Themes stressed in the resistance efforts focused around the dire effects the dam would have on them, their modest request for a hearing, their will-

*Except where otherwise noted, this case study is based on Hilhorst (2000, pp. 33–53).

ingness to "play by the rules," the symbolic and material importance of land ("land is life"), and a none-too-subtle suggestion that failure would lead to violence. The Bontok and Kalinga peoples of the area had a historical tradition of head-hunting that was evoked indirectly in one Catholic bishop's letter to the president. Furthermore, they institutionalized their resistance in 1975 with the establishment of a multilateral peace pact, a traditional means of regulating relations among normally contentious villages. Residents from one hundred fifty villages and many outside supporters attended a church-sponsored conference at which the peace pact was created and signed, consolidating their resistance against the government.

The government responded to the peace pact among the villages by suspending work on Chico II, but shortly thereafter, hoping to divert the opposition, it began work on the fourth dam at another site in Kalinga. The strategy was ill advised, however, as villagers from the area that would have been affected by Chico II continued to oppose the project in support of those to be affected by Chico IV. To fragment the opposition, the government sent the Presidential Assistant on National Minorities (PANAMIN) to the region to hand out money, rice, and other valued goods. PANAMIN, in an effort to exploit competition among communities and further fragment organized opposition, also distributed arms to a village that was in conflict with two villages in the resistance movement. These efforts had little effect, as villages continued their obstruction of surveying work and their petitions to the president. The government responded by intensifying military activities in the area, raiding villages and detaining approximately 100 villagers, mostly women, in an unknown camp. As village representatives attempted to locate the detainees, they expanded their network of supporters, recruiting several senators and NGOs in Manila.

The villagers recognized, however, that their capacity to resist the military was limited, and when their efforts gained the attention of the New Peoples' Army (NPA), they welcomed the offer of assistance. The NPA was the armed branch of the Communist Party of the Philippines (CPP), which had adopted a Maoist strategy of guerrilla war in the countryside as a spearhead for revolution. Although CPP cadres were based in the region, their ranks were heavily drawn from Manila-based, educated activists who had been influenced by increased interest in indigenous Philippine cultures. The NPA cadres won great popularity among the villagers opposing the dam when they attacked military forces stationed in the area. This popularity led both men and women from the affected villages to join the NPA and form local contingents.

In addition to military support, the NPA spent its time in education and organization. NPA cadres linked the peoples' local struggle against the dam to the broader issues of combating the feudal structures of Philippine society on a national level. They also assisted in establishing local organizations and planning strategies for legal aspects of the struggle. The villagers also continued to have the support of the churches, whose respectability enabled the struggle to acquire wide support among groups with diverse political orientations. The exposure to both groups influenced the nature of villagers' arguments, tying the primary focus of opposition to the dam to larger issues. In addition to themes of loss of land and cultural destruction, specific linkages to class-based interests were made between the electricity to be produced by the dam and its wealthy industrialist beneficiaries. Resisters were also quick to tie the dam and the destruction of their culture to their minority-group ethnic identity, asking if they were not "being considered non-Filipinos? Or are we third class?"

By the same token, NPA cadres were also influenced by the villagers. The Kalinga NPA chapter thought that the dam was more important than the struggle against feudalism and wanted to include indigenous ideas in the organizing efforts. To this end they proposed the creation of an Anti-Dam Democratic Alliance (ADDA) to include a broad array of anti-dam activists. The regional secretariat of the CPP rejected the proposal, fearing that the ADDA would eventually replace the NPA in the struggle. The debate pivoted around the issue of the feudal character of the dam. If the dam was simply a regional issue, then there was little need for national mobilization against it. If, however, the dam were an expression of the feudal character of Philippine society (in the case of the dam, with the government as landlord), then the regional opposition could be legitimately integrated into a nationwide and centrally coordinated resistance movement. In effect, the dam resistance produced debates of an ideological character within the CPP and the NPA, particularly among those members from the regions to be affected by the dams. In many senses, these individuals became what Gramsci characterized as "organic intellectuals," that is, people originally from the community who hold positions in the larger society and who are committed to and work for local issues.

The protest movement expanded considerably between 1980 and 1986, aided by the addition of another related issue, a government-sponsored timber exploitation initiative in nearby Abra province. The movement acquired an increasingly regional character and further assistance through legal organizations at both local and regional levels. In 1984 the Cordillera Peoples' Alliance (CPA) emerged out of the coalescing of a core of 25 collaborating resistance organizations, and in a year the membership doubled, bringing together village organizations, NGOs, human rights groups, antidictatorship groups, and the media. The major emphasis of the CPA was Cordillera regional unity and self-determination. The struggle attracted considerable international support, whose lobbying efforts finally led to the World Bank's suspending financial support for the dam. Within a short time, the Aquino government that had replaced the defunct Marcos regime, officially cancelled the Chico Dam projects.

The exposure of Cordillera activists to international discourses on indigenous rights also strengthened the regional movement's concerns with differences between highlands and lowlands. Post-Chico agendas began to be increasingly focused on indigenous rights and regional autonomy. The evolution of the movement produced a variety of competing discourses, all articulated by urban elite leadership with ties, based on varying degrees of legitimacy, to local village agendas. The dilemma of the movement was found in the fact that the government's agenda for the region, including the now-cancelled dam, provided a common ground for resistance but not a common identity that could encompass the differences within the region. The identification with the region provided the basis for resistance to the ambitions of the government but did not produce an overarching regional identity, and the unity of the Cordillera Peoples' Alliance eventually fragmented.

Increasingly today, national and state governments are giving way to private sector development interests in the planning, financing, and construction of large infrastructural projects. Private sector development interests can be national, international, or multinational. The very mobility and anonymity of capital make it difficult to isolate as belonging to national or international levels of action. Furthermore, private sector–driven DFDR presents a different set of challenges to resistance movements because corporations are not subject to the same restraints and guidelines imposed by multilateral lenders that states are. That is, resistance movements can challenge the state to live up to guidelines for resettlement agreed upon as terms of a loan from a multilateral agency such as the World Bank. With private sector development, despite apparent attention to guidelines, there is generally little evidence that corporate compliance with international human rights standards and development policies and procedures is forthcoming, despite intense media campaigns pledging respect for environments and cultures (Feeney, 2000). NGOs and DFDR resistance movements have undertaken selected campaigns to boycott the products of companies involved directly in DFDR projects as well as those involved indirectly through funding guarantees (see International Rivers Network case study).

The International Scale of Action

DFDR resistance movements have increasingly participated in global dialogues on development policy as well as on changes in practice in specific institutions. DFDR resistance movements and their NGO allies were among those who pushed successfully for the establishment of the World Commission on Dams, the final report of which vindicated a great many of the claims made by resisters over the years. In this sense, DFDR resistance movements are important contributors to what many see as a fundamental transition in the terms of the global development discourse.

For many years, when the World Bank and other development institutions financed large infrastructural projects involving resettlement, the costs of large-scale development projects were calculated in economic terms, and the resettlement associated with the projects was generally underfunded, poorly staffed, and haphazardly planned by the borrower nations constructing the projects. Social impacts of such projects were deemed to be negligible or unavoidable. In the 1970s poor planning and implementation as well as staunch local resistance to the Bank-assisted Sobradinho Dam in Brazil and the Chico Dams in the Philippines underscored the need for the formulation of explicit resettlement policies within the Bank (Cernea, 1993, pp. 19–20).

Greater interest also emerged within the Bank for projects addressing the alleviation of rural poverty (Shihata, 1993). This shift was due to the intensity of rural protest and resistance as well as the Bank's public embarrassment at the catastrophic consequences of resettlement by development projects it had funded. Large multilateral development banks (MDBs) are not monolithic structures. Like national governments, MDBs are complex, internally diverse organizations composed of individuals and groups with particular specialties and interests. DFDR resisters at all levels can actually find within MDBs sympathizers and allies in their struggles. Individuals whose responsibilities within MDBs focus on indigenous peoples or the environment frequently militate behind closed doors on behalf of the rights of people to be affected by DFDR. The results of these efforts can be seen when MDBs such as the World Bank, the Inter-American Development Bank, and the Asian Development Bank create guidelines for resettlement. Although these guidelines recommend that DFDR be avoided where possible, they are developed clearly within the framework of the model of development that necessitates such large-scale projects. In the final analysis, MDBs are in the business of lending money to fund projects. The model of development they adhere to and their internal incentive structures tend toward favoring larger projects because they involve larger loans (Rapp, 2000).

The exposure of these project failures and the media portrayal of resisters as Davids going up against the Goliaths of the state and the World Bank contributed to the pressure for the formulation of a set of resettlement policy guidelines within the Bank (cf., Rich, 1994). The result was Operational Directive 4.30: Involuntary Resettlement (World Bank, 1990). O.D. 4.30 called for minimizing resettlement; improving or restoring living standards, earning capacity, and production levels; and resettlee participation in project activities, the resettlement plan, and the valuation and compensation for assets lost (World Bank, 1990, pp. 1–2). Although these guidelines were hailed as an important step toward the reduction of damages, costs, and losses incurred by resettled peoples, their implementation in borrower nations has been consistently problematical. The Bank's response to this problem was to advocate the formulation and implementation of resettlement legislation in borrower nations, which produced policy changes in several developing nations, such as Brazil, Colombia and Mexico, as well as policy changes in development agencies such as the Organization for Economic Cooperation and Development and the Inter-American Development Bank (Cernea, 1993, p. 32; Shihata, 1993). However, a number of nations saw the O.D. 4.30 guidelines as an infringement on national sovereignty. Furthermore, adoption of formal policies, either by the World Bank or borrower nations, is no assurance of adequate implementation. In addition, the degree to which projects financed by private capital must adhere to these now-modified guidelines and procedures established by the Bank is far from clear. The World Bank commissioned an independent report on the Sardar Sarovar Project in the Narmada Valley in India, (Morse & Berger, 1992), which recommended cessation of the project pending major improvements in environmental and social monitoring and implementation. The reaction of India's government was to reject further World Bank funding of the project. The government insisted that the project would proceed with even higher standards in the areas of environment and resettlement than those mandated by the Bank, but that has not proven to be the case according to resisters (see Narmada case study, this chapter). Subsequent efforts to alter the guidelines of O.D. 4.30, seen by human rights and environmental groups as attempts to weaken safeguards, particularly for indigenous peoples, were met with the previously discussed "cascade" of protest.

DFDR resistance, however, has influenced change within the World Bank. Resisters and their allies in NGOs and social movements have for many years succeeded in communicating their position, backed by solid documentation, through declarations at numerous international meetings and conferences, including the Manibeli Declaration of 1994; the Curitiba Declaration at the

First International Meeting of Dam Affected Peoples and Their Allies in Curitiba, Brazil, in 1997; the Walker Creek Declaration at the International Seminar on Strategies for Dam Decommissioning in 1998; and most recently the Rasi Salai Declaration of 2003. NGOs also continue with their Multilateral Development Bank Campaign, putting pressure on nations that donate funds to development banks to withhold funds for the dams and other projects that displace people against their will.

These and many other earlier efforts have been aimed in part at revealing some of the disastrous consequences of multilateral-funded development projects and obligating these institutions, especially the World Bank, to become more responsive to the specific concerns of DFDR resistance and to social and environmental concerns generally. NGOs have severely criticized the performance of MDBs and other international agencies in DFDR projects with the aim of reforming the internal guidelines and policies to which they can then be held accountable. Activists and scholars began keeping close watch on policy formulation in these institutions to guard against the dilution or weakening of any policy relating to DFDR. More access to information about Bank projects was demanded and the Bank complied.

Another significant reform that developed out of these efforts and the widespread adverse publicity from the Bank-funded development disasters was the World Bank Inspection Panel. Based on an emerging "accountability politics," the Inspection Panel process enables local communities impacted by Bank-funded projects to file complaints and call for independent investigations into the Bank's compliance with its own social and environmental policies (Clark, Fox, & Treakle, 2003). The creation of the Inspection Panel in 1994 introduced into World Bank governance policies the political concept that the institution itself should be held accountable to the people who are directly affected by projects it finances. The Inspection Panel is made up of three members who are independent of the Bank and possess expertise in development issues. They are appointed by the board of executive directors for nonrenewable five-year terms. Between 1994 and 2003 the Inspection Panel heard 28 complaints from affected peoples in Bangladesh, Brazil, Chad, China, Ecuador, India, Nepal, Paraguay, the Philippines, and Uganda regarding dams, pipelines, forestry projects, power generation, and structural-adjustment lending. Regarding the panel's performance, Clark, Fox, and Treakle (2003) conclude that claimants were generally pleased with the panel process and felt they had been treated with respect and objectivity. However, despite some improvements that were made during the panel process, due in part to the attention of the media, local officials, and Bank staff, most claimants stated that their situations began to deteriorate after the panel process terminated.

Notwithstanding the gains made in obtaining better public information regarding Bank projects and the creation of the Inspection Panel, the late 1990s and early years of the present century saw a disturbing reformulation of many safeguards, including a weakening of environmental, indigenous peoples, and resettlement policies. While the Bank has denied that the reformulation of these safeguards has weakened them, it appears that the Bank was responding to claims by borrower nations that the policies constituted an infringement on their national sovereignty. A further issue that emerged in the 1990s was the trend in privatization that has also been seen by many to threaten the gains made in strengthening World Bank resettlement policy. Peter Bosshard, who used to be with the Swiss NGO The Berne Declaration and is now with International Rivers, said "The guidelines on the environmental analysis of IFC [International Financial Corporation] and MIGA [Multilateral Investment Guarantee Agency] projects are less strict and comprehensive than the World Bank's Operational Directive. The assessments can be done later in the project cycle, when critical decisions about the project have been taken and the analysis of alternative options does not make sense" (Khagram, 1999, p. 307).

Grassroots organizations, NGOs, and social movements involved in DFDR resistance have also acquired or developed legal personnel, expertise, and general knowledge that enable them to sue projects for violations of national civil and human rights laws as well as international accords. The aforementioned growth of international human rights norms has supplied a series of conventions and covenants that, while difficult to enforce in local circumstances, can be used to portray projects as being in violation of internationally accepted standards. The European Convention on Human Rights (1950); the International Covenant on Civil and Political Rights (1966); the Universal Declaration of Human Rights; the United Nations Declaration on the Rights to Development; the Declaration on the Rights of Persons Belonging to National or Ethnic, Religious or Linguistic Minorities; the articles of the International Labour Organization; and the United Nations Declaration on the Rights of Indigenous Peoples all provide articles and protocols that can be used to portray projects as being in violation of human rights on the international stage. There are now much more active efforts to use these and other documents to demand reparations for past injustices as well (Johnston, 2000).

Case Study: The Sardar Sarovar Dam and the
Narmada Bachao Andolan

Like many of India's tribal groups, the people of the Satpuda Ranges, which include the Narmada Valley, have a tradition of resistance to any attempts by outsiders to compromise their autonomy and their resource base. Their villages are isolated, and over the years, little in the way of governmental infrastructure or services was provided (Parasuraman, 1999, p. 232). After India achieved independence in 1948 the region was generally ignored by the state government, but the idea of damming the Narmada River dates as far back as 1946. Initial studies for the project were carried out promptly, but the project was stymied because the provinces that eventually became the states of Gujarat, Maharashtra, and Madhya Pradesh fell into disputes about sharing the waters. The Narmada Water Disputes Tribunal was established in 1969 to deal with the conflict, submitting its final report in 1978 (Baviskar, 1992, p. 232). Soon thereafter, the government of Gujarat started the planning process for the Sardar Sarovar Project (SSP).

The SSP is but one part of the Narmada Valley Project (NVP), which projects the construction of ten major dams on the Narmada and twenty others on its tributaries. The project plans also included another 135 medium and 3,000 minor dams (W. F. Fisher, 1995, p. 13). The Sardar Sarovar Dam is the second largest of the project in terms of submerged area and displaced population (Baviskar, 1992, p. 233). The dam is projected to provide irrigation water for 1.8 million hectares of land. The dam is also intended to provide drinking water for 4,720 villages and 131 towns while generating 1,450 megawatt hours of electricity annually. The damming of the Narmada will submerge roughly 37,000 hectares of land and displace an estimated 163,500 people (W. F. Fisher, 1995, p. 13; Parasuraman, 1999, p. 179). Preliminary work actually began in 1961 under Prime Minister Nehru who, as mentioned earlier, considered dams to be "the temples of development." Construction was considerably accelerated after the World Bank decided to fund part of the project in 1985.

The estimates of benefits to be generated and costs to be incurred by construction of the dam are hotly contested by a variety of people representing many interests. Economic costs are criticized for being grossly underestimated. Estimates of the human and environmental costs are, it has been argued, vastly miscalculated and based on low estimates of the number of people to be affected and a lack of understanding of the nature of the cultural disruption that the tribal people in particular will suffer in dislocation. The alleged benefits in the form of irrigation and drinking water are also said to be vastly unrealistic (W. F. Fisher, 1995, p. 17). Critics have also argued that there were no provisions for appropriately informing the people to be affected, much less any remotely adequate plans for their humane and constructive resettlement.

Protests against the dam appeared shortly after the Narmada Water Disputes Tribunal final report in 1978. Organized by a leading Congress Party politician, major protests and rallies focused on the issue of displacement in the region of Nimar in Madhya Pradesh, where large numbers of people were facing resettlement. The Nimar Bachao Andolan (Movement to Save Nimar) was largely supported by merchants and farmers and worked through the established structures of party politics. However, the Congress Party politician had essentially used the movement to further his own political career, and after the elections in 1979, he abandoned the organization and it collapsed (Baviskar, 1992, p. 237). In 1980 two volunteer organizations started working with the populations to be impacted. Arch Vahini began efforts to improve resettlement conditions, and the Rajpipla Social Service Society helped in legal actions related to land. Although they had only some limited successes, these organizations constituted the initial steps toward the formation of a people's movement (Parasuraman, 1999, p. 236). A second stage of resistance developed in 1987 after the Indian government gave clearance for accelerating work on the project and slightly more than 2000 families were displaced and resettled. The government neither informed nor consulted the affected people prior to relocating them because it believed that the tribal peoples would not have understood the issues even if they had been given the information (Parasuraman, 1999, p. 237).

In 1985 Medha Patkar, a social scientist and activist from the Tata Institute for Social Sciences in Mumbai (see discussion earlier in this chapter) began living and working in the project-affected villages of Maharashtra. She helped the people to form an organization; shortly after this, activists in the Nimar region reorganized the nontribals as the Narmada Ghati Navnirman Samiti (Narmada Riverbank Renovation Committee) in Madhya Pradesh. At the same time the people of Gujarat organized the Narmada Asargrasta Sangharsh Samiti (Narmada Struggle Committee). The activists framed the issues in development terms based on the absolute lack of basic services in the villages. They began to organize village committees and taught committee members some basic literacy skills. They instituted adult education programs, convinced the government to provide teachers for schools, and established health care programs. They provided the villages information on the dam, including submergence levels, the numbers of people who would face dislocation, the resettlement and rehabilitation programs, and other issues (Parasuraman, 1999, p. 238). The villagers themselves began to collect comprehensive household data on land ownership, the number and kind of cattle and trees owned, and the amount of produce harvested from land, forests and rivers, as well as other information such as the size of houses and the materials used to build them, to inform the government so that adequate compensation levels could be set. Furthermore, the people, supported by the activists, demanded that the government recognize their right to information on all aspects of the dam and their right to resettle within their own state, and that it provide more comprehensive land surveys for adequate compensation, a comprehensive re-settlement plan, and the extension of resettlement and rehabilitation benefits to all those affected by the subsidiary projects of the dam such as the workers colony, canal, sanctuary, and compensatory forestation programs (Parasura-man, 1999, p. 239).

These demands essentially fell on deaf ears. The government claimed that the tribal peoples could not possibly understand the project planning process or the technical aspects of the land assessment or the CBA. The government also disputed some of the terms for adequate resettlement and land acquisition procedures demanded by the people. By the late 1980s it was clear that the government of India and the state governments were not willing to establish a coherent policy for compensation for a variety of losses to be incurred by the people. There was little certainty regarding the availability of adequate land for those to be resettled, and the visible misery of those that had already been resettled, along with the low prospects for resolving the issues, all led to the evolution of a position of total opposition to the SSP (Parasuraman, 1999, pp. 240-241). In late 1988 the local organizations working with affected villages held rallies in several towns, and total opposition to the SSP was declared. The organizations and the people were determined to stop the dam, citing as their reasons the need to save the environment, the economic and social well-being of the people to be resettled, and the goal of working toward sus-tainable forms of development. The local organizations united and formed the Narmada Bachao Andolan (Save the Narmada Movement), or the NBA. Their opposition was voiced in the slogan *Koi nahin hatega! Baandh nahin banega!* (No one will move! The dam will not be built!) (Baviskar, 1992, p. 238).

The NBA initiated a campaign of resistance on a broad front. In addition to efforts to mobilize the villages in the valley, the NBA established linkages with NGOs and social movements in both rural and urban areas throughout India. Urban NGOs participated in the NBA by carrying out media campaigns, disseminating information, fundraising, and holding solidarity events. Rural NGOs sent their members to participate in NBA events. The NBA also estab-lished cooperative relationships with international NGOs in order to pressure the international financial community to withdraw economic support from the project. In 1989 the Environmental Defense Fund, the Environmental Policy Institute, and the National Wildlife Federation urged the U.S. Congress to require the World Bank to stop funding the SSP. This pressure convinced the Bank to undertake an independent review of the environmental and displacement aspects of the project, producing a report that was highly critical of the project (Morse & Berger, 1992). The NBA also brought suit against the SSP in state courts, charging improper land acquisition, forcible eviction, state repression, and the denial of constitutionally guaranteed right to life (Baviskar, 1992, pp. 239–240). The NBA brought another more comprehensive case against the project in the Supreme Court of India in 1994. The rejection of that case in 1999 led the NBA to call for yet another *satyagraha* (a nonviolent mass social action event) and renewed efforts at resistance, including "save or drown squads" who wait behind the partially completed dam in villages below the expected submergence lines as the monsoon-swollen waters fill the reservoir.

The NBA gained the support of celebrities, including rock stars, prizewinning authors, and Indian Supreme Court justices, and also won a number of international environmental awards. Medha Patkar assumed the leadership of the movement and also won international acclaim for her tireless efforts on behalf of the people and the environment. With the increasing international fame, tensions between the local priorities of people in the valley and the broader agenda of the NBA appeared. Amrita Baviskar, a dedicated opponent of the dam, noted that the NBA often made decisions without consulting with the people in the valley (Patel & Mehta, 1995, p. 404). Other NGOs criticized the NBA for speaking of fair compensation in the villages but of environmental hazards, foreign debt, earthquakes, and other reasons to stop the dam in the cities (Dwivedi, 1998, p. 167). Some people within the valley considered the NBA to be as filled with empty promises as the dam authorities. Others felt that the NBA was exploiting them, urging them to resist rather than accept resettlement in order for the NBA to gain political capital in their struggle against the dam (Dwivedi, 1998, p. 167). Nonetheless, the NBA appeared to have the support of most of the people in the valley, and they continued their opposition in the form of meetings, marches, demonstrations, petitions, strikes, public confrontations with authorities, road blocks, hunger strikes, refusals to move, and "save or drown squads." The NBA adopted Gandhian resistance strategies, including the *satyagraha*. They also acquired a volunteer support group, Friends of River Narmada, which provided a sophisticated website chronicling the history of the movement and up-to-date information on the struggle, as well as information on opportunities to contribute resources and participate. There is also a Narmada Solidarity Network composed of six organizations from various cities in the United States.

As it has evolved, the NBA has widened its agenda beyond resistance against the SSP or even dams in general. Its original goals included the pursuit of sustainable forms of development, so the NBA joined with other organizations against destructive state and corporate development projects throughout India (McCully, 1996, p. 306). On the strength of her charismatic leadership and her knowledge, Medha Patkar was chosen to be one of the 12 commissioners on the World Commission on Dams (WCD) in 1998. Characteristically, when the final report of the WCD appeared in November 2000, it included an appended comment Patkar had written in which she forcefully noted that some basic issues inherent to the unjust and destructive development model, of which dams were just a symptom, were not given the importance they deserved in the final report (WCD, 2000, pp. 321–322).

While the Narmada struggle has, in the end, failed to stop the dam, there is no question that the formation of the NBA has profoundly affected the form and nature of resistance, as well as the future of dam construction, on a worldwide basis. As a Maharashtra villager asserts, "If there had been no protest movement, nobody would have got anything. At least now, many have received some land and compensation. I still refuse to leave my ancestral home. The government is incapable of providing us with just compensation. We are now aware of our rights. We have waged battles in the streets of all the major cities. We will continue to fight for our rights" (Mehta, 2008, p. 218). Even in failure, as Patkar has eloquently expressed, the NBA has served notice that dam construction can no longer proceed as usual. The global impact of the NBA has raised consciousness around the world about the potential for transformation when grassroots movements link with global agendas for change. The global recognition of the NBA and the struggle of the people of the Narmada Valley, as evidenced in the awards Medha Patkar has won, were major factors that led to the eventual creation of the WCD. The WCD, whose composition reflected the entire spectrum of perspectives on dams, largely validated the arguments put forth by the NBA and other dam resisters for many years. The conclusions of the WCD indicate that the NBA and other dam resisters have altered the terms of discussion and have indeed changed the way decisions about dam construction will be made in the future.

DFDR resistance movements have emerged in an era of extraordinary organized social action. In many ways less dramatic but far more organized than the countercultural and radical activism of the 1960s, DFDR resistance has been part of an expanded activist agenda that is much more issue focused. NGOs and electronic information technology, both relatively new phenomena,

From the doorway of the dwelling provided by the Sardar Sarovar relocation authority, a mother and child survey their bleak surroundings. (photograph by Kayana Szymczak)

A village in the Narmada Valley in Western India awaits inundation by the Sardar Sarovar Dam. (photograph by Dana Clark)

Tin barracks were provided for the people displaced by the Sardar Sarovar Dam. (photograph by Kayana Szymczak)

have been two important vehicles by which DFDR resistance and many other social and environmental concerns have been able to make inroads into the development agenda. Through multiple organizational forms and operating at multiple levels, from the local to the wider regions of global political discourse, DFDR resistance has been able to insert its concerns into more public arenas, drawing on greater support and developing greater influence in wider venues of power. The concerns that these organized forms of resistance address range from the defense of local rights to the rejection of development as measured purely in economic terms to questions of global human rights and environmental sustainability. Each level may focus on its own particular concerns but is capable of action to address concerns at other levels inclusively as well. The multiplicity of organizational forms and levels of action inevitably involve tensions and problems of coherence, consistency, and contradiction for all participants in the struggles against DFDR, as a number of the case studies have shown. However, thus far, the coherence between grassroots communities, cooperating NGOs, national social movements, and transnational networks has been sufficient to gain for them the right to sit at the negotiating table for many projects of national scale and enough political and social power to influence the policies of multilateral development organizations.

CHAPTER EIGHT

The Risks and Results of Resistance to Resettlement

Just as any action produces a reaction, resistance to DFDR produces concrete outcomes. Regardless of whether the resistance succeeds or fails in halting displacement or at least improving resettlement, there are other outcomes that bring consequences for the community or region that has confronted the development project. The outcomes or results of resistance may or may not fall within the original agenda or goals of the movement. Although for reasons made clear in Chapter 5, I hesitate to refer to these outcomes as losses or gains, costs and benefits; references of this order do not seem inappropriate as long as there is no attempt to render a balance sheet so as to determine whether resistance is a viable option from an economic standpoint. Further, since outcomes are abstracted from the array of DFDR resistance experiences, they can be considered only as potential or possible results in any given situation.

The Costs of Resistance

Since DFDR resistance movements frequently confront vastly more powerful forces—either the state or major concentrations of private capital—there may be considerable risks and costs involved. At the most basic and most profound level, there can be serious personal risks in resisting. DFDR resistance can be very dangerous. Resisters and their leaders risk death and bodily harm in certain circumstances. DFDR resistance leaders have been murdered by both agents of the state and private mercenaries. Peaceful demonstrators, including women, have been grievously abused and beaten (M. Black, 2001). Detention for an indeterminate period of time without due process is also one of the risks of resistance. Recently in Mexico at least 5 people have been killed in protests against the construction of La Parota Dam in the state of Guerrero. In India in March 2007, protests against the establishment of a Special Economic Zone (SEZ) that would have affected over 40,000 people in Nandigram unleashed a violent attack by police and ruling party cadres that killed at least 14 ("Red-hand Buddha," 2007), with estimates of the dead reaching as high as 50 ("Nandigram Turns Blood Red," 2007). Reports of sexual assault and rape of women protesters were common in the narratives of survivors (Sen, Chattopadhyay, Ghosh, Murmu, Mollik, & Marik, 2007). In Guatemala in 1982, military and paramilitary forces killed about 400 Maya Achi men, women, and children from communities resisting resettlement for the Chixoy Dam (Colajacomo, 1999, p. 68; Johnston, 2005, 2009).

As mentioned in Chapter 1, in the highly charged post-9/11 climate, opposition to state programs or policies may lead to accusations of terrorism, with all the potential abuses that label may entail. Although authoritarian governments with fewer legal restraints may be more likely to employ violent methods, such methods are not unheard of in ostensibly democratic regimes either. Regardless of constitutional safeguards, neither formal nor informal security forces at the local level may be particularly constrained in their treatment of resisters. Ethnic, religious, caste, or class prejudices may also buttress the ideological justification for such abuse.

There may also be considerable economic costs to resistance. Resistance has opportunity costs. Economically, resistance requires the mobilization and expenditure of labor and other resources in novel ways, diverting time, energy, and resources from other important tasks and stressing communities that may already be struggling to meet normal needs. Resistance requires human and economic resources for organization, communication, and mobilization, few of which may be present in sufficient surpluses in project-affected regions to underwrite the costs of resistance. The time, energy, and resources necessary for organizing resistance movements can strain both household and community capacities.

Urban people have jobs or work with regular time requirements that they must attend to in order to support themselves and their families. Rural peoples, at certain periods or seasons in the year, may have time to devote to meetings, organizing activities, demonstrations, and other resistance activities, but it is usually limited and at some point, under the pressure of producing their own subsistence, they must return to normal activities. Diverting time and labor from these normal activities thus brings the costs of not producing sufficiently and the risk of impoverishment and marginalization. Such costs can be reduced or avoided if resistance activities are spaced throughout or occur during slack times in the agricultural calendar.

Where resettlement is already under way, resisters may run the risk of exclusion from the benefits that people who have accepted resettlement receive, thus prolonging their period of indeterminacy long after other people have been resettled and are hoping to begin reconstructing their lives. Again, these risks have to be balanced against the abysmal record of resettlement projects in actually restoring lives to pre-resettlement standards, much less improving them. However, being the last in line for or excluded from even bad resettlement projects may place people in very difficult circumstances. People who have participated in failed resistance movements may find themselves even further behind and with fewer resources than those who accepted resettlement from the beginning, no matter how poorly implemented the resettlement project may be. Differential experiences and benefits between accepters and resisters may also bring the cost of social disarticulation in resettled communities. Resisters can become scapegoats for inadequate state support.

Even successful resistance may appear to have some political and economic costs in terms of long-term relationships with sectors that supported the development project. Resistance may create problematic relations with local and regional elements of power and/or authority structures that might have benefited from the project's success. As seen in the case of San Juan Tetelcingo, the defeat of the dam planned for that region of Guerrero has assured the Nahuatl people that they can remain on their land. One of the important features of their resistance campaign was an alternative agenda of locally prioritized development projects for which a much more modest expenditure than the cost of the dam could be employed. However, now almost ten years later, it would appear that one of the costs of their victory is forgoing future state development assistance. Despite the fact that the 22 communities that formed the vanguard of the resistance movement fall within a zone targeted for federal aid for the marginalized, they have received no federal assistance (Garcia, 2000).

While members of resisting communities unquestionably run the greatest risks, there may also be some economic or political risk experienced by those who work in collaboration with or support of these efforts. In Chile in 1995, the Pehuenche Indians' resistance to resettlement from the construction of two dams, the Pangue and the Ralco on the Bio Bio River, as well as pressure from Chilean and international advocacy groups, prompted the International Finance Corporation (IFC), part of the World Bank Group, to hire Dr. Ted Downing to carry out a study of the social impacts of the Pangue Dam. Downing also evaluated the performance of the Pehuen Foundation, which the IFC and ENDESA, the national electricity corporation, had created to address the socioeconomic impacts of the dams (all information on this case is drawn from Johnston & Garcia-Downing, 2004, pp. 214–219).

In his evaluation Downing found that the Pehuen Foundation had not fairly compensated the displaced people and had failed to meet the social, environmental, and resettlement obligations required by the Pangue Project. He further asserted that the Pangue Project had violated the political and civil rights of the Pehuenche by withholding key information regarding the validity of the soon-to-be built Ralco Dam. Downing submitted his report to the IFC in May 1996, a summary of which was delivered to ENDESA. Rejecting the summary, ENDESA threatened to sue both Downing and the IFC if they released the report to the public or, more specifically, to the Pehuenche Indians, even though permission for public release had been explicitly stipulated in Downing's contract.

The IFC acquiesced and censored the report, whereupon Downing filed a human rights complaint with the World Bank. Two months later the Bank's lawyers rejected the complaint, and when Downing filed another complaint alleging an IFC cover-up, that was also dismissed. However, the result of Downing's efforts to require the Bank to make his findings public, again as stipulated in his contract, was a threat from the IFC of a lawsuit garnishing his assets, income, and future salary if he revealed the contents, findings, or recommendations of his evaluation.

A month later Downing was informed that the IFC would not pursue legal measures against him if, in making his report public, he added a statement that it was not an official IFC document. However, in the 18 months that had passed since delivering his report, this critical information on human rights violations by the Pehuen Foundation was still not available to the public. In addition, since the public review period for the Ralco Dam had expired during that 18-month period, important information on the foundation's lack of technical means to mitigate future displacement from that project had also been denied the impacted people and the Chilean public when they most needed it to make an informed decision (Johnston & Garcia-Downing, 2004, pp. 214–219).

The involvement of outside advocates in dam resistance has occasioned difficulties as well on issues of strategy. In the aftermath of several deaths of protesters and fearful that the Mexican state and the Comision Federal de Electricidad (CFE) were developing a hard-line approach to resistance, Scott Robinson, an anthropologist with 25 years of experience in the field of displacement and resettlement, presented to a meeting of the communities to be affected by the La Parota Dam in Mexico a negotiation strategy for better resettlement conditions and suggested they use this strategy rather than resistance. However, peasant groups had been mobilized for resistance and had developed their own hard-line attitude regarding resettlement.

The banner of these protestors against the La Parota Dam in Mexico reads, "We're not leaving, ok?" (photograph by Monica Montalvo)

Protestors drape a banner over a piece of heavy construction equipment at the site of La Parota Dam in Mexico. (photograph by Scott Robinson)

Ironically, in 1992 Robinson was commissioned by the World Bank to film and produce a documentary video program he eventually called *Hay unos mas vivos que otros* (Some are more clever than others) that documents the history of broken promises and negative impacts in Mexican dam construction and resettlement. The CFE did not like the original version and complained to the World Bank. Robinson was obliged to cut out the controversial testimonies that CFE found offensive. Recently, the video was distributed to the anti–La Parota group, and they liked it so much that they sent a copy to the Guerrero state governor with the suggestion that he watch it to gain a better perspective on their position. However, because Robinson had advocated negotiations to improve resettlement rather than resistance with an increasingly hard-line government, he is now persona non grata in the affected communities. But his video is considered a valuable resource and continues to circulate among protesters (Robinson, personal communication, November 4, 2007).

Success or Failure

The success or failure of resistance movements is not the only measure by which positive outcomes can be assessed. Failure to halt a development project does not always mean that positive outcomes are not forthcoming. The question of successful resettlement in those relatively few cases where it can be claimed is one possible outcome. Recognizing the difficulty inherent in establishing a set of criteria against which such a multidimensional social process, one that frequently transpires over many years and sometimes decades, might be assessed for success, a small number of projects have purportedly enjoyed partial success at one stage or another of development and are often held up as beacons of light in the otherwise dismal record of DFDR.

Partridge, for example, considered that the Arenal Hydroelectric Project in Costa Rica succeeded in improving the standards of living and returning control over their own lives to the resettled people five years after the implementation of the project (all information on Arenal is drawn from Partridge, 1993). The Arenal Hydroelectric Project involved the construction of a dam 70 meters high that would produce a reservoir of 85.5 square kilometers and necessitate the displacement and resettlement of about 2,500 people (roughly 500 families). The final cost of the project was US$179 million, almost twice the original estimated cost of $91 million.

The area in which the project is located was characterized by the "humid tropics cattle-ranching complex," consisting of three developmental phases. The first phase involved the colonization of the tropical forest by migrants who used slash-and-burn agriculture to begin small farms. The second phase involved the absorption of these smallholdings by large cattle ranchers who continued clearing the forest for pasture. The third phase resulted in the depopulation of the region as land was taken over for pasture and both farming and employment opportunities decreased. The region to be affected by the dam was fully in the third phase, having lost roughly a fourth of its population. The principal economic activity was cattle ranching, with little or no commercial agriculture. Subsistence agriculture was declining as well. In other words, the region's potential for supporting the existing population was in rapid decline.

When the dam project was approved, resettlement planning began two years before actual construction began. The first two to three years (1976–1979) were difficult for the new communities. The resettled people cleared land and planted traditional crops such as maize, manioc, plantains, and bananas. Seeds and cuttings were made available to the farmers as soon as their new plots had been allocated. The agricultural system in the new settlements was initially the traditional slash-and-burn method. Subsequently, new vegetable, tree, and pasture crops that had been fieldtested during the construction phase began to be cultivated, particularly a new variety of coffee. Individual farmers obtained loans from the National Bank of Costa Rica to intensify production, and the farmers as a group organized a marketing cooperative. Income from coffee increased by roughly 100 percent over pre-resettlement levels. New grasses for cattle fodder also enabled farmers to increase cattle herds from one animal pastured per hectare to three. A new road constructed by the ICE linked the new communities to market centers and fostered the development of several small dairy farms.

Income from these initiatives stimulated the purchase of additional farmlands, the construction of outbuildings on farms, the purchase of vehicles, and the construction of a rural school building with no assistance from the government. The success of the families in the farming sector nourished success in the commercial sector. Shopkeepers and their families benefited from the increased levels of cash income in the communities. Levels of fixed capital and inventory values in the new communities have ranged between 50 percent and 200 percent greater than in the old settlements. Furthermore, social organizational features developed in the new communities in the form of a school committee, a sports committee, and the continuation of the Catholic Church committees. Finally, the population of the new communities remained stable, halting the flight of people from an area they perceived as unable to sustain them.

Partridge attributes the successes achieved in the project to three basic steps in the preparation process. Good data collection and community studies carried out by social scientists resulted in a resettlement plan that was both realistic and practical. He also emphasized the importance of consultation with the people to be relocated and their meaningful participation in the preparation process. Also significant in the success of Arenal was the strategy of establishing the new farms on the basis of traditional crops and technology, allowing the farmers to continue with known practices for the initial period of adjustment. After three years, innovations were introduced when people were more able to assume risks, and the results significantly enhanced income generation, leading to long-term acceptance of the new settlements (Partridge, 1993, p. 367). These positive results at three years notwithstanding, Scudder asserts that long-term success cannot be evaluated for at least two generations (2009).

Two World Bank publications (Cernea & McDowell, 2000; Picciotto, van Wicklin, & Rice, 2001), while acknowledging that major problems remain for people uprooted by development projects, maintain that improvements are being made in resettlement in DFDR planning and implementation. The impoverishment risks and reconstruction (IRR) model developed by Cernea provides a significant tool for the prediction, diagnosis, and resolution of problems associated with DFDR (Cernea & McDowell, 2000). A study of five major Bank-funded dam projects by the World Bank's Operations Evaluation Department (OED) concludes that while better planning has occurred, it has not led generally to better involuntary resettlement (Picciotto, van Wicklin, & Rice, 2001). The OED sees the key to success as the borrower country's genuine commitment to the resettlement process as a development opportunity, but the public agencies charged with resettlement have not responded adequately to the task. The OED study also finds that income restoration strategies, whether based on land-for-land or other options, have not in general been successful (Picciotto, van Wicklin, & Rice, 2001).

In the face of such a dismal record, resistance, even if it is doomed to fail, is very often seen to be the only viable option for people threatened with displacement and resettlement. Failed resistance efforts can still gain a measure of success if they empower the resisters to bargain for improving the terms and conditions of resettlement. Many resistance movements at the local level initially ask for no more than recognition of their rights to adequate compensation for their losses and reasonable conditions of resettlement. The reluctance or inability of the state and/or private capital to dignify or implement these quite reasonable requirements is very often responsible for the escalation of tensions and outright resistance to projects. When resistance escalates, it begins to increase project costs through direct outlays, delays, bad publicity, and loss of political credibility with donor agencies. Thus, even if movements fail, if their activities threaten to increase the costs sufficiently, they can gain bargaining space to improve the terms and conditions of resettlement.

In effect, mere participation in resistance movements can bring clear benefits. Particularly resistance movements that emerge from local responses and require the participation of local people provide invaluable experience in dealing with outside agencies and institutions. For groups that have historically been ignored or marginalized by the state and its agencies, resistance movements provide a form of political socialization in which local people become much more acquainted with state agencies and bureaucracies and their procedures. Moreover, they become much more aware of their rights as citizens and the means to defend those rights within the framework of national constitutions and international accords. They may also acquire allies that will continue to work with them after the DFDR dispute is over. The acquisition of allies such as NGOs may make available other resource pools, injecting new skills, technology, and access to specialized economic resources into the local context. These allies, skills, and resources all may prove useful in future dealings with the state. For example, in Brazil several people in the national leadership of MAB emerged from local contexts in the early days of the struggle and have become very skilled over the years in organizing and negotiating at national and international levels. In effect, because of their participation in resistance movements, whether they succeed or fail, people become much more knowledgeable and much more skillful in dealing with local and national agencies and bureaucratic structures (Oliver-Smith, 1991, 2006). Regardless of whether the project is completed or halted, the state and/or large-scale private enterprise become larger presences in the local context than they were prior to the project. With the expansion of these institutions and their increasing impact on local lives and communities, the skills and resources for dealing with them that are acquired in resistance will prove valuable to local people in the future.

If resistance is successful in helping to stop a project, retaining control over land and remaining in one's home environment are major positive outcomes for the local group. However, the validation of the perspective and effort that project cancellation signifies for the resisting group takes on special significance as well. Since those most subject to resettlement are frequently from indigenous or other minority groups, successful defense of homeland can take on great significance to a group that has historically been ignored or oppressed by the dominant society (Khera & Mariella, 1982; Scudder, 2005; Waldram,

1980). The successful defense of human rights of self-determination, of rights to land, or of rights to religious freedom that may be embodied in resistance to resettlement constitutes a form of self-affirmation that can serve as a stimulus leading to a florescence of local culture and greater local autonomy. The demands that resistance movements voice for greater citizen participation in decision-making, for access to information, and for respect for civil and political liberties can also signify progress toward a more responsive and representative society in which the opinions of the less powerful are heard. Moreover, successful DFDR can add credence to arguments for more sustainable, more appropriate models of development, emphasizing projects that focus on benefits for local populations. These efforts have been taken up by the recently formed (and previously mentioned) regional associations of dam affected peoples for the Latin American region and in Mexico, specifically.

From the perspective of NGOs, allied social movements, and transnational networks, stopping the project is a major goal in itself but is not the end of the struggle. Although the conflict may last for years, even decades, stopping the project is just one battle in a many-fronted war against certain models or approaches to development and the institutions associated with them. Whether a project is halted or proceeds, local NGOs may continue to work with the communities, while international organizations may move on to tackle other cases of DFDR. Most certainly, national and international NGOs will continue to employ both the example and the perspectives gained in each case to struggle for MDB reform, greater transparency, and more sustainable forms of development. The experience of the anti-dam movement over the last thirty years, but of particular intensity in the last fifteen, has proven instructive in the struggle to alter approaches to development. The milestone meetings of dam affected people from around the world and their declarations from Manibeli, Curitiba, and Rasi Salai (see below) represent a form of global mobilization through networking and external support. Many of the movement's arguments and contentions were validated by the Morse Report and the final report of the World Commission on Dams and serve as major examples for resistance to other forms of unsustainable and undemocratic development.

The Rasi Salai meeting, briefly mentioned in Chapter 2, in particular demonstrates the vigor of the anti-dam movement. In late November 2003 representatives of dam affected communities and their allies from 62 nations met for five days in an encampment constructed on the banks of the Mun River near the village of Rasi Salai, Thailand. The purposes for their meeting were to strengthen the movement of peoples against large dams, build solidarity among dam affected peoples, and share experiences and develop strategies for the defense of rivers, environments, and communities facing destruction or displacement by the construction of large dams. Entitled "Rivers for Life," the Second International Meeting of Dam Affected Peoples and Their Allies took place on land that is being restored to life after being flooded by a dam whose gates had finally been opened, allowing the river to flow freely after years of protest and demands for compensation and decommissioning by the villagers of Rasi Salai and their allies. The villagers, who are all members of the Thai peoples' movement the Assembly of the Poor, constructed for the conference bamboo houses and meeting rooms that the community will use in the future as a school to educate the public about river ecology. The meeting, which brought together more than 300 participants in what has become a truly global social movement, was organized by the Assembly of the Poor, the Southeast Asia Rivers Network, and the International Rivers Network in association with an international agenda committee that included representatives from human rights and environmental NGOs from Brazil, India, Mexico, Mozambique, Nepal, Pakistan, the Philippines, South Africa, Sweden, Thailand, Uganda, and the United States. More than 70 representatives from impacted communities came from those nations and many more, including Bangladesh, Botswana, Cambodia, China, Colombia, Costa Rica, Ghana, Guatemala, Honduras, Indonesia, Japan, Lesotho, Malaysia, Panama, Paraguay, Poland, Senegal, and Zimbabwe. Other participants included foundation program officers, human rights and environmental law activists, and two WCD commissioners.

One of the principal goals of the meeting was to evaluate the progress of the international dams movement since the First International Meeting held in Curitiba, Brazil, in 1997. The Curitiba meeting was one of the first forums in which the World Bank's internal evaluation of large dams was severely questioned, leading eventually to the formation of the WCD. Therefore, one of the major goals of the Second International Meeting was an evaluation of the WCD process and its strengths and weaknesses, particularly in light of the recent backlash against the WCD from dam-building nations such as India, China, and Turkey and the misrepresentation of the commission's findings by the dam-building industry. Certainly, the failure of the World Bank to follow progressive WCD recommendations was a central issue for discussion and action.

Initial plenary sessions of the meeting focused on the interrelated issues of the resurgence of large dam construction and the evaluation of the international dams movement. The evaluation of the current state of the anti-dam movement was carried out through presentations by regional delegations and workshops on movement building, local and national campaigns, the WCD, and international financial institutions, many focused on assessing the effectiveness of campaigns in meeting the array of goals established at the First International Meeting of Dam Affected Peoples. Clear advances, it was noted, in the international movement have been achieved in successfully challenging the dam industry, governments, and financial institutions in the technical, political, and moral spheres. The movement has supported affected and threatened communities and allies in achieving participation in decision-making processes and in determining their own future in specific cases. These efforts and others have strengthened ties between indigenous peoples, grass-roots movements, and NGOs and between Northern and Southern civil society. The key achievement of the international movement since the Curitiba meeting is the WCD, which provides a framework for democratic, transparent, and accountable decision-making processes in dam project planning and im-plementation, including displacement and resettlement issues.

The majority of the meeting's activities were dedicated to workshops on a wide variety of themes. Some workshops focused on tactical and strategic concerns such as fund raising, dealing with export-credit agencies, the World Bank and dams, dam decommissioning processes, multistakeholder consul-tations and strategies for success, local information exchange, and lobbying, negotiation, and mass mobilization. Other workshops were concerned with broader issues regarding energy planning, dam economics, climate change and water resources, hydro and carbon trading, and alternatives to dams. Still others combined both information and strategizing in human rights focused discussions regarding indigenous peoples and dams; free, prior, and informed consent for indigenous peoples; peoples' struggles and national and inter-national law; community-based research methodologies; and reparations for dam affected peoples.

The meeting culminated in the unanimous endorsement of the Rasi Salai Declaration, redacted and issued in the ten languages employed in the work-shops and sessions, affirming the commitment to intensify the struggle against destructive dams, to work toward sustainable and appropriate methods of water and energy management, and to strengthen and broaden the movement through alignments with others that struggle against the current neo-liberal development models and policies and for global social and ecological justice. If the Rasi Salai meeting is any indication, the face and substantive agenda of environmental quality/social justice advocacy continue to evolve, with inter-national activists playing more of a supportive role and community-based representatives taking the lead in establishing agendas, securing assistance, and negotiating meaningful remedy.

A plenary session at the Second International Meeting of Dam Affected Peoples and Their Allies in Rasi Salai, Thailand, in November 2003. (photograph by Anthony Oliver-Smith)

A workshop on local organizing at the Second International Meeting of Dam Affected Peoples and Their Allies in Rasi Salai, Thailand, in November 2003. (photograph by Anthony Oliver-Smith)

A ceremony on the banks of the Mun River included launching small leaf boats with candles into the current to close the Second International Meeting of Dam Affected Peoples and Their Allies. (photograph by Anthony Oliver-Smith)

Present and Future Threats

The overall environment of development planning and funding is rapidly changing, particularly with regard to issues at the core of DFDR that impact social and environmental justice advocacy in the evolving nature of the local-global politics of social and environmental advocacy. In the public sector, internationally there has been a return to a culture of large-scale projects that displace large numbers of people and radically alter environments. The World Bank's adoption in 2002 of new policies that favor "high risk, high gain" kinds of projects represents a disturbing trend and a particularly acute threat. Essentially turning its back on the 1990s environmental reforms that favored a more cautious approach to high-risk infrastructure projects, the Bank was rejecting its "risk averse" approach and beginning to favor large hydropower, forest, oil, gas, and mining projects in high-risk environments (Bosshard, Brull, Horta, Lawrence, & Welch, 2003). However, the mindset has escalated even beyond individual megaprojects to the development of projects that subsume entire regions, even subcontinents, in vast networks of interrelated infrastructure that will further energy production, transportation, commerce, and resource extraction.

Interestingly, in the roughly seven years since the adoption of the new "high risk, high reward" policy, only two new high-risk projects, the Nam Theun 2 Dam on the Mekong and the Bujagali Dam on the Nile, have been approved for loans by the Bank. Despite the small number of high-risk projects funded by the Bank, it has returned to the debate as a cheerleader for large dams, lobbying strongly at international conferences, industry events, and bilateral meetings for big hydropower. Led largely by its Water Resources Management Group, the World Bank's promotion of large dams, which has been reengaged with a "missionary zeal," may prove to be as key a factor in the expansion of the number of high-risk projects as the Bank's actual funding of them (Bosshard, 2007, p. 19).

Although not a World Bank project, India's vast river-linking scheme, in which all the major rivers of that nation would be tied into one enormous network, is emblematic of the kind of project that threatens both people and environments. Indeed, the river-linking scheme defies every major recommendation of the WCD. Since the nineteenth century, linking India's rivers has been promoted as the solution to a variety of problems, including drought, flooding, irrigation, energy, and transportation. For much of the last century the undertaking was considered too vast to be seriously considered. In 1980 the Indian Ministry of Water Resources established the National Water Development Agency and framed the National Perspective for Water Development, which envisioned the water-linking proposal as providing 31 large-scale connections for rivers throughout all of India. Still, little was done on the project until October 2002, when India's Supreme Court ordered the completion of the interlinking of rivers project by 2014 (Bandyopadhyay & Perveen, 2004).

The project is expected to cost US$120 billion and will link 37 Himalayan and peninsular rivers in an enormous South Asian water grid that will include 12,500 kilometers of canals, 35 million hectares of irrigated land, and the generation of 35 gigawatts of hydropower. The river-linking scheme will impact 25 of India's 29 states, as well as the nations of Nepal, Bhutan, and Bangladesh (International Water Management Institute), which means that approximately one billion people will be affected. Touted by some as the answer to India's problems of western droughts and northeastern floods, others frame it as the most destructive project in the history of the world. The inundation of vast tracts of forests, disturbance of wildlife, enormous displacement of communities and cultures, changes in water quality and microclimatic conditions, and public health consequences are anticipated ("India's River-Linking Scheme," 2003). Civil society began organizing a short time after the announcement of the Supreme Court decision, and efforts to stop the advance of the project are now active in India and among international human rights and environmental groups.

Equally grandiose is the megaproject known as the Plan Puebla Panama (PPP), recently renamed "Proyecto Mesoamerica." The PPP is a 25-year, US$20 billion dollar program to create a development corridor from the Mexican state of Puebla to the nation of Panama. Included in the plan would be the nine southern states of Mexico and all seven Central American nations, covering a total population of 65 million people, most of whom are extremely poor. The PPP consists of eight components: energy production, commerce and competitiveness, sustainable development, transportation, telecommunications integration, human development, tourism, and prevention and mitigation of natural disasters. The PPP is designed to boost economic growth, reduce poverty, and nourish human capital as well as the natural environment (Plan Puebla Panamá, 2007). The plan includes the building of more than 8,000 miles of new or improved highways, more than 1,000 miles of new electrical lines to distribute power generated by gas and a still unknown number of dams, and six enormous "development zones" for maquiladora plants and processing facilities (Call, 2002). A mammoth infrastructure of ports, highways, airports, and railway lines will link the region's petroleum, energy, maquiladora, and agricultural industries to the North American and global markets (Plan Puebla Panama, n.d.).

Critics see the project as one vast scheme to open up the entire Mesoamerican region to private foreign investment and expand the Free Trade Area of the Americas (FTAA). The PPP is seen as based on an unsustainable model of development that exploits the human and natural resources of the region for the interests of big business rather than those of local communities. Human rights activists have serious concerns about massive displacement of communities by dams and other infrastructure, as well as maquiladora development that will trigger large-scale migration, particularly to the southern half of Mexico where wages are 30–40 percent lower than in the rest of the country. Environmental organizations protest that the PPP will enable private resource extraction industries focusing on the extraction of primary materials (timber, minerals, oil, and water), which will degrade the environment for private profits that will leave the country, with little benefit for local communities. These concerns have generated campaigns by more than 500 NGOs, community organizations, cooperatives, unions, and other groups against the sponsoring Inter-American Development Bank and the various states of the region, to resist the advance of the project. (Plan Puebla Panama, n.d.).

In addition to the emergence of these truly mammoth undertakings with all their human rights and environmental dangers, there are other disturbing challenges in the public sector that continue to confront communities threatened or displaced by development projects. For example, the repositioning of dams by the World Bank, nation-states, and industry associations as environmentally benign, socially productive, efficient technologies is particularly disquieting. The weakening of World Bank guidelines regarding both the protection of indigenous people affected by development projects and involuntary resettlement is also alarming to vulnerable communities and their supporters (Downing & Moles, 2001) since it diminishes the regulatory and legal protection that such groups need in their struggles against displacement.

The weakening of the Bank's guidelines on involuntary resettlement generates especially great concern. Since the guidelines on involuntary resettlement (officially, Operational Directive 4.30) were first issued in 1980, they have been revised four times. The latest version changes them from a binding operational directives format to Operational Policies (ops), Bank Procedures (bps), and Good Practices (gps). The new format consists of op/bp 4.12 on Involuntary Resettlement. ops and bps are binding on Bank staff and borrowers but gps are not (Clark, 2009). The changes ultimately established in op/bp 4.12 that concern critics most are those that diminish the protections available to vulnerable people and communities while at the same time enhancing procedures and processes that make it easier and more efficient for development planners to displace people. Key among these concerns is the failure of the new policies to protect people from indirect impacts. The new policy explicitly protects against direct economic and social impacts that result from Bank-financed projects, but it omits mention of indirect impacts. It is frequently the indirect impacts of development projects—loss of jobs, loss of access to resources, environmental degradation—that people who have not been resettled suffer and that go unnoticed in development plans. Since indirect impacts are not explicitly marked in the new policy, the Bank and borrowers are free to argue that they are not covered in op/bp 4.12.

A further concern centers on the differences between restoration and improvement in standards of living of displaced communities. The 1990 version of the guidelines stipulated that displaced and resettled people were entitled to receive benefits from the project and should have their standard of living improved. The new version of 2001 asserts that "displaced persons *should be assisted* in their efforts to improve their livelihoods and standards of living or at least restore them, in real terms, to pre-displacement levels or to levels prevailing prior to the beginning of project implementation, whichever is higher" [emphasis mine] (World Bank, 2001). This language, rather than *mandating* improvement, *recommends* ("should be") assistance in local efforts to improve levels of well-being. The weakening of the improvement aspect is in direct contradiction to most findings of researchers on resettlement impacts. Scudder, in his exhaustive volume on large dams, insists that restoration policies are abject failures and lead to greater impoverishment (2005). On the basis of a similar assessment of compensation as a failed policy, Cernea recommends widespread project benefit-sharing with affected peoples, in effect making them investors and beneficiaries of project outcomes (2009).

By the same token the guidelines protecting indigenous peoples are also of particular concern since they do not adequately address either recommendations from indigenous peoples or international documents relating to international human rights law and indigenous rights law, informed consent, and territorial rights. The process of free, prior, and informed consultation is also a major cause for concern among indigenous peoples. The language and application now employed by the World Bank are ambiguous. The use of the phrase "free, prior, and informed" suggests more than it actually means. Usually associated with the right to free, prior, and informed consent before any action is taken that will affect people, these words lose a great deal of their import when applied to the term "consultation." In a special session at the 2005 United Nations Permanent Forum on Indigenous Issues (UNPFII), representatives from the World Bank and the IFC presented the Indigenous Peoples (IP) policy recently approved by the World Bank board of directors. The presentation acknowledged that the final approved version of the IP policy was unlikely to satisfy most indigenous peoples since it required "free, prior, and informed consultation" for development project approval rather than the "free, prior, and informed consent" espoused by indigenous peoples and their allies.

Representatives of indigenous peoples rejected the idea of free, prior, and informed consultation, which the World Bank defined as "a culturally appropriate and collective decision-making process subsequent to meaningful good faith consultation and informed participation regarding the preparation and implementation of the project" (World Bank, 2005). Indigenous peoples' representatives felt that under these conditions, free, prior, and informed consultation is fundamentally a negotiating process. By that interpretation, the only option that indigenous peoples have is to work to improve the conditions of a project involving their land and resources, a project that they have no power to stop. The indigenous participants and their NGO allies attending the UNPFII expressed their extreme disappointment and directed sharp criticism at the World Bank and IFC representatives.

The prevailing political economic climate currently does not bode well for people confronting displacement by development projects. The increasingly apparent cooperation between the state and private capital in the acquisition of land for private development projects is of particular concern. As seen in the PPP's emphasis on maquiladora production facilities or the case of the Pfizer production plant in New London, Connecticut, to cite two familiar examples, this relationship represents a serious threat to anyone whose property can be demonstrated to have more economically efficient uses than mere residence, but particularly for indigenous and other traditional peoples whose land tenure is not formalized or lies outside the domains of the market and private property.

Indeed, the lack of clarity in the responsibilities that privately funded development projects have to affected peoples is cause for concern. As the power of international capital is granted exemptions from or is increasingly able to ignore or override state regulatory restrictions, wholesale displacements of communities by private investments may become more commonplace. As these projects advance and indigenous and traditional peoples become increasingly integrated into and impacted by both the state and the market, the nature of conflicts over displacement and resettlement may acquire greater relevance for the class and power relations of the sociopolitical systems in which they take place. In effect, since the early 1990s, when the national and international balance of forces between capital and labor swung more decidedly in capital's favor, the willingness and the ability of the state to provide social democratic protection to citizens has been diminishing. The state is now shifting from being a prime mover of these projects to becoming a willing partner, aider, and abettor of private capital in the displacement process.

Local people and activists are acutely aware of the reduction of state power in development initiatives and are now framing their struggle in more global terms. The testimony of a young woman affected by the Sardar Sarovar Project, whose attempts to meet with government (sarkar) officials to present demands were consistently frustrated, articulates a clear understanding of current political realities. "I have also understood why we never came face to face with the sarkar who can take decisions because the actual sarkar is far away in Manila and Washington or now consists of the companies who rule the roost. It is no longer the people we elect who take the decisions" (Ramkuwar, 2009, p. 279).

The state's declaration of Special Economic Zones (SEZs) as areas where taxation, labor, and environmental laws and regulations are more liberal than other regions of the nation demonstrates the consolidation of this role of partner, aider, and abettor and is sparking conflicts over displacement and resettlement around the world. According to the World Bank, there are more than 3,000 projects under way in SEZs in 120 countries around the world. Thus, despite the obvious confrontation between classes in DFDR resistance, the articulation of cultural and environmental concerns expressed by communities has downplayed issues of class conflict. After all, dominant discourse had always presented the projects as being promoted by the state for the development of the nation, and the discourses of resistance focused on the rights of the indigenous, the poor, and the marginalized, whose welfare had been left out of the national community by political elites. However, the trend toward privatization may reveal that behind the cultural or environmental concerns, resistance movements are becoming more fundamentally class conflicts. The links between political and economic elites have always been close, but today's neo-liberal ideology portrays the interests of private capital and those of the nation as identical. The role of the state, then, is simply to guarantee a favorable institutional environment for capital to pursue its reproduction and expansion. Industries may pay lip service to the guidelines contained in legislation, but many governments today either willfully turn a blind eye to infractions or are too weak to ensure compliance with regulations, leaving communities with no recourse or access to justice (Rebbapragada & Kalluri, 2009, p. 266). Thus, the increasing privatization of development projects, essentially unconstrained by international displacement and resettlement guidelines or human rights accords, subordinates the human and environmental rights of numerous indigenous and other minority groups to the agendas of corporate interests and the logic of the market.

Privatization of large-scale development projects thus presents local communities with serious consequences, largely because of the lack of constraints and accountability that current political economic models favor. However, globalization is not gravity, and market logics are not the laws of physics (Collins, 2003). Neither has the force of natural law and both are cultural phenomena that admit to wide variation in both interpretation and application. And thus, despite neo-liberal denials of intervention in matters of the economy, both globalization and the market are susceptible to alteration through the political process.

Conclusions

Resistance to DFDR in most cases constitutes a clear expression of a sense of real or potential injury and loss of rights. In any given context, there may be individuals who attach themselves to resistance movements because they see the potential for personal gain, but most participants associate themselves with resistance movements for more complex motives. People resist resettlement for a wide array of reasons: quite practical, material issues over land, resources, property, livelihood, or, in other words, control over the means of production; more ideologically oriented concepts such as tradition, ethnic identity, or religion; or a combination of all of these issues (Oliver-Smith, 1977, 2006).

Regardless of the specific issues being contested in a given case, behind these concerns lies a concept of rights. People resist because they recognize that certain basic, legitimate rights are being abridged. Resistance is often a demand that rights be recognized. Principal among these rights is the right of self-determination, the right—as defined in international law by the Charter of the United Nations (and embodied in the Universal Declaration of Human Rights [Resolution 2200A]) and as it exists within local conditions—to control one's own life and future. Even if we cannot establish that such a right exists as a cultural universal, it seems ethically dubious for us to claim such a right for ourselves and not recognize it as applying to others. The threat of DFDR amounts to the potential loss of the right of self-determination, in effect, the loss of relative control over self and community (Scudder & Colson, 1982). Although the degree of control over conditions is always partial in the best of circumstances, DFDR creates a "community which does not effectively control its own affairs . . . and in which a feeling of powerlessness is pervasive" or, as Kushner terms it, "an administered community" (1988, p. 29).

Resistance to DFDR, then, must be considered a legitimate expression of the defense of the right of self-determination, as well as a defense of land, religion, or identity. People also reject the loss of autonomy and the extreme form of political domination that resettlement both signifies and enacts, and their resistance questions whether resettlement can ever be development or empowering. Their resistance is, in some fundamental form, an act of self-empowerment, however partial or temporary that empowerment may be.

In that process of self-empowerment, resisters at all levels speak directly to powerholders and policy-makers. The messages they seek to communicate are not difficult to understand, but they do require a perspective that is capable of reevaluating suppositions, often deeply embedded, about the nature, quality, and scale of the development process, forms of governance and power sharing, and majority-minority relations. The messages that resisters communicate include the following:

- The legitimacy of the right of the state to relocate people and appropriate property with or without compensation must be reexamined.
- Appropriate and just forms and levels of compensation and investment must be determined in consultation with affected people. Outside standards employed to establish levels and forms of compensation will not

be appropriate unless approved in full consultation with the people to be resettled.

- If development is to become a democratic process, local rights must be recognized, because development-project effects are felt first at the local level.
- Development must be defined qualitatively as well as quantitatively. Development defined qualitatively includes the freedom to define local priorities democratically. Development projects must therefore include the authentic participation of local people in strategic planning and implementation.
- Resistance speaks of local needs and priorities.
- People with deep local knowledge are often better at predicting DFDR outcomes than external experts. Respect local knowledge as a source for viable, less destructive alternatives.
- Resistance speaks clearly about project deficiencies. Project problems do not originate with and are not the fault of the resettled people.
- The method and focus of decision-making must shift from purely economic criteria to a more dialogic form of participatory decision-making.
- Resistance is a rejection of the dominant society's cultural construction of the poor, of ethnic minorities, of peasants as incapable, powerless, and unworthy of consideration.
- Resisters join with others in seeking to democratize their societies.
- If national purpose is the justification for development projects, then national purpose has to be defined publicly and pluralistically, and projects have to be demonstratively inclusive. A national purpose that is not inclusive is not democratic. A national purpose that requires sacrifices only from those least able to absorb them for the benefit of those who least need them is authoritarian, regardless of the supposed democratic character of the regime.
- Resistance is, in effect, a demand for accountability and responsibility from government, from development agencies, and from multilateral development banks for actions taken in the name of social policy and development.

The role DFDR resistance movements are now taking in the broader realms of global political discourse may start at local levels but in many cases soon becomes part of a larger movement for both redressing the human rights abuses that occur in DFDR and altering contemporary development policy and practice. There are obvious points of tension that can occur between, on the one hand, a population threatened with resettlement that resists to gain a stronger negotiating position for better resettlement conditions and, on the other hand, allies at other levels who may have more systemic goals that reach beyond the local context to question the dominant models of development. For local communities involved in resistance, embracing such far-reaching goals requires the realization of a coincidence of interests and the construction of shared meanings that provide a common ideological basis for undertaking action in collaboration with others who are, more often than not, socioculturally, economically, and geographically distant from them. Local resistance dramas "in the shadow land . . . at the outer edge of the realm of politics . . ." thus may become internationalized and participants in the changing arena of global political culture" (Falk, 1983, p. 25, as cited in Wilmer, 1993, p. 39).

Apart from stopping actual displacement and resettlement, the major challenge facing DFDR resistance is maintaining the coherence among the agendas, goals, and discourses of the participants at all levels of the struggle. There will never be perfect coherence or perfect articulation, but enough political consistency has been achieved thus far to begin to alter the terms of debate in the field of international development toward greater recognition of human rights and environmental sustainability. When the local struggles of resistance to resettlement are cast in national debates attracting the attention of national and international NGOs and multilateral and international institutions, local resistance movements become active participants in a larger global dialogue. In effect, resistance to resettlement is helping to reframe the entire contemporary debate on development, the environment, and human rights, a debate that shows considerable signs of expanding and of increasing its relevance to both national development and human rights policy, as well as international standards.

For example, DFDR affected-peoples are developing novel strategies in defense of their rights in their relations with the state and the global capital market by invoking international human rights covenants. Political power is emerging in supranational organizations, NGOs, and private institutions to expand the claims for disempowered subjects under the law (Clark, Fox, & Treakle, 2003; Fox & Brown, 1998). Project-affected communities provide a point of convergence at which the human rights and environmental movements can create an arena for an expanded international civil society (W. F. Fisher, 1995). This convergence entails a critique of development models that accept the necessity of relocating people but also places in doubt the scale of development interventions that create major disruptions for people, their ways of life, and their environments. Further, the discourse at this convergence also reassesses the extent of state sovereignty and invokes changes in global political culture.

There is currently an active debate among powerful interests on the role of dams and other large infrastructural projects. On the one hand, renewed efforts by national governments and private interests to promote development projects with DFDR components but without significant legal and economic protection are threatening increasing numbers of people and communities. Despite widespread criticism, the actual practice of development continues to favor large infrastructural expansion and economic growth over ecological and cultural concerns (Flyvbjerg, Bruzelius, & Rothengatter, 2003; Josephson, 2002).

On the other hand, these trends have been met by such initiatives as the World Commission on Dams (2000), the Extractive Industries Review (2004) and the Equator Principles (2003), all aimed at creating what Jonathan Fox has called "accountability politics" to ensure socially and environmentally responsible development (Fox & Brown, 2003, p. xii). The previously mentioned World Bank Inspection Panel, which allows people affected by Bank-funded projects to file complaints and request independent investigations into its compliance with its own social and environmental guidelines, is another element in the quest for accountability, although its results since its creation in 1993 have been uneven (Clark et al., 2003). Furthermore, gaining prior informed consent from the people to be affected by projects (Goodland, 2004) and strengthening the legal basis of and procedures for payment of reparations for injuries and costs imposed on individuals and communities by projects have recently emerged as strategic priorities (Johnston, 2000, 2009).

As the debates on development evolve in the twenty-first century, the concerns about continued infrastructural and economic growth will continue to be countered by concerns about more environmentally sustainable and more democratic forms of development, particularly at the local level. Development projects have increasingly become the sites at which these interests and issues are contested and played out through different models of development by individuals and groups from a variety of communities, both local and nonlocal. As Fisher has noted, to a certain extent the rhetorics of social justice and material well-being are espoused by both parties, but their understandings of the deeper philosophical meaning of development as a social goal and the means by which that goal should be achieved are markedly different. The internal heterogeneity of both the development industry and those who propose alternative visions is reflected in the meanings, means, and implications of development that each side embraces (W. F. Fisher, 1995, p. 8).

Reigning development models, which promote large-scale infrastructural projects, transform social and physical environments and espouse the concept of "the greatest good for the greatest number" while promising to safeguard local rights and well-being. Such a position assumes, though the record generally does not support such an assumption, that the less powerful will benefit eventually from well-designed and well-implemented resettlement programs. For some, given the framework of current political economic structures and conditions, realism dictates acceptance of this development ideology despite its manifest failures. But on the other side are those who insist on the priority of the rights of the less powerful and the significance of cultural and environmental diversity over what they consider to be ecologically risky and economically questionable projects.

This debate about development, what it is and how to do it, spans a broad spectrum of issues and encompasses many scales, ranging from local struggles to national aspirations to world systems. However, approaches that emphasize local rights and concerns also address issues central to global social and ecological well-being. The variability inherent in local cultures and environments provides the means by which both nature and human beings achieve resilience and the capacity to adapt to both internally and externally induced change (Holling, 1994). Local and global survival depends, therefore, on the continuity of cultural and biological variability. The model of development that subjects all humanity to a uniform, large-scale, capital-intensive, technology-driven approach, articulated through the state and the market, can actually lead to a reduction of resilience and adaptability in the face of social and environmental perturbations.

Diversity is the foundation of the process of adaptation that enables all forms of life to evolve in the face of changing circumstances. The direct concerns of DFDR resisters work to conserve the variability and diversity of local cultures and environments. The significant correlation between high biodiversity and high cultural diversity (Oviedo, Maffi, & Larsen, 2000, p. 11) that suggests a kind of "double diversity" based on a mutual reinforcement between cultural and biological variation is clearly endangered by the enormous scale of many infrastructural development projects. In resistance to DFDR, local people defend not only their rights and well-being—they defend ours.

Bibliography

Acselrad, H., & da Silva, M. das Gracas. (2000, August). *Social conflict and environmental change at the Amazon Tucurui Dam region*. Paper presented at the meeting of the International Rural Sociology Association Meetings, Rio de Janeiro, Brazil.

Activists put IRN on the map. (1988). *World Rivers Review, 3*(3), 1.

Adams, J. (1996). Cost-benefit analysis: The problem, not the solution. *The Ecologist, 26*(1), 2-4.

Agrawal, A., & Redford, K. (2006). *Poverty, development and biodiversity conservation: Shooting in the dark?* Working Paper #26. Bronx, N. Y.: Wildlife Conservation Society.

Aguirre Beltran, G. (1973a). Editorial, acción indigenista. *Boletín del Instituto Nacional Indigenista,* 235.

Aguirre Beltran, G. (1973b). Teoría y práctica de la educación indígena [Theory and practice of indigenous education]. *Collección Sep-Setentas,* (No. 64).

Aguirre Beltran, G. (1972). El fin del Indigenismo no es el Indígena: es Mexico. *El Dia,* (pp. 8-12). Mexico.

Albert, B. (1992). Indian lands, environmental policy and military geopolitics in the development of the Brazilian Amazon *Development and Change, 23,* 35-70.

Altman, I., & Low, S. (1992). *Place attachment. Human behavior and environment: advances in theory and research* (Vol. 8). New York: Plenum.

Altshuler, A., & Luberoff, D. (2003). *Megaprojects: The changing politics of urban public investments.* Washington, D.C.: The Brookings Institution.

Alvares, C., & Billorey, R. (1987). Damning the Narmada: The politics behind the destruction. *The Ecologist, 17*(2/3), 62-75.

Anderson, B. (1983). *Imagined communities: reflections on the origin and spread of nationalism.* London: Verso.

Appa, G., & Patel, G. (1996). Unrecognised, unnecessary and unjust displacement: Case studies from Gujarat, India. In C. McDowell, (Ed.), *Understanding impoverishment: The consequences of development induced displacement* (pp. 139-150). Providence and London: Berghahn Books.

Arnold, D. (1996). *The problem of nature: Environment, culture and European expansion.* Oxford: Blackwell.

Arquilla, J., & Ronfeldt, D. (n.d.). Cyberwar is coming! *Comparative Strategy, 12*, 2.

Aryal, M. (1995, July–August). Dams: The vocabulary of protest. *HIMAL*, 11–21.

Asian Development Bank. (1998). *Handbook on resettlement: A guide to good practice.* Manila, Philippines.

Ault, S. K. (1989). *The health effects of involuntary resettlement: Status of present knowledge and needs assessment, Report prepared for the task force on involuntary resettlement, American Anthropological Association.* Washington, D.C.: American Anthropological Association.

Autumn, S. (1994). Anthropologists, development and situated truth: The uses of debate. *Human Organization, 55*(4, 480–485).

Bandyopadhyay, J. (1992). From Environmental Conflicts to Sustainable Mountain Transformation: Ecological Action in the Garhwal Himalaya. In D. Ghai, & J. Vivian (Eds.), *Grassroots environmental action* (259–280), London: Routledge.

Bandyopadhyay, J. & Perveen, S. (2004). The doubtful science of interlinking. Retrieved from www.indiatogether.org/2004/feb/env-badsci-pi.htm

Bartolome, L. (1992, April). *Fighting leviathan: The articulation and spread of local opposition to hydrodevelopment in Brazil.* Paper presented at the 41st annual conference of the Center for Latin American Studies: Involuntary Migration and Resettlement in Latin America, Gainesville, Fla.

Bartolome, M., & Barabas. A. (1990). *La presa Cerro de Oro y el ingeniero El Gran Dios, Tomo II*, Mexico DF: Instituto Nacional Indigenista.

Bartolome, M., & Barabas, A. (1973). *Hydraulic ethnocide: The Mazatec and Chinantec people of Oaxaca, Mexico.* Copenhagen: International Work Group for Indigenous Affairs.

Basso, K. (1988). 'Speaking with names': Language and landscape among the western Apache. *Cultural Anthropology, 3*(2), 99–130.

Batliwala, S., & Brown, L. D. (2006). *Transnational civil society: An introduction.* Bloomfield, Conn.: Kumarian Press.

Bauman, Z. (1989). *Modernity and the Holocaust.* Ithaca, N.Y.: Cornell University Press.

Baviskar, A. (1992). Development, nature and resistance: The case of the Bhilala tribals in the Narmada Valley (Unpublished doctoral dissertation). Cornell University, Ithaca, N.Y.

Beck, U. (1995). *Ecological politics in an age of risk.* London: Frank Cass.

Beck, U. (1992). *Risk society: Towards a new modernity.* Thousand Oaks, Calif.: Sage Publications.

Bellah, R. N., Madsen, R., Sullivan, W. M., Swidler, A., & Tipton, S. M. (1985) *Habits of the heart: Individualism and commitment in American life.* New York: Harper and Row.

Bellinghausen, H. (2000). Problem in Montes Azules is more about war than fires. La Jornada, Mexico DF. Retrieved from www.nettime.org/lists-Archives/nettime-1-0005/msg00040.html

Bennett, J. (1996). *Human ecology as human behavior.* New Brunswick, N.J.: Transaction Publishers.

Bensman, D., & Lynch, R. (1987). *Rusted dreams: Hard times in a steel community.* New York: McGraw Hill.

Bercovitch, J., & Houston, A. (1996). *Resolving international conflicts.* Boulder, Colo.: Lynne Reinner Press.

Berger, P. (1976). *The pyramids of sacrifice.* New York: Doubleday.

Berman, M. (1982). *All that is solid melts into air.* New York: Simon and Schuster.

Berry, J. W., & Annis, R. C. (1974). Acculturative stress: The role of ecology, culture and differentiation. *Journal of Cross-Cultural Psychology, 5*(4), 382–406.

Biery-Hamilton, G. (1987). *Coping with change: The impact of the Tucurui Dam on an Amazonian community.* (Unpublished doctoral dissertation). University of Florida, Gainesville.

Bilharz, J. A. (1998). *The Allegany Senecas and Kinzua Dam: Forced relocation through two generations.* Lincoln: The University of Nebraska Press.

Bishop, R. C., Champ, P. A., & Mullarkey, D. J. (1995). Contingent valuation. In D. Bromley (Ed.), *Handbook of environmental economics* (pp. 629–654). Cambridge, Mass.: Blackwell.

Black, M. (2001). The day of judgement. *New Internationalist, 336,* 9–28.

Black, R. (2001). Environmental refugees: Myth or reality? *UNHCR Working Papers, 34,* 1–19.

Blaser, M., Feit, H. A., & McRae, G. (Eds.). (2004). *In the way of development: Indigenous peoples, life projects and globalization.* London and New York: Zed Books.

Bode, B. (1989). *No bells to toll: Destruction and creation in the Andes.* New York: Charles Scribner's Sons.

Bodley, J. (1994). *Cultural anthropology: Tribes, states and the global system.* Mountain View, Calif.: Mayfield Publishing Company.

Boggs, C. (1976). *Gramsci's Marxism.* London: Pluto Press.

Bohannan, P. (1959). The impact of money on an African subsistence economy. *The Journal of Economic History, 19*(4), 491–503.

Bolaños, O. (2008). *Constructing indigenous ethnicities and claiming land rights in the lower Tapajos-Arapiuns region, Brazilian Amazon.* (Unpublished doctoral dissertation). University of Florida, Gainesville.

Bosshard, P. (2007). *The sustainability of the World Bank's infrastructure lending.* A Report for the Charles Stewart Mott Foundation. Berkeley Calif.: International Rivers Network.

Bosshard, P., Brull, J., Horta, K., Lawrence, S., & Welch, C. (2003). Gambling with people's lives: What the World Bank's new high-risk/high reward strategy means for the poor and the environment. Retrieved from http://action.foe.org/content .jsp?content_KEY=2961

Boutté, M. I. (2002). Compensating for health: The acts and outcomes of atomic testing. *Human Organization, 61*(1), 41–50.

Breaking new ground. (2002) Mining, Minerals and Sustainable Development (MMSD) Final Report. London: International Institute for Environment and Development.

Brecher, J., Costello, T., & Smith, B. (1999). *Globalization from below: The power of solidarity.* Boston: South End Press.

Brechin, S. R., Wilshusen, P. R., Fortwangler, C. L., & West, P. C. (2002). Beyond the square wheel: Toward a more comprehensive understanding of biodiversity conservation as social and political process. *Society and Natural Resources, 15*(1), 41–64.

Bretton Woods Project. Bretton Woods Institutions: Background to the issues. Retrieved from http://www.brettonwoodsproject.org/background/index.shtml

Brooks, R. L (Ed.). (1999). *When sorry isn't enough: The controversy over apologies and reparations for human injustice.* New York: New York University Press.

Brown, B., & Perkins, D. D. (1992). Disruptions in place attachment. In I. Altman, & S. Low (Eds.), *Place attachment* (279–303). New York: Plenum Press.

Call, W. (2002). Resisting the Plan Puebla-Panama, Global Exchange. Retrieved from http://www.globalexchange.org/countries/americas/mexico/ppp/318.html.pf

Capka, J. R. (2004). Megaprojects—they are a different breed. *Public Roads, 68*(1), 2–9.

Carpenter, D. M., & Ross, J. K. (2007). Victimizing the vulnerable: The demographics of eminent domain abuse. Arlington, Va.: Institute for Justice.

Carson, R. (1962). *Silent spring.* Boston: Houghton Mifflin.

Caruso, E., Colchester, M., Mackat, F., Hilyard, N., & Nettleton, G. (2003). *Extracting promises: Indigenous peoples, extractive industries and the World Bank.* Moreton-in-Marsh, U.K.: Forest Peoples Programme and Baguio City, Philippines: Tebtebba Foundation. Retrieved from http://bankwatch.ecn.cz/eir/reports/vol6_3.pdf

Celestino, E. S. (1999, August). *Nadando contracorriente en el Balsas.* Paper presented in the seminar-workshop on Forced Relocation from Disaster Risk, Universidad Autonoma de Colima, Mexico.

Cernea, M. M. (2009). Financing for development: Benefit sharing mechanisms in population resettlement. In A. Oliver-Smith (Ed.), *Dispossession and development: The crisis of forced displacement and resettlement* (pp. 49–76).

Cernea, M. M. (2003). For a new economics of resettlement: A sociological critique of the compensation principle. *International Social Science Journal, 55*(17), 37–45.

Cernea, M. M. (1999). *The economics of involuntary resettlement: Questions and challenges.* Washington, D.C.: The World Bank.

Cernea, M. M. (1997). The risks and reconstruction model for resettling displaced populations. *World Development, 25*(10), 1569–1588.

Cernea, M. M. (1993). Anthropological and sociological research for policy development on population resettlement. In M. M. Cernea, & S. E. Guggenheim (Eds.), *Anthropological approaches to resettlement* (pp. 13–38). Boulder, Colo.: Westview Press.

Cernea, M. M. (1990). Poverty risks from population displacement in water resources development. HIID Development Discussion Paper (No. 355). Harvard University, Cambridge, Mass.

Cernea, M. M. (1988). Involuntary resettlement in development projects. Washington, D.C.: The World Bank.

Cernea, M. M., & Guggenheim, S. (1993). *Anthropological approaches to resettlement.* Boulder, Colo.: Westview Press.

Cernea, M. M., & McDowell, C. (2000). *Risk and reconstruction: Experiences of settlers and refugees.* Washington, D.C.: The World Bank.

Cervantes Gomez, J. (1990, November 29). Inundará 34 pueblos nahuatlacas la presa de Tetelcingo. *El Universal,* p. 1.

Chadha, A. (1999). The anatomy of dispossession: A study in the displacement of the tribals from their traditional landscape in the Narmada Valley due to the Sardar

Sarovar Project. In P. J. Ucko, & R. Layton (Eds.), *The archaeology and anthropology of landscape* (pp. 146-158). London: Routledge.

Chambers, R. (1997). *Whose reality counts? Putting the first last*. London: Intermediate Technology Development Group.

Chambers, R. (1970). *The Volta resettlement experience*. New York: Praeger Publishers.

Chernela, J. (1988). Potential impacts of a proposed Amazon hydropower project. *Cultural Survival, 12*(2), 20-24.

Christiansen, U. R. (2001). In C. Lefebvre, & S. K. Olsen (Eds.), *URC HC*. [A catalog published in connection with the exhibition by U. R. Christiansen, & H. Christiansen at the Venice Biennale]. Copenhagen: Danish Contemporary Art Foundations.

Clark, D. (2003). Singrauli: An unfulfilled struggle for justice. In D. Clark, J. Fox, & K. Treakle (Eds.), *Demanding accountability: Civil society claims and the World Bank Inspection Panel* (pp. 167-190). Lanham, Md.: Rowman and Littlefield.

Clark, D. (2009). *An overview of revisions to the World Bank resettlement policy*. In L. Mehta (Ed.), Displaced by development: Confronting marginalization and gender injustice (pp. 195-224). Delhi, India: Sage.

Clark, D., Fox, J., & Treakle, K. (Eds). (2003). *Demanding accountability: Civil society claims and the World Bank Inspection Panel*. Lanham, Md.: Rowman and Littlefield.

Cleaver, F. (1999). Paradoxes of participation: Questioning participatory approaches to development. *Journal of International Development, 11*, 597-612.

Colajacomo, J. (1999). The Chixoy Dam: the Maya Achi genocide: The story of a forced resettlement. *Indigenous Affairs, 3-4*, 64-79.

Colchester, M. (1999). Sharing power: Dams, indigenous peoples and ethnic minorities. *Indigenous Affairs, 3-4*, 4-54.

Collins, J. (2003). *Threads: Gender, labor and power in the global apparel industry*. Chicago: University of Chicago Press.

Colson, E. (1999). Gendering those uprooted by development. In D. Indra (Ed.), *Engendering forced migration: Theory and practice* (pp. 23-39). New York: Berghahn Books.

Colson, E. (1971). *The social consequences of resettlement: The impact of the Kariba resettlement upon the Gwembe Tonga*. Manchester, U.K.: Manchester University Press.

Comaroff, J., & Comaroff, J. L. (2001). Millenial capitalism: First thoughts on a second coming. In J. Comaroff, & J. L. Comaroff (Eds.). *Millenial capitalism and the culture of neoliberalism* (pp. 1-56). Durham, N.C.: Duke University Press.

Comissao Regional dos Atingidos de Barragem. (1988). [Leaflet]. Brazil.

Consejo Autonomo de Ricardo Flores Magon. (2002). Retrieved from http://www.jornada.unam.mx/2004/07/19/oja87-magon.html

Consejo Autónomo Ricardo Flores Magón, Sobre la Reserva Integral de la Biosfera de Montes Azules. (2002, March 25) Retrieved from http://cedoz.org/cgi-bin/htmldoc/site/print.php?doc=502

Contreras, A. (1995). *La marcha historica*. Cochabamba, Bolivia: Centro de Documentacion e Informacion-Bolivia.

Conuel, T. (1981). *Quabbin: The accidental wilderness*. Lincoln, Mass.: Massachusetts Audubon Society.

Cordillera Peoples Alliance/International Rivers Network. (2001). *Dams in the Cordillera*. Berkeley, Calif.: International Rivers Network.

Coronil, F. (2001). Toward a critique of globalcentrism: Speculations on capitalism's nature. In J. Comaroff, & J. L. Comaroff (Eds.), *Millenial capitalism and the culture of neoliberalism* (pp. 63–87). Durham, N.C.: Duke University Press.

Corrucini, R., & Kaul, S. (1983). The epidemiological transition and anthropology of minor chronic non-infectious diseases. *Medical Anthropology, 7*, 36.

Cowen, M. P., & Shenton, R. W. (1996). *Doctrines of development*. London and New York: Routledge.

Crocker, D. A. (1991). Toward development ethics. *World Development, 19*(5), 457–483.

Cronon, W. (1983) *Changes in the land: Indians, colonists and the ecology of New England.* New York: Farrar, Strauss and Giroux.

Crossley, M. (1986, April 26). Ancient Olmec site unearthed in Mexico. *The Washington Post*.

Curle, A. (1971). *Making peace.* London: Tavistock Publications.

Dasgupta, P., & Maler, K. G. (1989). Social cost benefit analysis and soil erosion. In F. Archibugi & P. Nijkamp (Eds.), *Economy and ecology: Towards sustainable development* (pp. 221–260). Boston: Kluwer Publishers.

Davidheiser, M. (2000). *Negotiations between unequals: A review of the literature.* Unpublished manuscript, University of Florida, Gainesville.

Davidheiser, M. (n.d.). *The Navajo-Hopi land dispute and Navajo relocation resisters: Place attachment, the construction of meaning and identity and adaptation to change.* Unpublished manuscript.

De Vries, G. (2000). *Post-disaster reconstruction and income diversification in La Mosquitia, Honduras.* Unpublished master's thesis, University of Florida, Gainesville.

de Wet, C. (2009) Does development displace ethics? The challenge of forced resettlement. In A. Oliver-Smith (Ed.), *Development and dispossession: The crisis of forced displacement and resettlement* (pp. 77–96).

de Wet, C. (2006). Risk, complexity and local initiative in involuntary resettlement outcomes. In C. de Wet (Ed.), *Development-induced displacement: Problems, policies and people* (pp. 180–202). Oxford and New York: Berghahn Books.

Dhagamwar, V., Thral, E. G., & Singh, M. (1995). The Sardar Sarovar Project: A study in sustainable development? In W. F. Fisher (Ed.), *Toward sustainable development: Struggles over India's Narmada River* (pp 265–288). Armonk, N.Y., and London: M.E. Sharpe.

Dove, M. (1983). Theories of swidden agriculture and the political economy of ignorance. *Agroforestry Systems, 1*, 85–99.

Downing, T. E. (2002). Creating poverty: The flawed economic logic of the World Bank's revised involuntary resettlement policy. *Forced Migration Review, 12*, 13–14.

Downing, T. E., & Kushner, G. (Eds.). (1988). *Human rights and anthropology.* Cultural Survival Report (24). Cambridge, Mass.: Cultural Survival Inc.

Downing, T. E. & Moles, J. (2001). The World Bank denies indigenous peoples their right to prior informed consent. *Cultural Survival Quarterly 25*(4), 68–69.

Drucker, C. (1985). Dam the Chico: Hydropower development and tribal resistance. *The Ecologist, 15*(4), 149–157.

Drydyk, J., & Elliot, R. (2001). International policy guidelines for development-induced displacement: A critical review. Ethics of Development-Induced Displacement project, York University, Toronto, Canada.

Duncan, D. E. (2001, June 14). San Francisco bust. Morning Edition [Radio broadcast]. Washington, D.C.: National Public Radio.

Dwivedi, R. (1999). Displacement, risks and resistance: Local perceptions and actions in the Sardar Sarovar. *Development and Change, 30,* 43–78.

Dwivedi, R. (1998). Resisting dams and development: Contemporary significance of the campaign against the Narmada projects in India. *European Journal of Development Research, 10*(2), 135–179.

Dwivedi, R. (1997). *Why some people resist and others do not: Local perceptions and actions over displacement risks on the Sardar Sarovar.* Working Paper Series (No. 265). The Hague: Institute of Social Studies.

Edelstein, M. R. (1988). *Contaminated communities: The social and psychological impacts of residential toxic residue.* Boulder, Colo.: Westview.

The equator principles: A framework for banks to manage environmental and social issues in project financing. (2003). Retrieved from http://www.equator-principles.com

Eriksen, J. H. (1999). Comparing the economic planning for voluntary and involuntary resettlement. In M. M. Cernea (Ed.), *The economics of involuntary resettlement: Questions and challenges* (pp. 83–146). Washington, D.C.: The World Bank.

Eriksen, K. T. (1994). *A new species of trouble: Explorations in disaster, trauma and community.* New York: W. W. Norton.

Escobar, A. (2000). Culture sits in places: Reflections on globalism and subaltern strategies of localization. *Political Geography, 20,* 139–174.

Escobar, A. (1999). After nature: Steps to an antiessentialist political ecology. *Current Anthropology, 40*(1), 1–30).

Escobar, A. (1991). Anthropology and the development encounter: The making and marketing of development anthropology. *American Ethnologist, 18*(4) 658–682.

Espeland, W. (1999, October). *Value matters.* Paper presented at the conference The Cost-Benefit Analysis Dilemma: Strategies and Alternatives, Yale University, New Haven, Conn.

Espeland, W. (1998). *The struggle for water: Politics, rationality, and identity in the American Southwest.* Chicago: University of Chicago Press.

Ettenger, K. (1998). A river that was once so strong and deep: Local reflections on the Eastmain Diversion, James Bay Hydroelectric Project. In J. M. Donahue, & B. R. Johnston (Eds), *Water, Culture and Power* (pp. 47–71). Washington, D.C.: Island Press.

Evans, W. (2001). 'Women with the strength of the earth' keep Biobio Dam at bay. *World Rivers Review, 16*(3), 6–7.

Fahim, H. (1983). *Egyptian Nubians: Resettlement and years of coping.* Salt Lake City: University of Utah Press.

Falk, R. (1983). *The end of world order.* London: Holmes and Meier.

Fantasia, R. (1988). *Cultures of solidarity.* Berkeley: University of California Press.

Farmer, P. (2004). An anthropology of structural violence. *Current Anthropology, 45,* 305–325.

Feeney, P. (2000). Globalization and Accountability: The corporate sector in involuntary displacement and resettlement. *Forced Migration Review, 8,* 22–24.

Feit, H. (2004). James Bay Cree's life projects and politics: Histories of place, animal partners and enduring relationships. In M. Blaser, H. A. Feit, & G. McRae (Eds.), *In the way of development: Indigenous peoples, life projects and globalization* (pp. 92–110). London and New York: Zed Books.

Ferguson, J. (1990). *The anti-politics machine: Development, depoliticization and bureaucratic power in Lesotho.* Cambridge, U.K.: Cambridge University Press.

Ferree, M. M. (1992). The political context of rationality: Rational choice theory and resource mobilization. In A. D. Morris, & C. M. Mueller (Eds.), *Frontiers in social movement theory* (pp. 29–52). New Haven, Conn.: Yale University Press.

Fisher, J. (1996). Grassroots organizations and grassroots support organizations: Patterns of interaction. In E. Moran (Ed.), *Transforming societies, transforming anthropology* (pp. 57–102). Ann Arbor: The University of Michigan Press.

Fisher, R., & Ury, W. (1981). *Getting to yes: Negotiating agreement without giving in.* New York: Penguin Books.

Fisher, W. F. (2009). Local displacement, global activism: DFDR and transnational advocacy. In A. Oliver-Smith (Ed.), *Dispossession and development: The crisis of forced displacement and resettlement* (163–180). Santa Fe: SAR Press.

Fisher, W. F. (1999). Going under: Indigenous peoples and the struggle against large dams: Introduction. *Cultural Survival Quarterly, 23*(3), 29–32.

Fisher, W. F. (1997). Doing good? The Politics and anti-politics of NGO practice. *Annual Review of Anthropology, 26,* 439–464.

Fisher, W. F. (Ed.). (1995). *Toward sustainable development: Struggles over India's Narmada River.* Armonk, N.Y., & London: M.E. Sharpe.

Fisher, W. H. (1994). Megadevelopment, environmentalism, and resistance: The institutional context of Kayapo indigenous politics in central Brazil. *Human Organization, 53*(3), 220–232.

Fixico, D. L. (1990). *Termination and relocation: Federal Indian policy.* Albuquerque: University of New Mexico Press.

Flyvbjerg, B., Bruzelius, N., & Rothengatter, W. (2003). *Megaprojects and risk: An anatomy of ambition.* Cambridge, U.K.: Cambridge University Press.

Fortwangler, C. (2003). Social justice, biodiversity, conservation and protected areas. In S. R. Brechin, P. R. Wilshusen, C. F. Fortwangler, & P. C. West (Eds.), *Contested nature: Power, protected areas, and the dispossessed-promoting biodiversity conservation with social justice in the 21st century.* New York: SUNY Press.

Foucault, M. (1990). *The history of sexuality: Volume I, an introduction.* New York: Vintage Books.

Foweraker, J. (2001, February 19). *Towards a political sociology of social mobilization in Latin America.* Paper presented at the conference Latin American Sociology and the Sociology of Latin America, University of Florida, Gainesville.

Foweraker, J. (1995). *Theorizing social movements.* London: Pluto Press.

Fox, J. A., & Brown, L. D. (Eds.). (1998). *The struggle for accountability: The World Bank, NGOs and grassroots movements.* Cambridge, Mass.: The MIT Press.

Free Burma Coalition. (n.d.). Unocal, A New Breed of Corporate Greed. Retrieved from www.freeburmacoalition.org

Fried, M. (1963). Grieving for a lost home. In L. Duhl (Ed.), *The urban condition: People and policy in the metropolis* (pp. 359–379). New York: Basic Books.

Gans, H. J (1962). *The urban villagers: Group and class in the life of Italian Americans.* Glencoe, Ill.: The Free Press.

Garcia, M. (2000). Alto Balsas, Una decada de lucha indigena. *Milenio Diario.com .mx.* www.mileniodiario.com.mx/anteriores/23102000/te3.htm

Garcia, M. (1999, August). *Estrategia de Prensa de los nahua del Alto Balsas, Guerrero, en contra de la construcción de la presa San Juan Tetelcingo, 1990–92.* Paper presented in the Seminario-Taller, Sobre Reubicaciones Forzosas por Riesgo a Desastres, Universidad de Colima, Colima, Mexico.

Garcia Canclini, N. (1993). *Transforming modernity.* Austin: University of Texas Press.

Geertz, C. (1966). Religion as a cultural system. In: M. P. Banton (Ed.), *Anthropological approaches to the study of religion* (pp. 1–46). New York: Frederick A. Praeger Press.

Geisler, C., & de Sousa, R. (2001). From refuge to refugee: The African case. *Public Administration and Development 21*(2), 159–170.

Gellert, P. K., & Lynch, B. D. (2003). Mega-projects as displacements. *International Social Sciences Journal, 175,* 15–25.

Ghai, D., & Vivian, J. (1992). *Grassroots environmental action.* London: Routledge.

Ghimire, K. (1994). Parks and people: Livelihood issues in national parks management in Thailand and Madagascar. *Development and Change, 25,* 195–229.

Gibson, D. (1993). *The politics of involuntary resettlement: World Bank supported projects in Asia.* (Unpublished doctoral dissertation). Duke University, Durham, N.C.

Giddens, A. (1990) *The consequences of modernity.* Cambridge, U.K.: Polity Press.

Giddens, A. (1984). *The constitution of society: Outline of the theory of structuration.* Berkeley: The University of California Press.

Gleick, J. (1987). *Chaos: Making a new science.* New York: Penguin Books.

Godrej, D. (2007, May). Daring to dream. *New Internationalist* (400). Retrieved from http://www.newint.org/features/2007/05/01/keynote

Goethe, J. W. von. (1963). *Goethe's Faust.* (W. Kaufmann, Trans.). Garden City, N.Y.: Doubleday and Company.

Goodland, R. (2007, October 23). How to aid destruction. *The Guardian.* Retrieved from http://www.guardian.co.U.K./commentisfree/2007/oct/23/comment.globalisation

Goodland, R. (2004) Free, prior and informed consent. *Sustainable Development Law and Policy, IV*(2), 66–75.

Goulet, D. (1971). *The cruel choice: A new concept in the theory of development.* New York: Atheneum.

Grabska, K & Mehta, L. (2008). Introduction. In K. Grabska, & L. Mehta (Eds.), *Forced displacement: Why rights matter* (pp. 1–25). New York: Palgrave MacMillan.

Gray, A. (1998). Development policy, development protest: The World Bank, indigenous peoples, and NGOs. In J. A. Fox, & L. D. Brown (Eds.), *The struggle for accountability: The World Bank, NGOs and grassroots movements* (pp. 267–301). Cambridge, Mass.: The MIT Press.

Gray, A. (1996). Indigenous resistance to involuntary relocation. In C. McDowell

(Ed.), *Understanding impoverishment: The consequences of development induced displacement* (pp. 99–122). Providence & London: Berghahn Books.

Greene, J. R. (1985). *The day four Quabbin towns died.* Athol, Mass.: The Transcript Press.

Greenwood, D. (1977). Culture by the pound: An anthropological perspective on tourism as cultural commoditization. In V. Smith (Ed.), *Hosts and guests: The anthropology of tourism* (pp. 129–138). Philadelphia: The University of Pennsylvania Press.

Gualdoni, F. (2006, April 25). La Gran Puerta de Asia: Panama busca ser el paso de las crecientes exportaciones chinas hacia el Mercado de EE UU. *El Pais.*

Guardianes de los rios: Guia para activistas. (2000). Berkeley, Calif.: International Rivers Network. Retrieved from http://www.internationalrivers.org/en/am%C3%A9rica-latina/mesoam%C3%A9rica/los-guardianes-de-los-r%C3%ADos

Guggenheim, S. (1993). Peasants, planners and participation: Resettlement in Mexico. In M. Cernea, & S. Guggenheim (Eds.), *Anthropological approaches to resettlement* (pp. 201–228). Boulder, Colo.: Westview Press.

Guha, R. (1997) The authoritarian biologist and the arrogance of anti-humanism: Wildlife conservation in the Third World. *The Ecologist*, 27, 14–20.

Guha, R., & Martinez-Alier, J. (1997). *Varieties of environmentalism: Essays north and south.* London: Earthscan.

Gurung, B. (1997). The perceived environment as a system of knowledge and meaning: A study of the Mewhang Rai of Eastern Nepal. In K. Seeland (Ed.), *Nature is culture: Indigenous knowledge and socio-cultural aspects of trees and forests in non-European cultures* (pp. 19–27). London: Intermediate Technologies Publications.

Haggard, S. (1990). *Pathways from the periphery: The politics of growth in newly industrializing countries.* Ithaca, N.Y.: Cornell University Press.

Hansen, A. (1993). African refugees: Defining and defending their human rights. In G. H. Cohen, & W. Nagan (Eds.), *Human rights and governance in Africa* (pp. 139–167). Gainesville: University Presses of Florida.

Hansen, A., & Oliver-Smith, A. (Eds.). (1982). *Involuntary migration and resettlement.* Boulder, Colo.: Westview Press.

Hartmann, J. (2003, February). *Power and resistance in the later Foucault.* Paper presented at the 3rd annual meeting of the Foucault Circle, John Carroll University, Cleveland, Ohio.

Harvey, D. (2001). Cosmopolitanism and the banality of geographic evils. In J. Comaroff, & J. L. Comaroff (Eds.), *Millenial capitalism and the culture of neoliberalism* (pp. 271–310. Durham, N.C.: Duke University Press.

Harvey, D. (1996). *Justice, nature and the geography of difference.* Oxford, U.K.: Blackwell.

Hechter, M. (1987). *Principles of group solidarity.* Berkeley: University of California Press.

Heijmans, A. (2001, June). *Vulnerability: A matter of perception.* Paper presented at the International Workshop-Conference, Vulnerability in Disaster Theory and Practice, Wageningen University, The Netherlands.

Henry, J. (1964). *Jungle people, a Kaingang tribe of the highlands of Brazil.* New York: Vintage Books.

Hewitt, K. (1997). *Regions of risk: A geographical introduction to disaster.* Essex, U.K.: Longman.

Hewitt, K. (1983). *Interpretations of calamity.* Boston: Allen and Unwin.

Hilhorst, D. (2004). Complexity and diversity: Unlocking social domains of disaster response. In G. Bankoff, G. Frerks, & D. Hilhorst (Eds.), *Mapping vulnerability: Disaster, development, and people* (pp. 52–67). London: Earthscan.

Hilhorst, D. (2000). *Records and reputations: Everyday politics of a Philippine development NGO.* (Doctoral dissertation). Wageningen University, Wageningen, The Netherlands.

Hjort, A. (1985). A critique of "ecological" models of land use. *Nomadic Peoples, 10,* 11–27.

Hobbes, T. (1998). *Leviathan.* Oxford, U.K.: Oxford University Press.

Holling, C. S. (1994). An ecologist's view of the Malthusian conflict. In K. Lindahl-Kiessling, & H. Landberg (Eds.), *Population, economic development, and the environment* (pp. 79–103). New York: Oxford University Press.

Holman, P. A. (1996). Refugee resettlement in the United States. In D. W. Haines (Ed.), *Refugees in America in the 1990s* (pp. 3–27). Westport, Conn.: Greenwood Press.

Human Rights Watch/Asia. (1995). The Three Gorges Dam in China: Forced resettlement, suppression of dissent and labor rights (7) 2.

Ignatieff, M. (2001). *Human rights as politics and idolatry.* Princeton, N.J.: Princeton University Press.

Igoe, J. (2004). *Conservation and globalization: A study of national parks and indigenous communities from East Africa to South Dakota.* Belmont, Calif.: Wadsworth.

India's river-linking scheme worries the region's journalists. (2003). Planet's Voice. Retrieved from http://www.planets-voice.org/_interface/news.shtml?x-921

Indra, D. (1999). *Engendering forced migration: Theory and practice.* Oxford and New York: Berghahn Books.

International Rivers Network. (2000). Discover Three Gorges. [Brochure]. Berkeley, Calif.: International Rivers Network.

International Union for the Conservation of Nature. (1980). *World conservation strategy.* Gland, Switzerland: IUCN/United Nations Environment Programme/World Wildlife Fund. Retieved from http://data.iucn.org/dbtw-wpd/edocs/wcs-004.pdf

International Union for the Conservation of Nature/World Commission on Protected Areas. (2004). The Durban action plan. Retrieved from http://www.iucn.org/themes/wcpa/wpc2003/english/outputs/durban/durbactplan.htm

International Water Management Institute. Retrieved from http://nlrp.imwi.org/Pdocs/PrjProposal.asp

Jackson, J L., Jr. (2001). *Harlemworld: Doing race and class in contemporary black America.* Chicago: University of Chicago Press.

Jacoby, K. (2000). *Crimes against nature: Squatters, poachers, thieves and the hidden history of American conservation.* Berkeley: University of California Press.

Jeffrey, J. L. (2000). *The siege of Zapata: Long term consequences of displacement in a border town.* (Unpublished doctoral dissertation). University of Florida, Gainesville.

Jing, J. (1999). Villages dammed, villages repossessed: A memorial movement in Northwest China. *American Anthropologist, 26*(2), 324–343.

Johnston, B. R. (2009). Development disaster, reparations, and the right to remedy: The case of the Chixoy Dam, Guatemala. In A. Oliver-Smith (Ed.), *Dispossession and development: The crisis of forced displacement and resettlement* (pp. 201–224). Santa Fe: SAR Press.

Johnston, B. R. (2005). Chixoy Dam legacies: Volumes 1–5. Center for Political Ecology: Santa Cruz, Calif. Retrieved from http://www.centerforpoliticalecology .org

Johnston, B. R. (2000, July). *Reparations and the right to remedy.* Briefing paper prepared for the World Commission on Dams. Retrieved from http://web.world bank.org/WBSITE/EXTERNAL/TOPICS/EXTSOCIALDEVELOP MENT/EXTINVRES/0,,contentMDK:20486322~menuPK:1242304~page PK:148956~piPK:216618~theSitePK:410235,00.html

Johnston, B. R. (1994). *Who pays the price: The sociocultural context of environmental crisis.* Covelo, Calif.: Island Press.

Johnston, B. R., & Garcia-Downing, C. (2004). Hydroelectric development on the Bio-Bio River, Chile: Anthropology and human rights advocacy. In M. Blaser, H. A. Feit, & G. McRae (Eds.), *In the way of development: Indigenous peoples, life projects and globalization* (pp. 211–231). London & New York: Zed Books.

Josephson, P. R. (2002). *Industrialized nature: Brute force technology and the transformation of the natural world.* Washington, D.C.: Island Press.

Joshi, V. (1991). *Rehabilitation, A Promise to Keep, A Case of SSP,* Ahmedabad, Gujarat: Tax Publications.

Jun, M. (2005). Will China's rivers survive the next 20 years? *World Rivers Review, 20*(4), 12–13.

Kanbur, R. (2003). Development economics and the compensation principle. *International Social Science Journal, 55*(175), 27–35.

Kapur, D., Lewis, J. P., & Webb, R. (1997). *The World Bank: Its first half-century.* Washington, D.C.: Brookings Institution Press.

Kearney, M. (1996). *Reconceptualizing the peasantry: Anthropology in global perspective.* Boulder, Colo.: Westview.

Kearney, M. (1995). The local and the global: The anthropology of globalization and transnationalism. *Annual Review of Anthropology, 24,* 54–65.

Kedia, S. (2009). Health consequences of dam construction and involuntary resettlement. In A. Oliver-Smith (Ed.), *Dispossession and development: The crisis of forced displacement and resettlement* (pp. 97–118). Santa Fe: SAR Press.

Kedia, S. (2002, May). *Assessing and mitigating the health impacts of involuntary resettlement: The Tehri hydroelectric dam project.* Paper presented at the International Symposium on Resettlement and Social Development, Nanjing, Jiangsu Province, China.

Kedia, S., & van Willigen, J. (2005). *Applied anthropology: Domains of application.* Westport, Conn.: Praeger Press.

Khagram, S. (2004). *Dams and development: Transnational struggles for water and power.* Ithaca, N.Y.: Cornell University Press.

Khagram, S. (1999). *Dams, democracy and development: Transnational struggles for power and water.* (Unpublished doctoral dissertation). Stanford University, Stanford, Calif.

Khera, S., & Mariella, P. S. (1982). The Fort McDowell Yavapai: A case of long-term resistance to relocation. In A. Hansen, & A. Oliver-Smith (Eds.), *Involuntary migration and resettlement* (150–178). Boulder, Colo.: Westview Press.

Kihisang Magbubukid ng Pilipinas (Peasant Movement of the Philippines). (2001). *Hacienda Looc.* Retrieved from www.geocities.com/kmp_ph/strug/looc/looc.html

Kirsch, S. (2001). Lost worlds: Environmental disaster, "culture loss," and the law. *Current Anthropology, 42*(2), 167–198.

Klicksberg, B. (2001). *Towards an intelligent state.* International Institute of Administrative Sciences Monographs, Vol. 15. Amsterdam, The Netherlands: IOS Press.

A knife in the water. (2008). Retrieved from http://www.internationalrivers.org/en/blog/glenn-switkes/knife-water

Koenig, D. (2001). *Toward local development and mitigating impoverishment in development-induced displacement and resettlement.* Final report prepared for ESCOR R7644 and the Research Programme on Development Induced Displacement and Resettlement, Refugee Studies Centre, University of Oxford, U.K.

Koenig, D. (1995). Women and resettlement. In R. S. Gllin, A. Ferguson, & J. Harper (Eds.), *The women and international development annual.* Boulder, Colo.: Westview Press.

Kothari, S., & Harcourt, W. (2004). Introduction: The violence of development. *Development, 47*(1), 3–7.

Kroll-Smith, S., & Floyd, H. H. (1997). *Bodies in protest: Environmental illness and the struggle over medical knowledge.* New York: New York University Press.

Kuhn, T. (1970). *The structure of scientific revolutions.* Chicago: University of Chicago Press.

Kumar, C. (1996). It's virtually politics: Information technology and transnational activism in the developing world. (Unpublished doctoral dissertation). University of Illinois at Urbana-Champaign.

Kushner, G. (1988). Powerless people: The administered community. In T. E. Downing, & G. Kushner (Eds.), *Human rights and anthropology* (Cultural Survival Report 24) (pp. 27–42). Cambridge, MA: Cultural Survival Inc.

Lawrence, R. (1986). Showdown at Big Mountain. *In These Times, 10,* 14.

Layard, R., & Glaister, S. (1994). *Cost-benefit analysis.* Cambridge, U.K.: Cambridge University Press.

Leal, A. (1991, January 2). La presa San Juan Tetelcingo, una amenaza a la sobrevivencia de 22 comunidades indigenas. *Uno Mas Uno,* p. 23.

Ledec, G., Quintero, J. D., & Mejia, M. C. (1997). Good dams and bad dams: Environmental and social criteria for choosing hydroelectric project sites. Washington, D.C.: The World Bank.

Legal Information Institute. (2005). Supreme Court of the United States, Kelo et al. v City of New London et al. Retrieved from http://.law.cornell.edu//supct/html/04-108.ZS.html

Leiderman, E. (1997, October). Environmental refugees from energy projects: Exploration, extraction, construction, operation and waste disposal. Paper prepared for the Symposium on Global Connections: Environmental Justice in the Americas and Abroad, annual meeting of the Geological Society of America, Salt Lake City, Utah.

Leiderman, E. (1995). Reviewing global awareness of environmental refugees: 1985–95. Paper prepared for the Symposium on International Change: Third World

Development—Why Is the Future Not What It Used to Be? University of New Hampshire, Durham, N.H.

Levine, A. G. (1982). *Love Canal: Science, politics and people.* Lexington, Mass.: Lexington Books-D.C. Heath and Company.

Levine, S., & Lurie, N. O. (Eds.). (1968). *The American Indian today.* Baltimore, Md.: Penguin Books.

Lifton, R. J. (1970). *Boundaries: Psychological man in revolution.* New York: Random House.

Lifton, R. J. (1967). *Death in life: Survivors of Hiroshima.* New York: Random House.

Ling, C. Y., & Ferrari, M. F. (1995, June–July). Golf wars. *Toward Freedom, 44*(3), 8–9.

Little, P. E. (1999). Political ecology as ethnography: The case of Ecuador's Aguarico River Basin. In *Serie Antropologia* (No. 258). Brasilia: Departamento de Antropologia, Universidade de Brasilia.

Lohmann, L. (1999). Forest cleansing: Racial oppression in scientific nature conservation. Cornerhouse Briefing 13.

Magee, P. L. (1989). Peasant political identity and the Tucurui Dam: A case study of the island dwellers of Para, Brazil. *The Latinamericanist, 24*(1), 6–10.

Mahalia, B. (1994). Letter from a tribal village. *Lokayan Bulletin, 11*(2/3).

Malkki, L. (1992). National Geographic: The rooting of peoples and the territorialization of national identity among scholars and refugees. *Cultural Anthropology, 7*(1), 24–44.

Mariella, P. (1989). *Land is like diamonds, money is like ice.* Paper presented at the annual meetings of the Society for Applied Anthropology, Santa Fe, New Mexico.

Marris, P. (1975). *Loss and change.* New York: Anchor Books.

Marshall, G. (1983). Some remarks on the study of working class consciousness. *Politics and Society, 12*, 3.

McAdam, D., McCarthy, J. D., & Zald, M. N. (1988). Social movements. In N. Smelser (Ed.), *Handbook of sociology* (695–737). Newbury Park, Calif.: Sage Publications.

McAdam, D. & Snow, D. A. (1997). *Social movements: Readings on their emergence, mobilization and dynamics.* Los Angeles, Calif.: Roxbury Publishing Company.

McCollough, D. (1977). *The path between the seas: The creation of the Panama Canal, 1870–1914.* New York: Simon and Schuster.

McCully, P. (1999). After the deluge: The urgent need for reparations for dam victims. *Cultural Survival Quarterly, 23*(3), 33–36.

McCully, P. (1997). *A critique of "The World Bank's experience with large dams: A preliminary view of impacts."* Unpublished manuscript.

McCully, P. (1996). *Silenced rivers: The ecology and politics of large dams.* London: Zed Books.

McDonald, M. D. (1993). Dams, displacement and development: A resistance movement in Southern Brazil. In J. Friedmann, & H. Rangan (Eds.), *In defense of livelihood: Comparative studies in environmental action* (79–105). West Hartford, Conn.: Kumarian Press.

McDowell, C. (1996). Introduction. In C. McDowell (Ed.), *Understanding impoverishment: The consequences of development-induced displacement* (pp. 1–9). Providence & Oxford: Berghahn Books.

Mehta, L. (ed.) (2009). *Displaced by development: Confronting marginalization and gender injustice.* New Delhi: Sage.

Mehta, L (2008). Why are human rights violated with impunity? Forced displacement in India's Narmada Valley. In K. Grabska, & L. Mehta (Eds.), *Forced displacement: Why rights matter* (pp. 201–221). New York: Palgrave MacMillan.

Melucci, A. (1988). Getting involved: Identity and mobilization in social movements. In B. Klandermans, H. Kriese, & S. Tarrow (Eds.), *International social movement research: Vol.1. From structure to action: Comparing social movement research across cultures* (pp. 329–348). London: JAI Press.

Mexico Solidarity Network. (2001, May 8–14). "Indigenous Law" sent to states for approval; CNI launches campaign for rejection. Mexico Solidarity Network Weekly News Summary. Retrieved from http://www.mexicosolidarity.org/news/summary010514.html

Minewatch. (2000). Women united and struggling for our land, our lives, our future. Proceedings of the First International Conference on Women and Mining. London: Minewatch.

Moore, B., Jr. (1966). *Social origins of dictatorship and democracy: Lord and peasant in the making of the modern world.* Boston: Beacon Press.

Moran, E. (Ed.). (1996). *Transforming societies, transforming anthropology.* Ann Arbor: The University of Michigan Press.

More dams in the works for Brazil. (1989). *World Rivers Review, 4*(3), 3,7.

Morse, B., & Berger, T. (1992). *Sardar Sarovar: Report of the independent review.* Ottawa, Canada: Resource Futures International.

Morvaridi, B. (2008). Rights and development-induced displacement: Risk management or social protection?. In K. Grabska, & L. Mehta (Eds.), *Forced displacement: Why rights matter* (pp. 50–70). New York: Palgrave MacMillan.

Mueller, C. M. (1992). Building social movement theory. In A. D. Morris, & C. M. Mueller (Eds.), *Frontiers in social movement theory* (pp. 3–25). New Haven, Conn.: Yale University Press.

Munn, N. (1990). Constructing regional worlds in experience: Kula exchange, witchcraft and Gawan local events. *Man, 25* (New Series), 1–17.

Murphy, R. (1994). *Rationality and nature.* Boulder, Colo.: Westview Press.

Myers, N. (1997). Environmental refugees. *Population and Environment, 19*(2), 167–182.

Nachowitz, T. (1988). Repression in the Narmada Valley. *Cultural Survival Quarterly, 12*(3), 22–24.

Nader, L. (1997). Controlling processes: Tracing the dynamic components of power. *Current Anthropology, 38,* 5.

Nader, L. (1996). A civilização e seus negociadores: A harmonia como técnica de pacificão. In M.L.L.B. de Menezes (Trans.), *XIX Reunião Brasileira de Antropologia* (pp. 43–63). Niteroi, Brazil: UFF, ABA.

Nader, L. (1994). *Coercive harmony: The political economy of legal models.* Unpublished manuscript.

Nandigram turns blood red. (2007, March 15). Economic Times. Retreived from www.economictimes.indiatimes.com

Nandy, A. (1998). *Exiled at home.* Delhi: Oxford University Press.

Nash, J. (1979). *"We eat the mines and the mines eat us": Dependency and exploitation in Bolivian tin mines.* New York: Columbia University Press.

New directions for river protection. (1987). *World Rivers Review, 2*(6), 2.

The new plantations. (1991, March 31). *Sixty Minutes* [Television broadcast]. New York: CBS News.

Niemoller, M. (n.d.). [Untitled poem]. United States Holocaust Memorial Museum, Washington, D.C. Retrieved from www.Ushmm.org/wlc/article.php?lanf =en&moduleId =10007392

Nussbum, M. C. (2007). *The clash within: Democracy, religious violence and India's future.* Cambridge, Mass.: Belknap Press/Harvard University Press.

Oates, J. F. (1999). *Myth and reality in the rain forest: How conservation strategies are failing in West Africa.* Berkeley: University of California Press.

O'Connor, J. (1998). *Natural causes: Essays in ecological Marxism.* New York: The Guilford Press.

O'Connor, M. (1999, October). *Distributional obstacles to aggregation: From Arrow's impossibility to resistance politics.* Paper presented at the conference The Cost-Benefit Analysis Dilemma: Strategies and Alternatives, Yale University, New Haven, Conn.

Office of the High Commissioner on Human Rights. (1986, December 4). *Declaration on the right to development.* Adopted by General Assembly resolution 41/128, United Nations. Retrieved from http://www.unhchr.ch/html/menu3/b/74.htm

Oliver-Smith, A. (2009a). Disasters and diasporas: Global climate change and population displacement in the 21st century. In S. A. Crate, & M. Nuttall (Eds.), *Anthropology and climate change: From encounters to actions* (116–138). Walnut Creek, Calif.: Left Coast Press.

Oliver-Smith, A. (2009b). Evicted from Eden: Conservation forced displacement and resettlement. In A. Oliver-Smith (Ed.), *Development and dispossession: The crisis of forced displacement and resettlement* (141–162). Santa Fe: SAR Press.

Oliver-Smith, A. (2009c). Introduction: Development forced displacement and resettlement: A global human rights crisis. In A. Oliver-Smith (Ed.), *Dispossession and development: The crisis of forced displacement and resettlement.* Santa Fe: SAR Press.

Oliver-Smith, A. (2006). Displacement, resistance and the critique of development: From the grass roots to the global. In C. de Wet (Ed.), S. Castles, & D. Chatty (General Eds.), Studies in forced migration: Vol. 18. *Development induced displacement: Problems, policies and people* (pp. 141–179). New York & Oxford: Berghahn Books.

Oliver-Smith, A. (2005a). Applied anthropology and development-induced displacement and resettlement. In J. van Willigan, & S. Kedia (Eds.), *Applied anthropology: Domains of application* (189–220). Westport, Conn.: Praeger.

Oliver-Smith, A. (2005b). Communities after catastrophe: Reconstructing the material, reconstituting the social. In S. Hyland (Ed.), *Building communities in the 21st century* (pp. 45–70). Santa Fe, N.M.: School of American Research Press.

Oliver-Smith, A. (2001). *Displacement, resistance and the critique of development: From the grass roots to the global.* Final report prepared for ESCOR R7644 and the Research Programme on Development Induced Displacement and Resettlement, Refugee Studies Centre, University of Oxford, U.K.

Oliver-Smith, A. (1996). Fighting for a place: The policy implications of resistance to resettlement. In C. McDowell (Ed.), *Understanding impoverishment: The consequences of development induced displacement* (pp. 77–98). Providence, R.I., & London: Berghahn Books.

Oliver-Smith, A. (1994). Resistance to resettlement: The formation and evolution of movements. *Research in Social Movements, Conflict and Change, 17*, 197–219.

Oliver-Smith, A. (1992). *The martyred city: Death and rebirth in the Andes* (2nd ed.). Prospect Heights, Ill.: Waveland Press.

Oliver-Smith, A. (1991). Involuntary resettlement, resistance, and political empowerment. *Journal of Refugee Studies, 4*(2), 132–149.

Oliver-Smith, A. (1982). Here there is life: The social and cultural dynamics of resistance to resettlement in post-disaster Peru. In A. Hansen, & A. Oliver-Smith (Eds.), *Involuntary migration and resettlement* (pp. 85–104). Boulder, Colo.: Westview Press.

Oliver-Smith, A. (1977). Traditional agriculture, central places and post-disaster urban relocation in Peru. *American Ethnologist, 3*(1), 102–116.

O'Neill, J. (1999, October). *Markets and the environment: The solution is the problem*. Paper presented at the conference The Cost-Benefit Analysis Dilemma: Strategies and Alternatives, Yale University, New Haven, Conn.

O'Neill, J. (1998). Cost-benefit analysis, rationality and the plurality of values. *The Ecologist, 26*(3), 98–103.

Ortner, S. B. (1995). Resistance and the right of ethnographic refusal. *Comparative Studies in Society and History, 37*(1), 173–193.

Osun, M. (1999). Zapatista report. Presented as a speech at the Indigenous Struggles panel at the Second National Conference on Mexico-U.S. Relations, Mexico Solidarity Network. Retrieved from http://www.thirdworldtraveler.com/Latin_America/Zapatista_Report_Z.html

Ott, M. C. (1972). Mediation as a method of conflict resolution. *International Organization, 26*, 595–618.

Oviedo, G., Maffi, L., & Larsen, P. B. (2000). *Indigenous and traditional peoples of the world and ecoregion conservation*. Gland, Switzerland: WWF-World Wide Fund for Nature. Retrieved from http://assets.panda.org/downloads/EGinG2oorep.pdf

Palit, C. (2009). Displacement, gender justice and people's struggles. In L Mehta, (Ed.), *Displaced by development: Confronting marginalization and gender injustice* (pp. 282–294). New Delhi: Sage.

Panama's president touts canal expansion. (2006, April 24). Associated Press.

Parasuraman, S. (1999). *The development dilemma: Displacement in India*. New York: St. Martin's Press.

Parkin, D. (1999). Mementos as transitional objects in human displacement. *Journal of Material Culture, 4*, 303–320.

Parkin, M. (2003). *Microeconomics* (6th ed.). Boston: Addison Wesley.

Partridge, W. (1993). Successful involuntary resettlement: Lessons from the Costa Rican Arenal Hydroelectric Project. In M. M. Cernea, & S. E. Guggenheim (Eds.), *Anthropology and involuntary resettlement: Policy, practice and theory* (pp. 351–374). Boulder, Colo.: Westview Press.

Partridge, W. (1989). Population displacement due to development projects. *Journal of Refugee Studies, 2*(3), 373–384.

Patel, A., & Mehta, A. (1995). What do the Narmada Valley tribals want? In W. F. Fisher (Ed.), *Toward sustainable development: Struggles over India's Narmada River* (pp. 381–421). Armonk, N.Y., & London: M.E. Sharpe.

Peluso, N. (1993). Coercing conservation: The politics of state resource control. In R. Lipschutz, & K. Conca (Eds.), *The State and social power in global environmental politics* (pp. 46–70). New York: Columbia University Press.

Penz, G. P. (1992). Development refugees and distributive justice: Indigenous peoples, land and the developmentalist state. *Public Affairs Quarterly, 6*(1), 105–131.

Penzich, C., Thomas, G., & Wohlgenant, T. (1994). *The role of alternative conflict management in community forestry*. (Working Paper No. 1. Community Forestry Unit, Forests, Trees, and People Programme Phase II, Forestry Division). Rome, Italy: Food and Agriculture Organization of the United Nations.

Perlman, J. E. (1982). Favela removal: The eradication of a lifestyle. In A. Hansen, & A. Oliver-Smith (Eds.), *Involuntary migration and resettlement: The problems and responses of dislocated peoples* (pp. 225–244). Boulder, Colo.: Westview Press.

Phinney, D. (Producer, writer). (n.d.). *Large dams, false promises* [Video]. U.S.: International Rivers Network.

Picciotto, R., van Wicklin, W., & Rice, E. (2001). *Involuntary resettlement: Comparative perspectives*. Vol. 2, World Bank Series on Evaluation and Development. Washington D.C.: World Bank.

Plan Puebla Panama (PPP) (n.d.) Retrieved from http://www.globalexchange.org/countries/americas/mexico/ppp/ppp.html

Plan Puebla Panama: Conectando Mesoamerica. (2007). Retrieved from www.planpuebla-panama.org/main-pages/organigrama.htm

Pleumarom, A. (1994). Sport and environment: Thailand's golf boom reviewed. *TEI Quarterly Environment Journal, 2*(4), 1–11.

Posey, D. (1996). The Kayapo Indian protests against Amazonian dams: Successes, alliances and un-ending battles. In C. McDowell (Ed.), *Understanding impoverishment: The consequences of development induced displacement* (pp. 123–138). Providence & London: Berghahn Books.

Possekel, A. (1999). *Living with the unexpected: Linking disaster recovery to sustainable development*. Berlin: Springer-Verlag.

Rajagopal, B. (2001, August 9). The violence of development. *The Washington Post*. p. A19.

Ramkuwar. (2009). "We will never forgive the government"—A personal testimony. In L. Mehta (Ed.), *Displaced by development: Confronting marginalization and gender injustice* (pp. 270–281). New Delhi: Sage.

Rapp, K. W. (2000). Yacyreta: A study of affected people's resistance to involuntary resettlement in the Southern Cone. *The Eastern Anthropologist, 53*(1-2), 223–257.

Rebbapragada, R. & Kalluri, B. (2009). The Samatha judgement: Upholding the rights of Adivasi women. In L. Mehta (Ed.), *Displaced by development: Confronting marginalization and gender injustice* (pp. 249–269). New Delhi: Sage.

Redclift, M. (1992). Sustainable development and popular participation: A framework for analysis. In D. Ghai, & J. Vivian (Eds.), *Grassroots environmental action* (23–49). London: Routledge.

Redclift, M. (1987). *Sustainable development: Exploring the contradictions*. London: Metheun.

Redford, K. (1991). The ecologically noble savage. *Cultural Survival Quarterly, 15*(1), 46–48.

Redford, K. H., & Painter, M. (2006, March). *Natural alliances between conservationists and indigenous peoples.* (Working Paper No. 25). New York: Wildlife Conservation Society.

Redford, K., & Sanderson, S. (2000). Extracting humans from nature. *Conservation Biology, 14*(5), 1362–1364.

Red-hand Buddha: 14 killed in Nandigram re-entry bid. (2007, March 15). *The Telegraph.* Retrieved from http://www.telegraphindia.com/1070315/asp/frontpage/story_7519166.asp

Redmond, C. L. (1999). *Human impact on ancient environments.* Tucson: University of Arizona Press.

Ribeiro, G. L. (1987). ¿Cuanto más grande mejor? Proyectos de Gran Escala: Una forma de produccion vinculada a la expansión de sistemas económicos. *Desarrollo Económico, 27,* 1–36.

Rich, B. (1994). *Mortgaging the earth: the World Bank, environmental impoverishment and the crisis of development.* Boston: Beacon Press.

Rio Tinto. (2001). *Murowa Project Newsletter.* Harare, Zimbabwe: Rio Tinto.

Risse, T., Ropp, S. C., & Sikkink, K. (Eds.). (1999). *The power of human rights: International norms and domestic change.* Cambridge, U.K.: Cambridge University Press.

Risse, T., & Sikkink, K. (1999). The socialization of international human rights norms into domestic practices: Introduction. In T. Risse, S. C. Ropp, & K. Sikkink (Eds.), *The power of human rights: International norms and domestic change* (pp. 1–3). Cambridge, U.K.: Cambridge University Press.

Rist, G. (1997). *The history of development.* London & New York: Zed Books.

Rivers for life: Inspirations and insights from the 2nd International Meeting of Dam Affected Peoples and their Allies. (2004). Berkeley, Calif.: International Rivers Network and Environmental Leadership Program.

Robinson, S. (1992, April). *Participation and accountability: Understanding the political culture of involuntary resettlement in Mexico.* Paper presented at the 41st annual conference of the Center for Latin American Studies, Involuntary Migration and Resettlement in Latin America, University of Florida, Gainesville.

Robinson, S. (n.d.). *Some are more clever than others: Dams in Mexico* [Video]. Private distribution.

Rodman, M. C. (1992). Empowering place: Multilocality and multivocality. *American Anthropologist, 94*(3), 640–656.

Rodriguez, R. (1990a, August 28). Copalillo se Opone a la Construcción de 2 Presas; Podrían Desaparecer 300 Comunidades: el Edil *Excelsior,* p. 1.

Rodriguez, R. (1990b, November 29). Rechazan 22 Pueblos Indígenas de Guerrero Abandonar Tierras Donde se Hará Una Presa *Excelsior,* p. 1.

Rosales, M. R. (2007). *The Panama Canal expansion project: Transit maritime megaproject development, reactions and alternatives from affected people* (Unpublished doctoral dissertation). University of Florida, Gainesville.

Rosales, M. R. (2005, March). The Panama Canal or the canal's Panama? *Envio,* p. 284.

Rose, C. M. (1994). *Property and persuasion.* Boulder, Colo.: Westview Press.

Rosenau, J. (1991). *Turbulence in world politics: A theory of continuity and change.* Princeton, N.J.: Princeton University Press.

Rothman, F. D., & Oliver, P. E. (1999). From local to global: The anti-dam movement in Southern Brazil, 1979–1992. *Mobilization: An International Journal, 4*(1), 41–57.

Rousseau, J. J. (2002). The social contract. New Haven, Conn.: Yale University Press.

Rousseau, S., & Meloche, F. (2002). Gold and land: Democratic development at stake. International Centre for Human Rights and Democratic Development. Retrieved from http://www.dd-rd.ca/site/publications/index.php?id=1345&page=3&subsection=catalogue

Roy, A. (1999). *The cost of living.* New York: The Modern Library.

Salisbury, R. (1989). *A homeland for the Cree: Regional development in James Bay, 1971–81.* Montreal: McGill-Queen's University Press.

Sanabria, H. (1993). *The coca boom and rural social change in Bolivia.* Ann Arbor: The University of Michigan Press.

Sanders, T. G. (1991). *Northeast Brazilian environmental refugees: Part II Where They Go.* (Field Staff Reports, No. 21). Hanover, N.H.: Universities Field Staff International and the Natural Heritage Institute.

Sawicki, J. (1991). *Disciplining Foucault: Feminism, power and the body.* New York: Routledge.

Schkilnyk, A. M. (1985). *A poison stronger than love: The destruction of an Ojibwa community.* New Haven, Conn.: Yale University Press.

Schmink, M. (1992). Amazonian resistance movements and the international alliance. In L. Kosinksi (Ed.), *Ecological disorder in Amazonia* (pp. 149–172). Paris & Rio de Janeiro: UNESCO/ISSC/Educam.

Schradie, J., & DeVries, M. (Directors). (2000). *The Golf War* [Motion picture]. Available from Bullfrog Films, P.O. Box 149, Oley, Pa. 19547.

Schwartzman, S., Moreira, A., & Nepstad, D. (2000). Rethinking tropical forest conservation: Perils in parks. *Conservation Biology, 14*(5), 1351–1357.

Scott, D. C. (1990, October 11). Mexican dam would displace thousands. *The Christian Science Monitor.*

Scott, J. (1998). *Seeing like a state: How certain schemes to improve the human condition have failed.* New Haven, Conn.: Yale University Press.

Scott, J. (1990). *Domination and the arts of resistance: Hidden transcripts.* New Haven, Conn.: Yale University Press.

Scott, J. (1985). *Weapons of the weak: Everyday forms of peasant resistance.* New Haven, Conn.: Yale University Press.

Scudder, T. (2009). Resettlement theory and the Kariba case: An anthropology of resettlement. In A. Oliver-Smith (Ed.), *Dispossession and development: The crisis of forced displacement and resettlement* (pp. 25–48). Santa Fe: SAR Press.

Scudder, T. (2005). *The future of large dams: Dealing with social, environmental, institutional and political costs.* London/Sterling, Va.: Earthscan.

Scudder, T. (1996). Development-induced impoverishment, resistance and river-basin development. In C. McDowell (Ed.), *Understanding impoverishment: The consequences of development induced displacement* (pp. 49–74). Providence & London: Berghahn Books.

Scudder, T. (1973). The human ecology of big projects: River basin development and resettlement. *Annual Review of Anthropology, 2,* 45–61.

Scudder, T., & Colson, E. (1982). From welfare to development: A conceptual framework for the analysis of dislocated people. In A. Hansen, & A. Oliver-Smith (Eds.), *Involuntary migration and resettlement* (pp. 267–287). Boulder, Colo.: Westview Press.

Sen, D., Chattopadhyay, K., Ghosh, K., Murmu, M., Mollik, S., & Marik, S. (2007). A brief report on Nandigram. Retrieved from http://sanhati.com/wp-content/uploads/2007/05/nandigram_deposition_final.pdf

Serra, M. T. F. (1993). Resettlement planning in the Brazilian power sector: Recent changes in approach. In M. M. Cernea, & S. E. Guggenheim (Eds.), *Anthropological approaches to resettlement* (pp. 63–86). Boulder, Colo.: Westview Press.

Shihata, I. F. I. (1993). Legal aspects of involuntary population resettlement. In M. M. Cernea & S. E. Guggenheim (Eds.), *Anthropological approaches to resettlement* (pp. 39–54). Boulder, Colo.: Westview Press.

Smith, A. D. (1986). State-making and nation-building. In J. A. Hall (Ed.), *States in history* (pp. 228–263). Oxford, U.K.: Basil Blackwell.

Smith, C. (1996). Development and the state: Issues for anthropologists. In E. Moran (Ed.), *Transforming societies, transforming anthropology* (pp. 25–56). Ann Arbor: The University of Michigan Press.

Smith, N. (1996). *The new urban frontier: Gentrification and the revanchist city.* London: Routledge.

Snow, D., & Benford, R. (1988). Ideology, frame resonance and participant mobilization. In B. Klandermans, H. Kriese, & S. Tarrow (Eds.), *International social movement research: Vol. 1. From structure to action: Comparing social movement research across cultures* (pp. 197–217). London: JAI Press.

Soros, G. (1998). *The crisis of global capitalism.* New York: Public Affairs.

Squires, G. D., Bennett, L., McCourt, K., & Nyden, P. (1987). *Chicago: Race, class and the response to urban decline.* Philadelphia: Temple University Press.

Stacey, R. D., Griffin, D., & Shaw, P. (2000). *Complexity and management: Fad or radical challenge to systems thinking?* London & New York: Routledge.

Stevens, S. (1997). *Conservation through cultural survival: Indigenous peoples and protected areas.* Washington, D.C.: Island Press.

Stewart, D., Drew, L., & Wexler, M. (1999). How conservation grew from a whisper to a roar—History of US conservation movement. *National Wildlife, 38*(1), 22–43.

Stiglitz, J. (2002). *Globalization and its discontents.* New York: W. W. Norton.

Stonich, S., & Bailey, C. (2000). Resisting the blue revolution: Contending coalitions surrounding industrial shrimp farming. *Human Organization, 54*(1), 23–36.

Striking a better balance: The final report of the Extractive Industries Review, vols. I, II, & III. (2004). Washington, D.C.: The World Bank.

Subramanyam, K. (2001, December 20). Counter terrorism [Editorial]. *Times of India.* Retrieved from http://timesofindia.indiatimes.com/articleshow/850184084.cms

Switkes, G. (2008a). Judge suspends studies for Amazon dam: Legality of world's third largest dam project questioned. International Rivers. Retrieved from http://www.internationalrivers.org/en/node/2732

Switkes, G. (2008b) Tribes fight to keep the Xingu alive. *World Rivers Review, 23*(2), 1, 15.

Switkes, G, & Aguirre, M. (1991).Voices from the rainforest [Video]. Berkeley, Calif. Retrieved from http://www.videoproject.com/ama-111-v.html

Szablowski, D. (2004). Who defines displacement? The operation of the World Bank resettlement policy in a large mining project. Ethics of Development-Induced Displacement project report, York University, Toronto, Canada.

Szablowski, D. (2002). Mining, displacement and the World Bank: A case analysis of Compañia Minera Antamina's operations in Peru. *Journal of Business Ethics, 39*, 247–273.

Tarrow, S. (1994). *Power in movement: Social movements, collective action and politics.* Cambridge, U.K.: Cambridge University Press.

Taussig, M. T. (1980). *The devil and commodity fetishism in South America.* Chapel Hill: University of North Carolina Press.

Terborgh, J. (1999). *Requiem for nature.* Washington, D.C.: Island Press.

The Three Gorges Dam in China: Forced resettlement, suppression of dissent and labor rights concerns. (1995). *Human Rights Watch/Asia 7,* 2.

Tilley, C. (1994). *A Phenomenology of landscape.* Oxford, U.K.: Berg.

Turner, T. (1991a). Representing, resisting, rethinking: Historical transformations of Kayapo culture and anthropological consciousness. In G. W. Stocking, Jr., (Ed.), History of anthropology: Vol. 7. *Colonial situations: Essays on the contextualization of ethnographic knowledge* (285–313). Madison: University of Wisconsin Press.

Turner, T. (1991b) Major shift in Brazilian Yanomami policy. *Anthropology Newsletter, 32*(6), 1, 46.

United Nations World Commission on Environment and Development. (1987). *Our common future.* Oxford, U.K.: Oxford University Press.

United States Holocaust Memorial Museum, Washington, D.C. Retrieved from https://secure.ushmm.org/wlc/article.php?lang=es&ModuleId=10007392& print=y

Visvinathan, S. (1990). On the annals of the laboratory state. In A. Nandy (Ed), *Science, hegemony and violence,* (pp. 257–288). Oxford, U.K.: Oxford University Press.

Waldram, J. (1980). Relocation and political change in a Manitoba native community. *Canadian Journal of Anthropology, 1*(2), 173–178.

Wali, A. (1989). *Kilowatts and crisis: Hydroelectric power and social dislocation in eastern Panama.* Boulder, Colo.: Westview Press.

Ward, R., & Prior, I. (1980). Genetic and sociocultural factors in the response of blood pressure to migration of the Tokelau population. *Medical Anthropology, 4,* 33–39.

Weeks, P. (1999). Cyber-activism: World Wildlife Fund's campaign to save the tiger. *Culture and Agriculture, 21*(3), 19–30.

Wehner, R. (2000, December 17). Rebels in the rain forest: Mexico's peace talks with Zapatistas complicated by fate of fragile environment. *San Francisco Chronicle.*

Welch, C. E., Jr. (2001). *NGOs and human rights: Promise and performance.* Philadelphia: University of Pennsylvania Press.

Werner, D. (1985). Psychosocial stress and the construction of a flood-control dam in Santa Catarina, Brazil. *Human Organization, 44*(2), 161–167.

When the rivers run dry: The World Bank, dams and the quest for reparations. (2007). International Rivers Network Briefing Paper. International Rivers Network. Retrieved from http://www.internationalrivers.org/en/latin-america/mesoamerica/ chixoy-dam-guatemala/when-rivers-run-dry

Why this newsletter? (1985). *International Dams Newsletter, 1*(1), 1.

Wilches-Chaux, G. (1994). El Sentido de la participación. In A. Lavell (Ed.), *Viviendo en riesgo: Comunidades vulnerables y prevención de desastres en América Latina* (137–158). San Jose, Costa Rica: FLACSO/La Red/CEPREDENAC.

Williams, P. B. (1997a). *A historic overview of IRN's mission.* Unpublished manuscript.

Williams, P. B. (1997b). *Confronting the international hydromafia: The experience of the International Rivers Network.* Unpublished manuscript.

Williams, R. (2005). *Culture and materialism.* New York & London: Verso.

Wilmer, F. (1993). *The indigenous voice in world politics.* Newbury Park, Calif.: Sage Publications.

Wolf, E. (1982). *Europe and the people without history.* Berkeley: University of California Press.

Wolf, E. (1972). Ownership and political ecology. *Anthropological Quarterly, 45,* 201–205.

Wood, E. M. (2002). *The origin of capitalism: A longer view.* New York & London: Verso.

World Bank. (2005). Revised operational policy on indigenous peoples, OP 4.10. In *The World Bank operational manual.* Washington, D.C.: The World Bank. Retrieved from http://web.worldbank.org/WBSITE/EXTERNAL/PROJECTS/ EXTPOLICIES/EXTOPMANUAL/o,,contentMDK:20553653~menuPK :4564185~pagePK:64709096~piPK:64709108~theSitePK:502184,00.html

World Bank. (2001). Operational policies 4.12: Involuntary resettlement. In *The World Bank operational manual.* Washington, D.C.: The World Bank. Retrieved from http://web.worldbank.org/WBSITE/EXTERNAL/PROJECTS/ EXTPOLICIES/EXTOPMANUAL/o,,contentMDK:20064610~menuPK :64701637~pagePK:64709096~piPK:64709108~theSitePK:502184,00.html

World Bank. (1994). *Resettlement and development: The Bankwide review of projects involving involuntary resettlement, 1986–1993.* Washington, D.C.: The World Bank (Environment Department).

World Bank. (1990). Operational directive 4.30: Involuntary resettlement. In *The World Bank operational manual.* Washington, D.C.: The World Bank. Retrieved from http://www.ifc.org/ifcext/sustainability.nsf/AttachmentsByTitle/pol_Resettle ment/$FILE/OD430_InvoluntaryResettlement.pdf

World Bank Operations Evaluation Department. (1996). *The World Bank's experience with large dams: A preliminary review of impacts.* Washington, DC: The World Bank.

World Commission on Dams. (2000). *Dams and development: A new framework for decision making.* London: Earthscan.

Zaman, M. Q. (1982). Crisis in Chittagong Hill tracts: Ethnicity and integration. *Economic and Political Weekly, 17*(3), 75–80.

Index

chaos theory, 73, 216
Chico Dams (case study), 217–220, 221
Chile, 174, 200, 235
China, 2, 36, 37, 42, 59, 135, 139, 180–183
Chinantecs, 172, 188, 197, 211
Chixoy Dam (Guatemala), 58, 152, 234
class, 1, 90, 95, 198, 234, 251–252
Clean Development Mechanism (CDM), 60
collective action frames, 53
Colombia, 222
Colson, Elizabeth, 90
Comisión Federal de Electricidad, 130, 209, 236
Comissão Pastoral da Terra (Pastoral Land Commission), 62
Comissão Regional dos Atingidos de Barragens (CRAB), 62–64, 100, 121, 177, 196, 199
commodification, 12
common property use rights, 89
communal labor exchange institutions, 61–62
Compañia Minera Antamina, 87
compensation, 31, 91, 149–150, 164, 177–179, 181–182, 192, 227, 229, 240, 250, 253
complex adaptive systems, 73
complexity theory, 72–73
Consejo de Pueblos Nahuas del Alto Balsas, 210
conservation, 37, 122–127, 132
Conservation International, 128–129
Constitutive Incommensurability, 148, 177–179
contingent valuation, 144, 148, 179
Coordinación Campesina Contra Embalses (CCCE), 138–139
Cordillera Peoples Alliance, 219–220
cost-benefit analysis, 28, 142–146, 148, 150, 177–178, 225
Costa Rica, 238–240
culture: extinction of, 169; and heritage, 176; and representation, 175
cultural resources valuation, 148–150
Curitiba Declaration, 222, 242
cyberactivism, 215

dams, 35–37, 117–118; as "temples of development," 225
democracy, 11–13
democratic regimes, 190
development: aggression, 2; alternatives to, 9, 14; cleansing, 2; costs of, 10; ethics of, 17–27; industry of, 16; models, tensions between, 7
development forced displacement and resettlement (DFDR): categories of affected people, 99–101
de Wet, Chris, 25–26
Discover Card, 59
"dislocation free zones," 154
dissipative structures, 73
diversity, biological and cultural, 257
dot-com economy, 154
Downing, Ted, 235–236
Dubois, Mark, 54
Dwivedi, Ranjit, 77, 93–95

Earth Summit, 211
economic analyses of projects, 141–142
economic models, western, 1, 132
economic rationality, 8
economies of scale, 8, 133–134
efficiency, 15–16, 133
electronic information technology, 38, 45, 65, 196, 213–217
ELETROBRAS, 62, 197
ELETRONORTE, 118–121, 175
ELETROSUL, 62, 100, 194
eminent domain, 17, 28, 132, 142, 154–156
Empresa Minera Tambogrande, 113
Enchente do Uruguai, A (The Flood of the Uruguai), 63
enclosure movement, 11
ENDESA, 235
Entidad Binacional Yacyretá, 201
environment: destruction of, 109–111; impacts on, 8, 114; and justice, 7; and movements, 38; refugees, 112
Environmental Defense Fund, 64, 228
Environmental Mining Council of British Columbia, 115
Environmental Policy Institute, 228

International Meeting of Dam Affected
People and their Allies, 54
International Monetary Fund (World
Bank Group), 1, 70
International Rivers: case study, 56–60,
57, 65, 68, 216, 220, 224, 243–246;
Network, 55
Itaipu Dam, 62, 196

Jal samadhi, 187
James Bay Cree, 192–193
"Jeremiad discourses," 184
Johnson, Ian, 216
Johnston, Barbara Rose, 150–151
joint use area, 167

Kalinga people, 218
Kanbur, Ravi, 150
Kaptai Dam, 171
Kayapo, 174–176, 198, 212–213
Kelo v. New London, 155
Khagram, Sanjeev, 13, 224
Kinzua Dam, 201
Kyoto Protocol, 60

laboratory state, 25
Lacandon forest, 127–130
land reform, 129
La Parota Dam, 208, 233–234, 236–238
Latin American Network Against Dams
and for Rivers (REDLAR), 209
leadership, 198–200
"legal persons," 86
legibility, 163
Lifton, Robert J., 87–88
Little, Paul, 49, 72, 80, 82, 189
loan conditionalities, 15
Locke, John, 16, 105
losses, access to resources, 147–148

Maheshwar Dam, 201
Malaysia, 13, 57
Malkki, Liisa, 168
Manhattan Minerals Corporation, 113
Manibeli Declaration, 152, 222, 242
Manila South Coast Development Corporation, 158

Mapuche, 174
Maquila, 155, 248, 251
Marcos, Ferdinand: regime of, 217
mariculture, 46
market, 31, 106, 132, 146, 154, 170
market-driven displacement, 26–27
Marshall Plan, 6
martyrdom, 186–187
Mayan people, 152
Mazatecs, 172, 197
megaprojects: 134–136; case study,
137–139
messianic resistance movement, 197
methods for research and action, 80–83
Mexico, 36, 127–131, 172–173, 188, 191,
197, 199, 205, 208, 209–212, 222, 233,
235, 236–238, 248
Mexican Movement of Dam Affected
Peoples and for the Defense of
Rivers (MAPDER), 209
Mexico Solidarity Network, 129
migration, voluntary, 3
Miguel Aleman Dam, 172
Mineral Policy Center, 115
mining, 37, 44, 111, 153
minorities, 47, 198
MISEREOR, 62
mosquito plague, 119–120
Montes Azules Biosphere Reserve (case
study), 127–130
Morse Report, 242
Movimento de Atingidos por Barragens (MAB), 61–66, 121, 196, 199,
207, 241
Movimento sem Terra (the Landless
Movement), 64, 197
multilateral development banks (MDBs),
39, 99, 221
multilateral development bank campaign, 223
Multilateral Investment Guarantee
Agency (MIGA), 224
multi-stakeholder processes, 50, 55,
69–72

Nahuatl People, 208–212, 235
Nam Theun, 2; dam, 247